Remembering the Past, Educating for the Present and the Future

Remembering the Past, Educating for the Present and the Future

*Personal and Pedagogical Stories of
Holocaust Educators*

Edited by
Samuel Totten

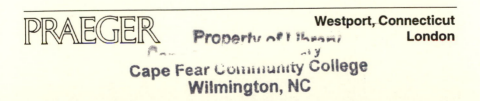

PRAEGER

Westport, Connecticut
London

Library of Congress Cataloging-in-Publication Data

Remembering the past, educating for the present and the future : personal and
pedagogical stories of Holocaust educators / edited by Samuel Totten.
    p. cm.
   Includes bibliographical references and index.
   ISBN 0–89789–709–9 (alk. paper)
   1. Holocaust, Jewish (1939–1945) – Study and teaching (Secondary).
 I. Title: Personal and pedagogical stories of Holocaust educators. II. Totten,
Samuel.
   D804.33.R48 2002
   940.53′18′0712 – dc21   2002067936

British Library Cataloguing in Publication Data is available.

Library of Congress Catalog Card Number: 2002067936
ISBN: 0–89789–709–9

First published in 2002

Praeger Publishers, 88 Post Road West, Westport, CT 06881
An imprint of Greenwood Publishing Group, Inc.
www.praeger.com

Printed in the United States of America

∞™

The paper used in this book complies with the
Permanent Paper Standard issued by the National
Information Standards Organization (Z39.48–1984).

10 9 8 7 6 5 4 3 2 1

Every reasonable effort has been made to trace the owners of copyright
materials in this book, but in some instances this has proven impossible.
The author and publisher will be glad to receive information leading to more
complete acknowledgments in subsequent printings of the book and in the
meantime extend their apologies for any omissions.

Contents

Contents

Introduction

Samuel Totten

Remembering the Past, Educating for the Present and the Future: The Personal and Pedagogical Stories of Holocaust Educators is composed of essays about Holocaust education by educators involved at the secondary level of schooling (grades 7–12). It was inspired by Carol Rittner and John K. Roth's *From the Unthinkable to the Unavoidable: American Christian and Jewish Scholars Encounter the Holocaust*. In the latter, such noted Holocaust scholars as Harry James Cargas, Franklin Littell, A. Roy Eckardt, Michael Berenbaum, Alice Eckardt, Richard Rubenstein, and others reflect on their encounters with the Holocaust and that which led them to dedicate their lives' work to wrestling with, and thinking, writing, and teaching about, the Holocaust. The stories are moving and thought-provoking, and the insights are illuminating. In a review I wrote of the book I said:

The individual and collective essays of this book work their way into the reader's mind and heart. Not only is one left with ample food for thought about a host of vitally significant issues, but a deep appreciation for these scholars who are such passionate and caring human beings. . . . [A]ll have been moved in significant ways by others' suffering and have committed their professional and personal lives to delving into a world of darkness. Many are doing so in the hope that their own and others' efforts will raise a clarion call to the fact that one of the worst sins is to be a bystander when others are taunted, tortured and murdered because they are marked as "different"—or as less than human.

This is a book that many readers, especially those who are engaged in study, scholarship, and/or activism in the fields of Holocaust, genocide, and human rights, will likely return to time and again. Not only will they revisit it for its many cogent discussions of critical issues, but for the inspiration that can be gleaned from the struggles and successes inherent in the stories of these remarkable human beings. (Totten, 1997, p. 144)

Ultimately, I hope that *Remembering the Past, Educating for the Present and the Future* serves much the same purpose for the reader as *From the Unthinkable to the Unavoidable* does for me.

In their chapters, the contributors to *Remembering the Past, Educating for the Present and the Future* relate the genesis of their interest in the Holocaust, and the evolution of their educative efforts. The latter includes but is not limited to their efforts to gain an ever-deepening knowledge about the Holocaust, their initial efforts to teach about the history of the Holocaust, their on-going teaching efforts and the changes they have made along the way, and their involvement in curriculum development, staff development, and other outreach projects. Various authors also include the insights and reactions of their students to this history.

All of the contributors have dedicated a great amount of time, energy, and commitment to learning and teaching about the Holocaust. Many have done so for well over 25 years. They are individuals who believe this history is imperative for the young and others to learn *and* to learn from. They are also committed to teaching it in a historically accurate and pedagogically sound manner. That is not to say that all go about teaching it in the same way, let alone for the same or even similar reasons. Indeed, if the individuals represented in this book were involved in a debate with one another, undoubtedly there would be many disagreements over what should be emphasized when teaching this history. In fact, one of the more curious (and telling?) aspects of this book is the vastly different rationales and motives that the different individuals have for teaching this history. For example, while some in the United States teach about the Holocaust because they believe that it is a watershed event in the history of humanity and firmly believe that students need to know this history in order to understand the world in which they live, others are of a firm belief that learning about the Holocaust is capable of helping students become more personally and socially responsible citizens. Still others believe that such a study is capable of reducing prejudice and intolerance. Understandably, the motives and rationales that educators have for teaching this history dictate—to a certain, if not large, extent—the aspects of the history that they emphasize.

Although there are great differences regarding these educators' motives and rationales, they all share several key characteristics:

first, they passionately care about the history, and particularly what happened to the victim populations during the Holocaust; second, they are dedicated to teaching about the Holocaust in the most pedagogically sound manner, and thus look askance at using frivolous activities (such as simulations that "provide the student with a sense of what the victims experienced") that result in the study of the history degenerating into not much more than fun and games; and third, they all deeply care that students come to understand that the Holocaust was not inevitable, but rather the result of the actions of perpetrators, collaborators, and many bystanders, and thus, while morally incomprehensible, the decisions, actions, and events *are* comprehensible. They also believe that there is a moral imperative to teach about the Holocaust, but to do so one must muster all of one's integrity, skill, mind, and heart in order to teach it in a way that does not minimize the complexity or the horror, but, at one and the same time, accomplishes that goal in a way that is both developmentally appropriate and true to the history.

In a project of this nature it is not always possible to include all the individuals one would wish—nor is it always possible for those invited to participate to actually do so. In regard to the former situation, space constraints precluded inviting many noted Holocaust educators. It is also worth noting that in order to offer a diverse set of stories and insights, an effort was made to seek individuals who have come to Holocaust education under vastly different circumstances and/or work in unique settings. Thus, unfortunately, individuals who would have been ideal contributors could not be included in the book. This is particularly true of those individuals working for the same organization or in the same state with similar curricula. When all is said and done, it must be understood that there are scores of outstanding educators in the United States and abroad who are teaching in powerful and unique ways about the Holocaust, and whose efforts, accomplishments, and stories are likely to be as powerful, unique, and significant as those related herein.

Be that as it may—and in light of the fact that there are thousands upon thousands of educators who teach about the Holocaust—readers are sure to wonder how the nine contributors to this book were selected. It was not an easy decision to make. That said, the following criteria established a starting point in the selection process:

- An individual had to have been involved in Holocaust education for at least a decade, and, ideally, much longer than that;

- An individual's experience in Holocaust education had to be, in one way or another, at the secondary level (grades 7–12);
- The individual needed to be extremely well versed in the history of the Holocaust;
- The individual had to be recognized as having made a significant contribution to Holocaust education; and
- The individual must have moved beyond the classroom in his/her endeavors (for example, developed major curricula on the Holocaust, published articles or books, created and implemented major staff development programs, served as a staff developer for a major institution whose focus was Holocaust education).

Next, I made the decision that contributors needed to be representative of a wide geographic range, and that it would be ideal to include a fairly equal representation of males and females, and backgrounds (Jewish, Christian, and/or unaffiliated).

Based on the above, I immediately developed an initial list of 25 noted Holocaust educators, and over a six-month period I added names to the list. Eventually, I had a list of approximately 50 educators to consider. Then, it was a matter of culling the list down — again, which was not easy in the least.

There were numerous people I asked to participate, but who chose not to do so for various reasons — the key reason, though, was that they were already overextended in their work. Among such individuals were: Jan Darsa, Margaret Drew, William Fernekes, Vladka Meed, and William Parsons.

Many people, including numerous contributors to this volume, have asked me, "What is the purpose of this book?" It is a good and fair question. Among the contributors who asked that question, some were worried that they would be part of a project that was, or at least seemed to be, self-serving. Tellingly, that was a major concern of mine from the inception of the project. I have always looked askance at those who use the Holocaust as a means to serve any purpose other than conducting research into the history, educating about the event, and/or learning from it in order to become more aware of what needs to be done to address contemporary human rights infractions, including — of course — genocide. Thus, from the outset my sense was that while the essays in the book needed to focus on the "personal" — that is, highlight the genesis and evolution of noted Holocaust educators' work — they also needed to be instructive or, if you will, didactic in nature. More specifically, from the start it has been my ardent hope that readers would glean valuable insights from what such dedicated educators (for example, the contributors to this book) have learned over the years in regard to tackling such a complex and terribly difficult and sorrowful topic in the classroom and beyond. It is also my hope that the book proves to be inspiring in that it encourages those who have not yet taught about the Holocaust to seriously consider the possibility of doing so. Further, I hope that in reading the essays, readers become more reflective individuals and educators. That is, I hope that those who are already teaching this history will reflect upon their pedagogical efforts and, in doing so, ask themselves if they are teaching it in the most efficacious and powerful ways—ways that are accurate and comprehensive and that avoid the simplistic, perfunctory, and gimmicky. Furthermore, I hope it leads to a bevy of questions for all readers, questions that result in pondering what it means to live in a world in which such a horrific tragedy could and was perpetrated. Finally, it is my ardent desire that as readers contemplate the words and thoughts of the contributors they ponder what it means to live in a world where genocidal acts continue, on a frighteningly and sickeningly regular basis, to further scar the face of humanity. The point is, then, anyone who, more or less, merely wanted to relate his/her story and not provide key insights into the whys and hows and the strengths and weaknesses of how he/she has gone about teaching this history was not included in the book.

It is important to note that this book originally contained eighteen, rather than nine, personal accounts by Holocaust educators. The other nine included many more educators at the university level and numerous stories of individuals who directed Holocaust education projects outside school systems, many of which were located in various cities across the globe. The manuscript, though, far exceeded the number of words and pages stipulated in the contract issued by the publisher, and thus there was no solution but to cut nine of the accounts. To prevent the disappointment of those who had taken the time and energy to write the accounts as well as to make their insights available to current and future Holocaust educators, the publisher kindly agreed to publish a separate book of accounts by college- and university-based Holocaust educators. In order to produce a book-length manuscript, I decided to ask two colleagues to join me in coediting the college/university book. Both readily agreed, and helped, initially, to develop a list of key college- and university-based Holocaust educators who could be invited to submit essays. The latter book is now being completed, and will include stories by such noted Holocaust scholars and educators as Christopher Browning, Sid Bolkosky, Deborah Lipstadt, Herbert Locke, and David Patterson.

Even with the development of the second book of college- and university-based educators, five essays from the original book were still to be left unpublished. All of the accounts were by those educators who were affiliated with Holocaust organizations outside of a school system. So, at the close of 2001, a proposal was submitted to a publisher who had voiced an initial interest in the manuscript. As luck would have it, the acquisitions editor who was initially keen on the idea left the publishing house for another position. The new acquisitions editor, who was also keen on it, finally was forced by the powers that be to decline the manuscript. The manuscript was next submitted to Lexington Books, and after five months of consultation in-house, Lexington agreed to publish the book. The latter will come out in 2003 under the title *Working to Make a Difference: The Personal and Pedagogical Stories of Holocaust Educators Across the Globe.*

Each person who was invited to write an essay for inclusion in *Remembering the Past, Educating for the Present and the Future* received the following note (and directions) from me:

The book will be composed of personal essays in which noted Holocaust educators at the secondary level of education and/or teacher education will delineate the genesis and evolution of their thought and work in this field.

In relating their personal stories, each author is expected to discuss, among other issues: how he/she became engaged in Holocaust education; those individuals and/or works that have most influenced him/her, and how; the major focus of his/her pedagogical efforts; the aspirations, barriers, successes and frustrations one has faced; his/her perception of the field, and where it needs to go from here.

In order to assure some semblance of continuity amongst the chapters, each author is to address the following questions: (1) What led you to initially begin thinking, teaching, speaking and possibly writing about the Holocaust? (2) How has your thought, knowledge base, pedagogy, and related efforts evolved over the years? (3) What has your primary goal(s) been as you proceeded in this work? (4) What individual(s) and/or scholarly work(s) vis-à-vis the Holocaust and/or the field of education has/have most influenced you in your work, and how? (5) Has there been a persistent and consistent focus in your thinking and practice regarding Holocaust education? (6) Has your work changed in practical terms as your thinking has evolved? If so, how? (7) What are the major obstacles, if any, you've come up against in your work? (8) What do you perceive as your major contributions to the field? (9) What are your perceptions of the field of Holocaust education—where it has been, where it is, and where it appears to be heading? and (10) What, in your mind, remains to be done in the field of Holocaust education?

Finally, each author was asked to provide a select bibliography of *his/her own* list of books, essays, articles, teachers' guides, and curricula that he/she perceives as being his/her most significant contributions to the field of Holocaust education. This list is located at the rear of the volume.

It has been an honor to work with so many intelligent, caring, and passionate educators. All of the contributors took time out of extremely hectic schedules to write and revise their essays for this book, and I am most grateful for that. While I do not necessarily agree with all of their perspectives regarding the teaching of the Holocaust, all of their stories have inspired me to work just that much harder in the field; and in doing so, to constantly ponder what it means to be an educator of the Holocaust, to never forget what the victims went through and why, what it means to be a bystander in a world where injustice and atrocities frequently occur, and to be as reflective as possible as I go about my work.

Again, it is my hope that this book will prove to be both an inspiration to current and future educators as well as a source of valuable insight and information regarding the teaching of the Holocaust.

L' Chaim.

REFERENCES

Rittner, Carol and Roth, John K. (Eds.) (1997). *From the Unthinkable to the Unavoidable: American Christian and Jewish Scholars Encounter the Holocaust*. Westport, CT: Praeger Publishers.

Totten, Samuel (1997). Book review of *From the Unthinkable to the Unavoidable: American Christian and Jewish Scholars Encounter the Holocaust*, edited by Carol Rittner and John K. Roth. *Educational Studies* 28(2) (summer):139–144.

Personal and Pedagogical Stories

Chapter 1

~

Accompanied by the Words of Witnesses: One Teacher's Encounter with the Holocaust

Rebecca G. Aupperle

The Diary of Anne Frank was the only mainstream Holocaust work during my schooldays in the 1960s, and though clearly more a chronicle of the coming of age of a young girl than an examination of the Holocaust per se, the words of this precocious adolescent fueled my interest and desire to learn more about this seminal event in history.

Why would the reading of a book such as *The Diary of Anne Frank* during my adolescence—a rather universal, if not pedantic, rite of passage—have such a profound effect on me? What was it about the words of the ingenuous teenage diarist that served as the catalyst that propelled me on a journey of inquiry, study, and teaching that would consume a substantial portion of my future professional and private life? Why did this parochial introduction to the Holocaust—certainly no scholarly work—captivate my interest in such a way that it became the rubric that would inform my future academic endeavors and guide my personal passions?

Over the years, people have repeatedly quizzed me about my interest in the Holocaust—inquiries invariably couched in the supposition that one would have to be Jewish in order to be interested in such a thing or be motivated by having relatives who were affected by this event. Being devoted to the study of the Holocaust even though I was not Jewish was not an issue for me. What others saw as enigmatic, I viewed as perfectly normal. Now, viewing the situation with the clarity that only many years bestow, I am beginning to arrive at a sense that the horror, disbelief, and outrage I felt about the Holocaust was an epiphany that uniquely coalesced with the values and approach to humanity with which I had been raised in the western Pennsylvania steel town of Latrobe, Pennsylvania.

My father, whose parents were immigrants from Italy, lived a blue-collar, small town life. Declining the numerous athletic and academic scholarship offers he received from colleges and universities throughout the country, he chose instead to attend college in his hometown. My mother, the grand-daughter of Czechoslovakian immigrants, was a well-read woman from whom I most certainly inherited my passion for reading. She was unrelentingly strict in shielding my sister and me from what she considered the seduction and pitfalls of popular culture, but intriguingly liberal in the topics (examinations of the human condition, especially the downtrodden, the poor, and those marginalized by society) and authors she encouraged and permitted us to read. In regard to the latter, for example, by the time I entered high school I had read John Steinbeck's *The Grapes of Wrath*, Pearl Buck's *The Good Earth*, and Harper Lee's *To Kill a Mockingbird*. Though blessed with intelligence, these folks, who were not worldly, comprised the microcosm in which I was raised; they did not travel, nor did they have occasion to mix with others of different races and religions. Indeed, Latrobe was a town virtually devoid of people of color and characterized by the various Christian denominations that populated it; not until many years after I had moved away did I surprisingly discover that there had been a tiny population of Jews and even a makeshift synagogue of which I had been totally unaware. Virtually all of my friends came from second-generation European families, and I was vaguely aware of the differences in the surnames of my Polish, Italian, Slovak, and Irish companions, but in the parochial school I attended we all blended harmoniously as we studied, respected our elders, and wended our way through the childhood rites of passage calibrated by the Roman Catholic religion—Sunday mass, First Holy Communions, Confirmations, graduations. Even Scouts, piano lessons, youth groups, dances were all funneled through the aegis of the church, a pattern that exponentially amplified during high school as I attended an all-girl convent academy where I was prepared to face young womanhood under the watchful ministrations of the Sisters of Mercy.

But despite the homogeneity that surrounded me socially and educationally, despite my parents' unyielding belief that their professed faith embodied the "true religion," I was extremely conscious of their accompanying profound conviction in a credo that respected all of God's creatures as equal and worthy. I have the most salient memory of my parents imbuing in me the ideology that every living person was the same in God's eyes—rich or poor; white, yellow, or black; Hindu, Jew, Muslim, or Catholic—and should be regarded by his fellow man with equal dignity. The school nurse from my elementary years, whose annual job it was to dutifully check my classmates' and my hearing, recounts the tale of directing us, as we donned headphones, to pretend that we were airplane pilots flying to any place in the world of our choosing. I stunned her by replying that my destination would be neither Disneyland nor grandma's house, but India—the first (and she assures me, the last) fourth grader to select a locale so distant and exotic. Even as a kid, I was intrigued by diversity and puzzled by intolerant and biased responses to differences. I saw nothing odd then about being entranced with the wonder of India as I see nothing peculiar today about my interest in the Holocaust. The belief system I inherited in the inviolability of God's creation of all men as equal was so strong, so powerfully instilled in me, that it never occurred to me to consider a person of a different color, race, religion, or ethnic tradition as inferior or an object of derision.

While an entire generation of my Christian contemporaries was being taught in school or from the pulpit that the Jews were directly responsible for Jesus' death and therefore deserved to be reviled as "Christ-killers" and as people who could never enter the kingdom of heaven, by some benign munificence I was spared this hateful, vindictive rhetoric by both my parents and teachers, a legacy for which I am enduringly grateful. During Bible history classes and the celebration of Holy Week, I was able to put the scriptural readings about the death of Jesus into what I now see was, for an impressionable kid, an appropriate, nonretributive context. When the entire student body made the much-anticipated trek up the main highway from our elementary school to the local monastic prep school to view the annual passion play, a reenactment of Jesus' last days from Palm Sunday through Good Friday and Easter, I was able to view the Jews not as vicious murderers of the Son of God but as confused and fallible humans, struggling to come to grips with God's promise to them. In my little girl's mind, I did not see Jesus as apart from the Jews, cast as the protagonist in a good guy/bad guy scenario. After all, Jesus was a Jew: His name was Jewish; he was born to Jewish parents; the entire world in which he was raised was Jewish; his early followers were all Jews, including Peter, who became the first pope. I assimilated the biblical narratives as a story of the Jewish religion fragmenting under a renegade leader with the fear and chaos that accompanied it, all exacerbated by the manipulation of the Romans. Had I been a sounding board at home for bigoted rantings against the

Jews, had I been exposed during my formative years to the type of hatred that throughout the centuries spawned the antisemitism that ended in horrific pogroms, unconscionable anguish for the Jewish people, and ultimately the Holocaust, chances are I would have been denied appreciation of the Jews' contribution to Christianity's salvation and the role we play as spiritual brothers. Maybe I, too, then would have become a bigot or an antisemite like those I met for the first time when I went away to college. Perhaps the accepting and unbiased outlook of my parents found its origins not only in their religious convictions, but also in their own experiences as members of immigrant families — having to endure being taunted as "greasy dagos" and "Hunkies" — situations certainly not remotely approaching the vitriol and physical attacks heaped upon the Jews by Christians, but a tiny taste of the prejudice the former had experienced for the past 2,000 years. The simple fact is that as an impressionable child this venomous bigotry did not rub off on me because I did not hear it at home. I feel quite certain that the nonracist, inclusive environment in which I was raised not only paved the way for my acceptance of the Holocaust as a topic to be embraced and studied, but also actually invited my interest to be piqued by the literary and humanistic appeal of a diary such as Anne Frank's.

Curiously, despite the universal human acceptance espoused by my parents, I have no remembrance of the Holocaust being discussed in my home, nor can I remember it serving as more than a footnote in my high school and college history textbooks. I now ask myself how it was possible that I attended school for 16 years without a topic of this magnitude being broached. How could the genocide of six million people and the lessons it engendered for humanity be withheld from a discussion of the history of the twentieth century?

TEACHING *THE DIARY OF ANNE FRANK*

As an undergraduate student I attended Clarion State College (now Clarion University of Pennsylvania) due to its reputation for preparing students in library science. Not far into my studies, I switched majors to secondary education. I chose to go into teaching because I had always loved school and venerated my teachers; they *knew* and they could teach me *to know*.

In an unusual twist, I began my teaching career in 1971 at the elementary school I had attended as a child, St. Vincent Parochial School in Latrobe, Pennsylvania, where my aunt still taught. There I taught reading, spelling, art, music, religion, and ancient history to sixth, seventh, and eighth graders. The following year I moved to New Jersey and accepted a position at Mary E. Volz School in Runnemede, where I have taught for the past 28 years. Recently, I have added teaching a class on the History of the Holocaust at Camden County College in Blackwood, New Jersey, to my teaching load.

It seemed completely natural for me, as I undertook my professional mission of teaching reading and language arts to 14-year-olds 28 years ago, to include Anne Frank's words in my curriculum. The anthology I initially used contained the unabridged dramatic version of *The Diary of Anne Frank* published in 1955 by Frances Goodrich and Albert Hackett (winner of the Pulitzer Prize), and subsequent texts I chose throughout the years invariably included either the play or excerpts from Anne's diary. I supplemented this with Ernst Schnabel's research on Anne and the other inhabitants of the Secret Annex following their capture in his book *Anne Frank: A Portrait in Courage*.

What was I trying to achieve by throwing the Holocaust into the mix with Edgar Allan Poe, Jack London, and Ray Bradbury? In addition to using Anne's diary as an age-appropriate tool for teaching, in part, the differences between the various literary genres of biography, autobiography, and drama, it became quickly apparent that this work provided an opportunity for my students to explore deeper ethical issues as well.

As I became more sophisticated in my approach to teaching the *The Diary of Anne Frank*, I would initially provide my students with a brief background on the Treaty of Versailles, the Weimar Republic, and Hitler's ascension to power in Germany. In regard to the latter, I explained the Nazi ideology, National Socialism's policies toward the Jews and other victims, and the final results of the Holocaust. I also prefaced our reading with a short biographical piece on Anne and then presented Anne's diary or its dramatization as the eyewitness report of an individual of my students' age who had lived through this incredible event.

By adding the Holocaust to my language arts curriculum, I acted on a purely emotional, intellectual, and spiritual response to my deeply felt instincts that this was a topic so important, so germane to an adolescent's understanding of humanity's reaction to otherness, that it had to be taught. What would it benefit my students to grasp the role of setting in *The Call of the Wild* or the use of onomatopoeia in *The Tell-Tale Heart* if they were denied opportunities to know and evaluate information about the world's past— opportunities that would help them grow to be valuable, contributing human beings as well as global citizens? How could we teach fairness, acceptance, and understanding to our children when there existed in their lifetime a record of one and one-half million children being murdered simply because they had been born into a certain religion?

In the early years of my teaching about the Holocaust, I labored in a virtual vacuum; self-taught and feeling incredibly alone, I flew by the seat of my pants. Finding myself a member of an educational community where I encountered (out of either fear, ignorance, or both) no other colleagues teaching this material, I consoled myself with the rationalization that if Anne's words had elevated me from the egocentric concerns of teenage life and prompted me to think about someone other than myself when I was their age, would they not speak to my students as well? I patched together a curriculum to suit my needs, endeavoring to give my students as much chronological and historical preparation as possible, but I was hindered by their (and frankly, my own) lack of knowledge of European history and the paucity of mainstream material on the subject. There were no centralized curricula, no courses for educators, no degrees to be had. I clipped book reviews and hoarded newspaper and magazine articles dealing with anything remotely pertinent; many of these materials reside in my archive to this day. Above all, I read—anything and everything I could lay my hands on related to the Holocaust—first-person accounts, literature, and historical pieces.

EXPANDING MY OWN AS WELL AS MY STUDENTS' UNDERSTANDING OF THE HOLOCAUST

During the 1980s, while still teaching in Runnemede, I felt the need to physically experience the places about which I was teaching, and thus I traveled to Europe where I visited the Anne Frank House in Amsterdam and walked the Normandy beaches of D day in France. While I also visited other areas of France, Switzerland, Germany, and Austria, my prime motivation was to see and experience the setting of Anne's work so that I could establish a more tangible connection for myself and my students with her words and situation. When I returned, not only with pictures of the Secret Annex, but with me in them—standing on the narrow, winding steps leading to her attic hiding place, ducking behind the bookcase that camouflaged the entrance, and in front of the wall on which she displayed her movie star pictures in the small bedroom she shared with Mr. Dussel—my students were better able to make the connection to Anne as a real person in a real place suffering the very real governmental as well as spatial and social restrictions that bound her.

Each year, tantamount to the sum of information gleaned from my private research, I increased the depth and scope of my unit on the Holocaust. I realized the necessity of making my adolescent students aware of who the Jews of Europe were (virtually unknown to my predominantly Christian students), what their culture was like before the war, and the kinds of vibrant lives they lived before they became victims. Before even speaking about the atrocities of the Holocaust, my aim was to facilitate an understanding of what was lost.

By beginning with historical background, including time lines and a chronology, key vocabulary terms, and maps of Europe, I progressed to an overview of the Jewish experience, including the history of antisemitism, explaining the evolution from religious antisemitism in ancient times to political antisemitism in the Middle Ages to the modern racial antisemitism of Hitler.

I followed this with an exploration of the nature of "man" as he responds to the issues of conformity, prejudice, intolerance, discrimination, scapegoating, and indifference that I paralleled to our own Jim Crow laws in the American South. My objective was to clarify a citizenry's response to the powerful political, social, and economic conditions at play that presaged the Holocaust (the impact of losing World War I, the humiliation felt by the imposition of the Treaty of Versailles, the instability of the Weimar Republic, galloping inflation, increasing antisemitism), all of which made Germany ripe to accept a leader such as Hitler.

My 14-year-olds, a tough audience not renowned for their embrace of multidimensional topics, were appreciative of the complexity of the issues involved and, especially gratifying to me, were motivated to elevate their discourse to a level that challenged their understanding of the cognitive dissonance inherent in the topic. Their responses, visceral yet sincere, not only mirrored my own confusion and horror so many years ago upon initially learning about the Shoah from Anne's diary, but also dramatically underscored what was to become the guiding thrust of my Holocaust pedagogy: how to engage my students in a study of the Holocaust that would be relevant to an adolescent 50 years after the event.

The Impact of the Survivors' Stories on My Students

I found the answer to this conundrum during the 1980s when I began making contact with the few survivors in the area, some of whose memoirs were starting to appear. Each story—whether that of a survivor of a death camp, a resistance fighter, or a hidden child—uniquely and rivetingly peeled away the layers of a discrete Holocaust experience, manufacturing a heartbreakingly pure record of a time that I believed could be made relevant to readers and listeners through the vehicle of words. I had a gut feeling that the words of these true chroniclers of the Holocaust must not go unheard by the generation of children now being raised and educated.

Clara Isaacman, hidden child survivor of the Holocaust and author of the memoir *Clara's Story*, visits my class yearly to share her testimony with my students. No matter the age or cognitive level of the audience, Clara has the unique ability to become a part of it, relating on an appropriate plane. She commences her presentation by discussing with the students simple concepts such as hunger, walls, fear, silence, fresh air. She leads them through an interactive exercise in which she contrasts the everyday, abstract meanings these words have for them and the vastly different concrete connotations they assumed for a child who was shut off from the world in hiding during the Holocaust. After engaging her listeners in this personal and illuminating way, Clara sets the scene with a brief review of Holocaust chronology, utilizing a map of Europe and/or time lines.

Clara relates the story of how she and her family members hid from the Nazis in Antwerp, Belgium, in 18 different places over a period of two and one-half years to issues such as antisemitism, persecution, emigration, deportation, murder, hiding, resistance, indifference, altruism, and rescue. She stresses concepts such as the ludicrousness of "hating" someone you don't even know because of a stereotype or because of their membership within a certain group, and the kindness and humanity displayed by the Righteous Gentiles who enabled Jews to survive.

My kids listen in awe as Clara relates an incident from her memoir about watching from her hiding place in a basement and seeing a young boy, one of her brother's classmates, fatally shot in the back by a Nazi soldier when he refused to obey the command to halt as he walked fearfully down an Antwerp street with a loaf of bread under his arm. Clara goes on to tell my students that seeing the child murdered in cold blood was horrible enough, but her horror grew as she continued to watch the street before her, peopled with hundreds of regular Belgian citizens on their way to work, walking north and south, up and back—people afraid to stop and give aid to this Jewish child, people too terrified to even remove his corpse from the street, people who just passed him where he lay. Despite her tender years, she knew all too well the reason for their inaction: their overwhelming fear not only of the uniforms of the Nazi soldiers, but that the guns in their holsters would be turned on them as well if they intervened.

The high point of interest for my kids is when Clara integrates pre- and postwar slides of herself, family, friends, and rescuers into her testimony. The stunning slides create a visual image not only of European Jewry before Hitler, but also a concrete image of what was lost. A moment of absolute heartbreak occurs when she points down a row of laughing, robust teenagers, swinging their legs from atop the wall on which they are perched, and calmly repeats, as she singles out each, the phrase: "This one died; this one died; this one died; this one died—all because they were born Jewish." The pictures and Clara's sensitive yet honest presentation give emotional and stark meaning to her words and to the stories of the one and one-half million Jewish children who did not survive.

The children's reaction to Clara is illuminating. In almost groupielike fashion, they cluster around her when she has finished; they sense her approachability and what the telling of her tale has cost her emotionally. Some ask if they may give her a hug, and much to her dismay, they invariably ask her age, trying to mentally calculate the historical mathematics. Many request Clara to autograph copies of her memoir that they have read. The following day in class they willingly write letters of appreciation to her, indicating the impact her words have made on them.

During a cultural heritage study that was peripherally attached to our exploration of the Holocaust, the grandfather of one of my students, in answer to his grandson's queries about his ethnic background, presented Jeff with a journal documenting his ancestor's lineage from Poland. As I paged through the extensive and meticulously kept family tree, I was stunned to discover that several of Jeff's relatives had died in the 1940s at Majdanek. At this point Jeff did not recognize the significance of the fact that his forebears, all Catholic, had met their end in a Nazi death camp. Using this unanticipated opportunity to speak to my class about the "other" victims, including political prisoners, I hoped to ignite his initiative to research the particulars of how his ancestors came to be interned in Majdanek. Jeff expressed his feelings about the surprising information he had uncovered and the widespread reach of the Nazi grasp in the following way:

I am an eighth grader who had never actually heard of the Holocaust until this year. Our reading teacher started teaching us about it, and I learned much more than I expected. When I discovered that members of my Polish

family had been in Majdanek, Ms. Aupperle was more shocked and excited than I was!

My existing family has no idea why my relatives were put in there, for
they were not Jewish. Whether they supported the Jewish community or
refused the Nazis for other reasons, it angers me knowing what horrors
they must have gone through, especially after we learned how the Nazis
felt that all people not of the Aryan "race" were subhuman. It angers me
as well that I'll never know or get to meet my ancestors who were murdered in Majdanek. . . . When I see what happened in the past, that part
of my family fell victim to it, and that similar genocides are happening in
the world today, I see what horrors humans are really capable of, and it
scares me.

Throughout this solitary exercise of teaching about the Holocaust, there occurred the occasional distraction of colleagues and
other school and community members questioning the necessity
or even the advisability of teaching this subject to middle school
students. I was bemused by studiously polite comments that very
transparently bespoke their inherent prejudices. To most people,
teaching Anne Frank was evidently acceptable, but deeper probing into the heart of the Holocaust elicited nervous remarks such
as: "You know, the Jews weren't the only ones who suffered in
World War II"; "Millions more died in Russia under Stalin than
under Hitler!"; and my favorite from a PTA member, born and raised
in Germany, who asserted during a parent discussion led by me
of why the Jews had traditionally been persecuted and then singled
out for annihilation, "Well, they had all the money!" There remained
two constants. I unwaveringly believed that teaching about the
Holocaust would enable young people to examine their beliefs about
the concepts of right and wrong, ethical choices, and personal responsibility to their fellow human beings; and I instinctively knew
that the best method of teaching my eighth graders about the
Holocaust was through the stories of people who had lived it. Age-
appropriate literature was the key. Buttressed with a solid back-
ground of historical fact, my students could access aspects of the
Holocaust through diaries (such as those by Hannah Senesh, Eva
Heyman, Mary Berg, Yitzhak Rudoshevski, and more recently,
Dawid Sierakowiak); memoirs (*Clara's Story* by Clara Isaacman,
Fragments of Isabella by Isabella Leitner, *Dry Tears: The Story of
a Lost Childhood* by Nechama Tec, *All But My Life* by Gerda
Weismann Klein, and, more recently, *I Have Lived a Thousand
Years: Growing Up in the Holocaust* by Livia Bitton-Jackson); and
personal testimony of its participants—testaments that were be-
ginning to bubble to the surface from a long-cloistered sea of primary Holocaust documents. Among the latter I have used such

materials as *Vedem: We Are Children Just the Same, the Secret Magazine of the Boys of Terezin* edited by Marie Rut Krizkova and Paul Wilson; *I Never Saw Another Butterfly: Children's Drawings and Poems from Terezin Concentration Camp, 1942–1944* edited by Hana Volavkova; *Final Letters: From Victims of the Holocaust* edited by Reuven Dafni and Yehudit Kleiman. I have also made use of several videos, including *Kitty Hart: A Return to Auschwitz, The Courage to Care*, and videotaped survivors' testimonies from Yale University's Fortunoff Archives for Holocaust Testimonies.

I wanted my students to experience a personal encounter via the real words of real people that only survivor testimony, both written and oral, provides—an encounter that elevates the Holocaust from the concept of the "unknowable" to a plane where it can be "presentable" (Doneson, 1999 p. F4) or known, even if the inhumanity responsible for its cause cannot be comprehended. To say that my students were captivated by the material is an understatement. They were flabbergasted, as was I, that the genocide of 11 million people, sanctioned by the state, could have happened several decades ago with the tacit consent of the populace. As an outgrowth of our study, they were motivated to express their responses in stunningly mature and insightful pieces of writing and art.

In answer to the query, "Why study the Holocaust?" my students' journal responses have included the following:

Who can help but see the similarities between the Holocaust and current social issues such as the "ethnic cleansing" of Muslims by the Serbs in Bosnia? Another example is the increase and popularity of hate groups such as neo-Nazis and "skinheads" among young people in our country; in our neighboring state of Pennsylvania we find the second highest number of hate groups in the nation. Just in school, I see kids of different races and religions hating each other because "He's Hispanic or Muslim," and "She's African-American." You can't escape the comparison.

Converse to the cruelty and horrible treatment of the victims by the Nazis, I also became aware that the Holocaust brought out the best and most noble characteristics in others. Righteous gentiles emerged, such as Miep Gies, Oskar Schindler, the Trocmes, and Raoul Wallenberg, who were willing to risk their lives to help Jews—not for money or fame—but out of a pure belief in the dignity of man. Is it possible that these two types of people could co-exist simultaneously?

EXPANDING MY HOLOCAUST EDUCATION ENDEAVORS

The years leading up to and into the 1990s were filled with my continuing teaching and study of the Holocaust. Though I had yet to encounter local colleagues with whom I could share my interests,

I attended Yom Hashoah (Holocaust remembrance) programs sponsored by the local Jewish federation, the annual Ida E. King Visiting Holocaust Scholar's lecture at the Richard Stockton College of New Jersey, and the long-standing Scholars' Conference on the Holocaust and the Churches founded by noted Holocaust scholars Franklin H. Littell and Hubert Locke. I also made several visits to the United States Holocaust Memorial Museum once it opened in 1993.

Over the course of the years I was influenced by the scholarship of Raul Hilberg, Yehuda Bauer, Leni Yahil, Lucy Dawidowicz, Martin Gilbert, Michael Berenbaum, and Christopher Browning. I also read the memoirs of Charlotte Delbo, Elie Wiesel, Isabella Leitner, Jean Amery, and Primo Levi. These great scholars and gifted writers caused me to examine more deeply the pedagogy that I was using to teach my students about the Holocaust.

As an example, I defy anyone to read the poems in *Auschwitz and After* that Charlotte Delbo has written about her incarceration in Auschwitz and not, in some way, empathize with the crystalline lucidity of her analogies that illuminate how the very act of her survival entailed a daily agony of repeated death. The power of the words of those who, as Wiesel has said, "had been there" convinced me that I was following the right path in using literature to affect a personal relationship between my students and the Holocaust.

As mandates to teach the Holocaust in schools began to be delivered by legislatures in several states (with my own state of New Jersey in the forefront), my interest was engaged by a concept that began to resonate throughout the context of Holocaust scholarship: by teaching the event, would we transform it? Paradoxically, I began to see this paradigmatically European and deeply, profoundly Jewish event being utilized to teach deeply American values. The Holocaust, not discussed for decades, now occupied the role of evil incarnate, and that paradigm began presenting itself ubiquitously in our society. When, during the O.J. Simpson murder trial, defense attorney Johnnie Cochran invoked the Holocaust by referring to detective Mark Fuhrman as a genocidal racist and a Nazi, a line was drawn in American consciousness regarding our understanding of the Holocaust and our willingness to accept it as metaphor. Robert Shapiro, another lawyer on the O.J. team and a Jew, condemned the comparison as deeply offensive, as did the father of one of the victims who was Jewish, bringing to a worldwide audience via the daily chronicles of CNN and Geraldo Rivera the debate over whether the Holocaust can ever, or should ever, be compared to other events. To me, the curiousness of this event is not the debate over the uniqueness or universality of the Holocaust (which continues to rage unabated among Holocaust scholars) or its appropriateness as an analogy, but the fact that the analogy was used at all. Would this have occurred 30 years ago, and would it have been as understandable to the mainstream jury/audience?

I was moved to consider the outpouring of American interest in the Holocaust during the last several decades, an interest that was all but absent immediately following the war. Such interest was readily attested to by the televised 1961 trial of Adolf Eichmann in Jerusalem; the 1978 *Holocaust* miniseries on television; the 1993 opening of the United States Holocaust Memorial Museum in Washington, D.C.; and Steven Spielberg's *Schindler's List* of the same year. Anne Frank today is ubiquitous, whereas she was a solitary voice back in the 1950s. Does the proliferation of materials and memorials create a salutary effect on our understanding of the Holocaust or a detrimental one? It is an issue over which Holocaust scholars and educators constantly wrestle.

For decades very few formally structured sources or institutions existed to carry out the work of Holocaust education. Now as the survivors pass on, the responsibility for this work is being assumed by committed historians, educators, second- and third-generation members of Holocaust families, and institutions of learning. This is admirable, but they (we) cannot speak with a survivor's voice of experience and authority. By necessity, this will change the substance of Holocaust education in certain respects.

One of my concerns is that with the advent of mandates for Holocaust education in five states in our country and recommendations for its inclusion in curricula from the legislatures of at least 15 others, the Holocaust will be misrepresented to students by well-meaning but ill-prepared teachers. There is also the question of whether Holocaust education is being accepted in many schools as a method of teaching kids the actual historical event of the Holocaust or a thinly disguised cover for tolerance education or multiculturalism and good citizenship. It is certainly laudable for schools to endeavor to teach these elements, but would their inclusion in a course about the Holocaust and genocide not result in a watering down of the actual subject?

I think it is safe to say that throughout the years, Holocaust scholarship has evolved from strictly historical accounts such as Raul Hilberg's *The Destruction of the European Jews* and Leni Yahil's *The Holocaust: The Fate of European Jewry, 1932–1945*, both masterful works of detail and organization, to an even more powerfully effective combination of history and literature. I remain convinced that the transition to an interdisciplinary approach in

the teaching of the Holocaust is a welcome and productive transformation. The inclusion of literature brings to the historical
account a personal immediacy with which students identify, a con-
creteness provided by the words of real people, not statistics, within
the context of historical accuracy.

Yet even this approach has undergone an evolution. The narrative of Anne Frank's experience as a Jew in hiding from the Nazis
during World War II, the study of which accounts for the majority
of Americans' exposure to the Holocaust (certainly the lightning rod
that illuminated my interest in the subject), barely skims the surface of the total experience of Jews during the Holocaust. It speaks
less of European Jewry and the Holocaust than it does of the matu-
ration of an adolescent girl. If we truly wish to present our students with a well-rounded, provocative study of the Holocaust—one
that is thoughtful and challenging—it is incumbent upon the educator to introduce narratives of others caught in the web of the
Nazis, stories other than Anne's, to illuminate the complex nature
of the Holocaust. This evolution in pedagogy, which I found myself adopting, requires educators to examine the nature of language
as used in written and oral survivor testimonies, language that
expresses the dichotomy between the durational memory of the
survivor and the common memory of the listener. I will return to
this topic later in my essay.

I awoke one morning to discover that what I had been doing for
nearly 20 years without being consciously aware of it was transforming my classroom into a minimuseum of the Holocaust—a
laboratory where young people could be exposed to books, videos,
articles, photographs, primary documents, and displays that would
agitate their thinking and engage them in an examination of their
ethical principles. At the same time I was nurturing relationships
with several survivors, second-generation members (the sons and
daughters of survivors), and liberators—people I later brought into
my classroom and workshop sites as speakers—that afforded me
and my students rare, firsthand insight into their personal experiences regarding the Holocaust.

Leah Kalina, a refined, compassionate woman who survived
Plaszow, Auschwitz, Bergen-Belsen, and a death march from
Mecklenburg, graced me with her friendship after she and I met
at a Holocaust gathering where I heard her give her testimony for
the first time. She was kind enough to tell her story at various
workshops I held for New Jersey teachers after my school had been
named a Holocaust Demonstration Site. In her gentle voice, Leah
told of being so driven with hunger in Auschwitz that when she
saw the pot with the day's soup ration being carried by, she

grabbed her small pail and scooped out a pitiful portion of the noxious liquid. This defiance of the rules earned her a daylong sentence of kneeling in the sun on gravel without being permitted to move or bend over. By the end of the seeming eternity of holding this painful position, her knees had been ground to bloody cuts and her back was a spasm of agony. But the remembrance that affected audiences most deeply and illustrated the lengths to which hunger could transform a person was the story of how, while in Plaszow, she and her two sisters, desperately worried about the emaciated condition of their fourth little sister, ate only two of their three daily portions of bread and hid the remaining piece, saving it for their youngest sibling. One day they discovered that the hiding place of their hoarded single piece of bread had been raided, and the precious food they hoped would save their little sister had been taken. Their anger and anguish turned to compassion when they encountered another girl in the barracks sobbing, according to Leah, as if she had lost the most expensive diamond in the world. She was crying, she confessed, because she was starving and had stolen their sister's piece of bread, the little sister who would soon be sent to the gas. The girl's remorse and Leah's compassion for this pathetic creature, driven to stealing molding bread from her bunkmates by an all-consuming hunger they both shared, spoke volumes about the humanity of each.

A Seminal Experience: The Vladka Meed Program— Traveling and Studying In Europe and Israel

But a piece was still missing in my encounter with the Holocaust—a void that could be filled by nothing less than an actual confrontation with the sites. In the early 1990s, I became aware of Vladka Meed's Teachers' Summer Fellowship program on the Holocaust and Jewish resistance sponsored by the Jewish Labor Committee, the American Gathering of Holocaust Survivors, and the American Federation of Teachers. Grateful to be accepted from among hundreds of applicants throughout the country, I packed my bag, joined the 45 other participants in New York, and embarked on a grueling three and one-half week odyssey that signaled the beginning of my formal Holocaust training and changed my life forever. The unique journey orchestrated by Vladka, a survivor who had been a courier for the resistance in the Warsaw ghetto, began with a face-to-face encounter with the death camps of Poland.

Vladka Meed is a smartly dressed, delicate-looking woman with a will of iron. After being in her company for only a very short time, it became obvious that there was one way to do things—and that was Vladka's way. Even at this stage of her life, removed from the Holocaust by 50 years, it was easy to observe in her the courage, intelligence, determination, and *chutzpah* that had qualified her, and served her well, as a courier for the resistance in the Warsaw ghetto. Marshaling a group of 45 teachers around Poland and Israel, many of whom had independent agendas or ideas, also required determination and *chutzpah*, and Vladka was up to the task. When she told us in her ladylike voice to listen, we listened. When she told us to be quiet, 45 adults followed her petite figure in silence like schoolchildren. Truth be told, we would have followed her to the ends of the earth had she requested it, our admiration for her was so great. When she told us to sing on the bus, we sang.

My most vivid memory of Vladka came near the end of the trip, as we approached the conclusion of our stay at Lohamei Haghettaot, the Ghetto Fighters' House in the northern Galilee. Vladka took the podium at the front of the room where, for a week, we had listened to lectures by survivors and resistance fighters and had taken part in teacher workshop sessions. I thought I was prepared for Vladka's testimony as we had heard many bits and pieces of her story, and of course, I had read her memoir, *On Both Sides of the Wall*. I was wrong. This tiny little woman, whose voice could barely be heard when she made an announcement on the bus, was transformed into a formidable speaker when she told the story of the Jews in the Warsaw ghetto.

Her testimony was a primer on physical and spiritual resistance. She told us she had been 16 when the Germans occupied Poland and her father became a broken man. Starvation, she related, began the first week in the ghetto, and many children became smugglers of food because of their diminutive size. Vladka's father died of pneumonia, but in a show of spiritual resistance, her mother continued to prepare her younger brother for his Bar Mitzvah. I was riveted as she described her beloved mother, her voice shaking in her rolling Polish accent, "I can see her now before mine eyes, her face all swollen from hunger. In America we are so worried about what we eat, about gaining too much weight."

She continued by saying that despite their food deprivation, her mother, out of respect, saved the best morsel of bread for the rabbi who secretly came to their home to give her brother Hebrew lessons.

Along with her tales of being a courier and a smuggler due to her ability to "pass" as Aryan "on the outside," Vladka told us she believed that the absence of research on the lives of Jews as a people and individuals hindered the understanding of resistance. She declared,

You can't have resistance unless you are raised with values and beliefs. The life of the Jews equals resistance, which took many forms: cultural activities, dealing with hunger, helping a neighbor, keeping your house clean, transferring knowledge to the young in secret schools—not only shooting a gun. Physical resistance in the ghetto was not justified because our aim was to survive.

Vladka's words, more than any scholarly history of resistance I had read, concretely delineated that in the face of the greatest deprivation, the Jews did not go like sheep to the slaughter. I now understood that the starving and weary Warsaw ghetto resistance members, splintered into 22 groups that constructed shelters, underground bunkers, and even tunnels leading to the Gentile portion of the city, couldn't have accomplished these small miracles unless they were fighting *for* something beyond mere physical existence. For them, to survive without their culture was no survival at all. Vladka's dedication to educating teachers not only about the Holocaust, but also the ideology of the resistance of the Jews, is a labor of love and determination.

It is impossible to overestimate the impact of my visit to Auschwitz, Majdanek, and Treblinka on my personal attempts to fathom the meaning of the Holocaust and, ultimately, on my teaching. Scorched like an immutable brand on my psyche is the sensation that seeped through me as we approached Auschwitz, a tangible feeling of anticipation descending, shroudlike, over every individual on the bus. Colleagues who only a moment earlier had been joking or even napping became subdued, but alert, in heightened expectation. I myself strained, as we rode through the bucolic Polish countryside, for a glimpse of the physical manifestation of evil that awaited. Auschwitz I today exists primarily as a museum, but the horror is there in the mounds of hundreds of thousands of pairs of shoes, combs, eyeglasses, suitcases, prostheses, human hair, and children's toys taken from the victims by the Nazis. These personal items, each a most intimate documentation of a human life that was eclipsed, are displayed in what were originally Polish (and later, German) army buildings that were not destroyed—as were the barracks, showers, and crematoria—at the approach of the Allies. I remember a surreal aura overtaking me, as if my conscious self had disengaged from my being and hovered overhead recording, automatonlike, as my physical body absorbed the impact of the place that has become synonymous with the Holocaust. Seeing Auschwitz I and the killing center at Birkenau was a watershed for me. The immediacy of tangible contact with the place I had been reading and studying about for so long was a visceral experience equaled only by the mental challenge of processing the reality that nearly two million people had been cold-bloodedly killed on this site strictly for the "crime" of being born Jewish. And I was suffused with a feeling of thanks to Vladka, who, by the collegial structure of her seminar, had ensured that I would no longer be performing my efforts in a void; I had been gifted with professional and personal colleagues with whom to process the experience of the trip and from whom to garner support, ideas, and encouragement about transmitting the lessons learned to students.

I felt an almost instant bond with a handful of knowledgeable and committed Pennsylvania and New Jersey teachers on the trip. As the days progressed, we found ourselves gravitating toward one another, discussing what we had seen and heard, bemoaning the fact that we felt on sensory overload. We had experienced so many meaningful historical sights—not just the camps, but Rapaport's Warsaw ghetto monument, the remains of the ghetto wall, the *Umschlagplatz* (departure site of trains to Treblinka), the demolished Jewish cemetery, and Mila 18 (the headquarters of the Jewish Fighting Organization in the Warsaw ghetto where Mordecai Anielewicz, leader of the resistance, perished)—that we often had little or no time to process it all. The same was true of the brilliant lectures we heard, one after another.

Our group's camaraderie grew as we pondered and debated issues such as the cognitive readiness of students to study the Holocaust. On our flight from Warsaw to Tel Aviv we would encounter a group of American high school students on a tour of the camps. We were shocked when they characterized Treblinka, which had affected us so powerfully with its abstract symbolism, as "boring" with "nothing to see." We relied on one another's wisdom and experience as we thought through the pedagogical processes of how best to present this material to students in a pedagogically sound, developmentally-appropriate way and their ability to accept and understand abstractions.

I am happy to say that several of these companions are today some of my dearest friends and Holocaust colleagues. As a result of my association with the Philadelphia contingent, I was asked to join the Holocaust Education Task Force of Pennsylvania—a group of educators, chaired by Elaine Culbertson, whose objective is to bring the lessons of the Holocaust to Pennsylvania schools. I work with them to this day, as well as with several New Jersey teachers

who serve as consultants to the New Jersey Commission on Holocaust Education. We represent the commission by speaking at
workshops and conferences as well as by taking part in other
projects. Our most recent efforts have been devoted to revising and
updating the New Jersey Holocaust and Genocide Curriculum for
grades 7–12.

The three death camps spoke to me in different ways. Auschwitz
humbled me with the knowledge that a paradigm for evil of this
magnitude really did exist. The famous inscription, *Arbeit macht
frei* (Work makes freedom), over the main entrance to Auschwitz I
appeared smaller than I had imagined it from pictures I had seen.
But I think at this point I was curiously anesthetized to what it
all meant—the personal belongings in the museum displays, the
barracks, the gas chambers—until my gaze found a name written
in whitewash on the side of a battered suitcase, a simple name and
address, a name in my mind that I multiplied by two million.

As for Majdanek, the actual proof was there: the most intact
former death camp, according to many historians. There we witnessed row after row of barracks containing huge bins with only
a portion of the 800,000 pairs of shoes discovered by the Allies at
liberation; the sheer number and diversity of shoes in style and
size was an awful assault and no less so was the suffocating heat
within the barracks.

Treblinka is located in the forest countryside approximately two
and one-half hours from Warsaw. Nothing remains of the death
camp today but grassy fields full of delicate little flowers. Here, in
the form of 17,000 stone markers jutting defiantly skyward, representing the Jewish communities that had been destroyed, was
tangible evidence that Hitler had very nearly succeeded in his mission of eradicating Polish Jewry. The day of our visit was extremely
hot, and fat flies hovered annoyingly around our heads as we said
Kaddish in Hebrew and English and lit memorial candles. Farther
along we came upon the site of what had been a cremation pit—
now a strange, large rectangular monument flush with the ground,
containing the remains of human bones and ash. This symbol of
murder and destruction, funereally black and stretching pool-like
in front of us, stood in jarring juxtaposition to the beautiful meadow
filled with wildflowers in which it resided. I was soon overcome with
the sickening awareness that the lushness of the growth was the
result of human fertilizer.

Upon leaving Treblinka, our group was detained for a short time
in the parking lot waiting for our bus. Today even former death
camps have parking lots. A handsome Polish family parked their
station wagon, kids and parents clambering out, attired in shorts

and tank tops. The father opened the rear door and out hopped a fluffy little dog that he immediately leashed and took for a bathroom break along the "road to heaven," the path on which the Jewish victims had marched to their deaths after disembarking from the cattle cars that had brought them to Treblinka. I was dumbfounded by this lack of sensitivity blatantly displayed at a memorial to 800,000 murdered Polish Jews. If there was ever a signal that education about the Holocaust was needed, this was it.

Numbed, I headed for Israel, flagellating myself with the ubiquitous questions: How could a genocide of this nature have occurred in the middle of the twentieth century in the heart of Christendom? How could human beings—Christian human beings—whose religious practices were governed by the tenet to "love thy neighbor," have hated "others" so much that they murdered millions of them? Feeling ineffable shame in the name of my Christian brethren who had perpetrated this act or who had stood idly by while it occurred, I conceded that despite my best efforts, I had known nothing of the Holocaust until I had lain my foot on the cemetery that was Polish soil, until I had smelled the death-soaked timbers that were Majdanek and Auschwitz, until I had gazed upon the Vistula River, imagining it as it had once run with rivers of Jewish blood. But despite my reeling sensibilities, despite my inexpressible feelings of shame and disgust, I stubbornly refused to relinquish the naive belief that by continuing to immerse myself in the study and scholarship of the Holocaust I could somehow come to understand it.

Emotionally limp from pondering the grim experience in Poland, I arrived in Jerusalem, site of the confluence of the three great monotheistic religions of the world, my head swirling with questions and uncertainties about belief in God, memorials, symbols, and how they all related to the Holocaust. I marveled at the ability of the Jewish community to establish continuity from the great synagogue in Poland to the historical, interwoven identity of Jews, Christians, and Muslims in Jerusalem. Also, the resistance or defiance of the Jews that arose even when hope was nearly lost— where had it come from? Continuity of community seems the most reasonable answer to what sustained them, because many ultimately lost their faith in God.

During the three weeks spent absorbing the culture of Israel at both Yad Vashem, Israel's major center for Holocaust study in Jerusalem, and Lohamei Haghettaot, the Ghetto Fighters' House in northern Israel, the centerpiece of our efforts was a rigorous course of study under the tutelage of some of the preeminent Holocaust scholars in the world, giants in the field whose seminal works have exerted a profound influence upon the whole of Holocaust scholarship. I reveled in the opportunity to interact with academicians of the stature of Raul Hilberg, Yehuda Bauer, Yisrael Gutman, and Martin Gilbert.

Professor Bauer, a renowned Israeli historian, argued that the Holocaust as an historical and human event is unique in terms of the murderers' motivation: a mission to rescue Germany, Europe, and the world from their supreme enemy, the Jews. He stated that in his mind the event that most closely parallels the Holocaust was the Armenian genocide by the Turks; yet, in its attempts to exterminate all Jews everywhere, he said he believes the Holocaust stands alone.

During another lecture, Bauer spoke on the *Judenrat* and life in the ghetto. The phrase "choiceless choices" seems the only applicable way to describe the situation wherein Jewish ghetto leaders were forced to deal with their occupying Nazi tormentors. He disagrees with Raul Hilberg's contention that all *Judenrati* were collaborators with the enemy. I was more swayed by Bauer's argument and moved to ponder his queries: Do you sacrifice yourself to save others? and Can you play God?

At the end of our seminars at Yad Vashem I remember writing on an evaluation sheet, "Can we clone this man's brain?"

Sir Martin Gilbert was introduced by Vladka as "our greatest living factual historian of the Holocaust." The official biographer of Churchill, recently knighted by the queen in his native England and just returned from Chechnya with refugees of the war in Bosnia, he highlighted the fact that the Shoah had continued for more than 2,000 days uninterrupted. Its length, he explained, enabled every element of protest to be bipartisan; in its absence, there was sufficient time to do whatever the Nazis wanted. He also called attention to the scientific element of the Holocaust. It didn't require large numbers of people to run a death camp, but it did require a great deal of support from the bureaucracy, clerks who recorded railway timetables, kept records, and so forth, the so-called "desk murderers" like Eichmann who would later claim they were only following orders and knew nothing of the end result.

In addition to the vital and enriching nature of these seminars, the highlight of my sojourn in Israel emerged from the opportunity to meet and hear the testimony of several survivors now living there. Among the many whose testimonies I was privileged to hear were Dov Freiberg, a survivor of the escape from the death camp Sobibor; Sima Skurkowitz, a survivor from Vilnius, Lithuania, whose attempts to preserve the heritage of the Holocaust include bringing to the public Yiddish folk songs and songs of the ghetto, which were written during the cruel days of oppression by Hitler; and Hannah Pick Goslar, a childhood friend and schoolmate of Anne Frank who was reunited with her prior to her death during the waning days of the war in Bergen-Belsen.

The testimonies of these survivors was so intimate, so private, so traumatic that some of them had to undergo special training with a psychotherapist in order to be able to tell their stories to an audience. Dov Freiberg says people might wonder why survivors want to keep talking about the "bad things," but he maintains he has an obligation to tell us, and we, as teachers, have an obligation to tell the children about the Holocaust. He felt that even that was not enough, so on weekends and holidays he wrote a book about his experiences in Sobibor, including his participation in the successful escape from the death camp. Dov said that, initially, he was afraid he would not be able to remember details to write his book, but when he wrote at night after work, the details came back to him so clearly that he was afraid that if he reached out to touch his mental picture he would be transported back to that time.

It is difficult to describe the profound effect Dov's words had on me. A soft-spoken, self-effacing, huggable looking grandfather, the retelling of his experiences in Sobibor was galvanizing both for its content as well as his unembellished, powerful narration.

Upon Arrival: Where are we? What kind of place is this? It looks too wonderful—Germans giving new clothes to children? [Kids' clothes confiscated by Nazis as they were sent to "showers."]

After One Week: We know we are in a place [that is at] the end of the world. People come in—no one goes out. The Germans have built a machine to kill people quickly; the machine was working 24 hours a day. The Germans—they think of all things.

About Torture: The Nazis made us act like a dog on all fours. I have no place on my body that was not beaten. I was bitten by a dog twice. They tried to put it between my legs, but I fought it: there is a big bite [mark] on my leg.

About Suicide: I was alone. In such a situation it was the worst thing in the world. I felt something on my face. I looked up and saw someone who had cut his hand [makes motion of slashing wrist], and the blood was spurting out.

I contemplated suicide. Then I had a dream about my mother. She gave me orders: "Stay here; it's good for you." After that I no more think about making suicide.

About Hope: We said we would never go to the gas chambers. Three times we tried to organize an escape, and three times we failed. I built myself an illusion; my illusion is one day I will get out of this camp. I secreted money. I learned to use a rifle when I worked for the Ukrainians so I would know how to do these things.

About Revolt: All the officers had been killed. They were the biggest murderers in the world; it was the greatest feeling in the world. Nobody of us had the chutzpah to be alive and run in a minefield. You didn't think about it; it was luck. I crossed the fence, the channel, the minefield, and ran to the forest. It was a wonderful sight. In the revolt we killed fifteen guards. Three hundred people ran away into the forest.

 For ten months I lived in the forest. I fought for survival. For awhile I was with a group of robbers. Thirty-six of us survived the war.

About Survival: In the forest you are a free man. You are like another animal. In Sobibor you are a dead man. When running away, all I could think was "Nobody will die in the gas chambers today."

Hannah Pick Goslar's testimony was delivered outside in the powerful setting of the Valley of the Communities. This area of Yad Vashem is landscaped as a map of Europe where 15,000 to 20,000 communities were affected by the Holocaust. Walls of enormous, rough-hewn boulders of Jerusalem stone create a series of canyons, each representing a region of Nazi Europe, the names of 6,000 destroyed communities inscribed in the stone monoliths. Under "Amsterdam" stood Hannah. She told of knowing Anne Frank before the war, of going to school and playing with her, and of Anne being what she called a "spicy" girl. She related that her mother always described Anne by saying, "God knows everything; Anne Frank knows everything better!"

I had seen Hannah in the film *Anne Frank Remembered* and felt a sense of familiarity with this handsome lady in the red dress and black hat who so willingly cast attention away from herself and spoke of her more famous counterpart. In her telling of her pitiful reunion with Anne during the waning days of the war in the hellhole of Bergen-Belsen, Hannah said that she knew that the "spicy" Anne had lost hope, which was evident by the blankness of her face, a condition referred to by many survivors as becoming a "*musselman*."

Hannah graciously agreed to pose in a photo of the two of us so that I could return to my class with a photo of one of the last surviving persons who knew Anne Frank.

All of the survivors' testimonies were heartfelt, wrenching, and shockingly immediate; each told a story that reverberated with first-person insight—a tale that no history book could tell—a story that, in addition to providing critical eyewitness information, granted credence to my personal ideology that more meaning could be garnered from the Holocaust through literature, both oral and written, than through mere history alone. Their stories concretely attested to the historical chronology of the Holocaust, the ideology of the perpetrators, the motivations of both bystanders and rescuers, and the experiences and responses of the victims; they tangibly demonstrated the difference between teaching *Anne Frank* and teaching the Holocaust.

It was during these emotional exchanges with survivors at Yad Vashem that I became interested in the topic of how survivors "survive survival." This was initially piqued when I had the opportunity to hear the testimony of Ruth Brand, an Auschwitz survivor. Her story of imprisonment at the hands of the Nazis, replete with horrific details of camp experiences, was stunning, but even more revealing were the comments to her from inmates when she arrived at Auschwitz: "Don't you see the chimneys with flames splashing out of them? They are burning your families now. From here, you only go out of the chimneys in smoke." Even in the face of that negativism, she did not abandon hope.

About Transport: We were walked to the train station to the cattle car. We were thrown in not like cattle with dignity, but like garbage. There was a pail for a toilet. In this car, people starved of hunger or thirst, gave birth, and died. We stopped in the middle of the night and saw Birkenau/Auschwitz; we were thrown out. We did not know where we were or what was happening, but we were aware of an unbelievable stench.

About Processing: We were told to undress. We refused. There were shootings, beatings, dogs. We undressed. They shaved the hair from every part of our body. They made us take a cold shower, and all our belongings were taken. When I hear people say, "I have nothing," I think you don't know what it means to have nothing—like when you were born—including your hair.

About Survival: How did I survive? Some sat down and died; some went to the electrified fence and finished it. I contemplated suicide. After I came out of the hospital, a girl gave me one glove. It was winter and cold, and another gave me a strip of rag for a scarf. There is humanity left, I thought, and I decided not to end it. We were left alive for a purpose: I will live and I will tell.

Ruth ended with a provocative anecdote. Upon arrival in Israel after liberation, she had assumed the business of dressmaking—wedding dresses in particular—and gave special consideration to young women who were otherwise financially unable to afford the requisite bridal gown for their marriage day. A client's mother, responding to Ruth's obvious delight in her *mitzvah* of making brides happy, asserted that she found it impossible to believe that the seamstress was a survivor. When Ruth asked why, the woman responded that she appeared far too happy and content to fit that role; she didn't appear to be sad at all. Ruth replied with her own question, "Why should I be sad when I'm alive?" She continued by explaining that even though every other member of her family perished, she believes that God spared her for a reason. "I made God as a partner, and I told Him, 'If I survive, I will tell.' If God wants us to live, they [the Germans] can throw us in fire and we will walk out alive." She further elaborated that despite a lifetime of mourning her lost loved ones, she felt she had achieved a victory over Hitler and the Nazi regime by rebuilding her life in Israel, making a family, and enabling others to commence their new lives on a note of happiness. She would not wear sackcloth and ashes.

Humbled by Ruth's recitation, I immediately questioned whether I, in the same circumstances, could summon the strength to adopt a similar positive dedication to making good come from something so evil. Intriguing to me was that several of my fellow audience members saw Ruth's declaration differently. They were highly offended by her unwavering insistence that she had been spared by God for a special purpose. One gentleman, a practicing Jew, took particular umbrage to her assertion and demanded, "Who does she think she is that God would spare her and allow a million and one-half innocent children to die?" I was stunned by the ferocity of their discomfort toward what I considered a rationalization that enabled her to "survive her survival." It was at that precise moment that the epiphany occurred: I had been teaching for years the words of survivors in an effort to get kids to achieve an understanding of the Holocaust, yet as a direct result of the unique learning scenario in which I now found myself, it became suddenly clear that regardless of the contextual framework in which Ruth (or any survivor) chose to couch her/his experiences and beliefs about the reasons for her/his survival, we would have been at a loss to comprehend. How could I best utilize personal testimony and memoir in the classroom to transmit the reality of the Holocaust—the culmination of which had occurred at the camps I had just visited—while assuring that survivors who ripped open the wounds in their souls and psyches to tell us what they had endured would be more than merely listened to—they would be understood?

I humbly submit that no one of us can ever truly "know" or "understand" what a survivor has endured; how, then, can we begin to empathize with the Holocaust experience if we cannot pierce the armor of misconceptions, uncertainties, and misinterpretations so often ascribed to survivor testimonies? A total realignment of the pedagogy I had employed for so many years in teaching about the Holocaust would not be arrived at blithely or easily. The individual whom I credit for singularly inspiring and motivating me as I traversed these choppy waters is Holocaust scholar Lawrence L. Langer, Professor Emeritus of English at Simmons College, who has made invaluable contributions to the field of Holocaust literature via the numerous books and articles of literary criticism he has authored and the seminal research he has conducted on survivor testimonies. In addition to benefiting from his publications, I was privileged to be his student during an exhilarating monthlong Summer Seminar for Teachers on the literature of the Holocaust, sponsored by the National Endowment for the Humanities, in which I was the beneficiary not only of his stunning intellect, but also his perspicacious insight into the spoken word of the survivor, which aimed at dispelling the romanticized theses that populate Holocaust pedagogy and so often skew the understanding of observers. These include, but are not limited to, the erroneous expectation that liberation from the Nazis granted victims a life sentence of unfettered joy; the manufactured idea of fate versus random circumstance; the day-to-day effect of durational memory; the limits of memory's ability to recreate the past; the notion of heroic behavior and the usage of labels of Christian martyrology; and most critically, the role of language in the presentation of both oral and literary Holocaust testimony. (For a more detailed discussion of such issues, see the following works by Langer: *Preempting the Holocaust*, *Admitting the Holocaust*, *Holocaust Testimonies: The Ruins of Memory*, and *Versions of Survival*.

In researching survivors' stories compiled by the Fortunoff Video Archive for Holocaust Testimonies at Yale University, Langer commented that the survivors are desperate to make us understand that their survival was not a matter of moral strength, but of blind chance. This is a difficult concept for the uninitiated to accept because it goes against what Langer calls "one of the deepest instincts in the civilized mind: the need to establish a principle of causality in human experience." (Langer, 1982, p. ix) Apparently, Ruth Brand seeks to find such a cause for her survival; yet many who hear her testimony are unable to deal with her belief that she was spared for a purpose, because her fate corresponds to no sensible format with which we are familiar.

Professor Langer made clear to me that the crucial issue in survivor testimony is language, and its usage presents a problem for survivors in telling their stories because language relies on the memory of traditional historical behaviors and expectations. In "real" life, we assign a common meaning to words such as cold or mud or hunger; we know these words to mean certain things because we have experienced them and they are filed in our memory banks. These same words possess entirely different, concrete, memory-specific definitions for survivors that are impossible for outsiders to ever understand. The mud at Auschwitz is not the annoying layer of wet dirt that clings to our shoes on a rainy day, dries, and breaks off in clumps to be swept away. It is the cloying, ever-present, calf-deep mire that surrounded the barracks and buildings of Auschwitz, exacerbated by the marshlike terrain and the foggy, moist Polish climate; muck that had to be negotiated in all weather; mud that sucked out the energy of victims who attempted to perform slave labor in its morass; mud that was the slimy, viscous remains of a landscape that had once supported the life of growing things but was now barren because the starving inmates had eaten the grass that had grown there. This is a meaning that only survivors know.

The issue of durational memory is explored in two of Langer's (1991 and 1998, respectively) books, *Holocaust Testimonies: The Ruins of Memory* and *Preempting the Holocaust*. In each, he discusses the testimony of Bessie K., who relates that on her way to the cattle trains, in a state of emotional paralysis induced by shock, she relinquished the bundle that in actuality was her baby when commanded to do so by a German. Bessie K. subsequently survived the Holocaust, came to America, remarried, had a family, and appeared to be living a fulfilling and satisfying life surrounded by family members. But as she sits on the couch with her husband during the interview with her children nearby, she summarizes her entire life by saying, "I think all my life I been [sic] alone." (Langer, 1991, p. 49) Even though she has created a new family, her physical survival is inextricably characterized by the death of her first child, an event to be endured her entire life. Langer calls this ". . . a consequence of atrocity that surfaces in numerous survivor testimonies—the condition of having missed one's intended destiny by surviving one's death. The death instant of her child is her own death instant, too, not in fantasy but in reality, a permanent intrusion on her post-Holocaust existence." (Langer, 1998, pp. 72–73) She has survived—yes—and on the surface appears to have achieved everything required for a complete and happy life, but as the audience, we must struggle to accept the reality that this fact alone does not liberate her from surviving the remainder of her life haunted by the suffering of this durational moment. "The difference between living and surviving," Langer informs us, "is living opens out into the future, governed by the expectation of fulfillment; survival draws its energy from the past, and is burdened by the unforgettable memories that offer little relief to the individual simply because he has survived them." (Langer, 1982, p.12)

Awareness of these issues alerted me to the fact that, as post-Holocaust readers of Anne Frank, we possess advance knowledge of Anne's horrific demise, information the young writer did not have. We are spared gruesome details of incarceration, transport, and life in a death camp, the absence of which no doubt contributes to the universality and palatable nature of her diary.

Elie Wiesel, however, provides us with a vivid delineation of the horror of these later experiences, information crucial in communicating to the listener or reader the role that such detailed knowledge plays in our easy acceptance of Anne's testimony. For example, in his exquisite and powerful memoir, *Night* (1969), Wiesel describes his nightmarish arrival at Auschwitz:

Never shall I forget that night, the first night in camp which has turned my life into one long night, seven times cursed and seven times sealed. Never shall I forget that smoke. Never shall I forget the little faces of the children, whose bodies I saw turned into wreaths of smoke beneath a silent blue sky. Never shall I forget those flames which consumed my faith forever. (p. 9)

And at Buchenwald, after leaving his ill father, who had collapsed outside during an air raid alert, he speaks to the depths of his personal loss:

I awoke on January 29 at dawn. In my father's place lay another invalid. They must have taken him away before dawn and carried him to the crematory. He may still have been breathing.

There were no prayers at his grave. No candles were lit to his memory. His last word was my name. A summons, to which I did not respond.

I did not weep, and it pained me that I could not weep. But I had no more tears. And in the depths of my being, in the recesses of my weakened conscience, could I have searched it, I might perhaps have found something like—free at last! (pp. 123–124)

I needed to enable privileged, nonminority students to see that there is no equation between the vicissitudes of our daily lives, no matter how grotesque we consider them, and being forced to pull the bodies of loved ones from the gas chambers. The bottom line of the challenge issued to me unknowingly by Ruth that day at Yad Vashem—a challenge I saw as the motivating core of my involvement with the Holocaust—was not merely how I could prepare my students to hear Holocaust testimony, but how I could make them active, intelligent, responsive listeners.

FOUNDING A HOLOCAUST DEMONSTRATION SITE

The years following my first trip to Eastern Europe and Israel were a nonstop blur of Holocaust-related activity. Whereas I had previously been spurred on by personal interest and the inquiries and responses of my students, I now found myself propelled, in the wake of a sudden interest in Holocaust education across the country, by the need to inform those educators who would be presenting this sensitive material to students. Pursuant to a grant I secured from the New Jersey Commission on Holocaust Education, my school was designated a Holocaust Demonstration Site. As director of this site, I opened my classroom for visitation to educators who wished to observe middle school Holocaust education in practice. I organized and hosted workshops, bringing together survivors, liberators, historians, authors, and members of the second generation to share their unique experiences and insights with teachers and administrators from southern New Jersey who desired to get their own Holocaust education programs up and running.

At one such workshop, William Zimmerspitz, who survived five years in Plaszow, Auschwitz, Oranienburg/Sachsenhausen, and Mauthausen, told the group of approximately 90 local educators how his adolescence had been terminated at age 13 when German soldiers liquidated the Jewish ghetto in Kraków where he and his family had been forced to live.

Of a roundup in which children were torn from their families, he said, "I can still hear the cries of those mothers in my ears. They were so loud they must have reached all the way up to the heavens." When his aunt refused to let her children be snatched away from her, she was shot to death in front of him, along with the baby in her arms.

William survived because he was young, strong, and brash, yet it is almost impossible today to imagine this highly intelligent, courtly, impeccably dressed gentleman living through the camps' indignities he described, including a death march out of Auschwitz to Germany.

It is hard for me and other survivors to talk about our experiences. . . . The hardest thing for us to understand was how these cultured people, well-educated Germans, could sink so low as to murder so many people. . . . There was no humanity. It is very important to let people know that whenever they see injustice or discrimination, they must speak out. They must not tolerate it.

At another workshop, Floyd Cochran, former director of propaganda for the Aryan Nations Church in Hayden Lake, Idaho, mesmerized his listeners with his narrative of being a recruiter and proselytizer for hate until 1992. Cochran told the audience of teachers what it was like to grow up a "hater," and about the process by which he became a member of the organized white supremacist movement in the United States. "I wasn't a member of a sports team. I wasn't a member of the band. I wasn't a member of the honor roll, but I was a white supremacist. That gave me some notoriety at high school; it gave me a sense of self-esteem." He told of racist recruiters' reliance on the seductive elements of belonging—music, flags, symbols, uniforms, and responsibility—to entice young people in the early stages of personal development into their fold.

That which caused Floyd Cochran to turn his back on 15 years in the racist movement is telling. When his first son was born with a cleft palate, he was told by his white supremacist colleagues that the child would have to be euthanized because he was a genetic defect. "I couldn't reconcile how, on the one hand, it was wrong to advocate killing my son, who had bothered nobody in life, and how it was all right for me to advocate killing people different than myself. So I left the Aryan Nations."

Cochran acknowledged that his departure from espousing racism and bigotry is a work in progress, and in an attempt to atone for the hatred, he spends his life on the road, lecturing young people, educators, church groups, and the military on the legitimate threat to our youth from white supremacist members whom he says are today more articulate than in the past, growing in strength, and appealing primarily to the 14–24 age bracket. Cochran's message was clear: As educators, we must be aware that racist ideas can influence a young person's perception of personal and cultural identity.

During this same period I also answered the call to speak at numerous colleges, universities, and religious and civic venues, including the American Society for Yad Vashem in New York, the New Jersey Human Rights Committee, the Annual Curriculum Conference for the Pennsylvania Department of Education, the Educational Media Association of New Jersey, the New Jersey Library Association Annual Conference, the National Alumni Conference of the Teachers' Fellowship Program on the Holocaust and Jewish Resistance in Washington, D.C., and others.

In addition to being awarded the Chapter of Four Chaplains Legion of Honor Membership for "service to all people regardless of race or faith" and the Anti-Defamation League Honey and Maurice Axelrod Pedagogical Award, I was invited by then-U.S. Secretary of Education Richard W. Riley to attend a three-day National Teacher Forum in Washington, D.C.

But my proudest moment was sharing the *bimah* (pulpit) at a Yom Hashoah observance in Cherry Hill, New Jersey, with Jan Karski, the Polish Gentile who took extraordinary risks to witness the horrors of the Warsaw Ghetto and warned the West in 1942 of Hitler's plans for the Jews.

In addition, I drove hundreds of miles to present in-service workshops to school faculties in New Jersey and in nearby states. I modeled lessons on using Holocaust literature in the classroom, shared my experiences teaching this subject to adolescents, dispensed Holocaust education materials, and served as a general resource to those scrambling to fulfill the 1994 New Jersey mandate for Holocaust education in the state's public schools.

Becoming a Mandel Fellow at the United States Holocaust Memorial Museum

The aforementioned activities were exhausting work, and despite the fact that I continued to teach full-time, I took advantage of the advanced learning opportunities on the Holocaust beginning to proliferate in this country—opportunities I had so longed for in the 1970s. Unsupported by an organization or university, I took sick days from work and attended conference after conference at my own expense, determined to plumb every learning avenue that had opened. Each summer was occupied by attendance at seminars and fellowships, the highlight of which was being named a Mandel Fellow by the United States Holocaust Memorial Museum (USHMM) in Washington, D.C.

The purpose of the Mandel Teacher Fellowship program is to develop a national corps of skilled teachers who can serve as leaders in Holocaust education in their schools, communities, and professional organizations. Up to 25 educators from grades 8 to 12 are designated yearly as Mandel Fellows, based upon their extensive knowledge of Holocaust history, successful teaching experience, and participation in community and professional organizations. The Mandel Teacher Fellowship program was held in Washington, D.C., at the United States Holocaust Memorial Museum and was designed to immerse the participants in advanced historical and pedagogical issues.

The intense, five-day program was composed of diverse elements: a private tour of the museum's permanent exhibition; a fascinating architectural tour of the museum; the presentation and sharing of presubmitted Holocaust lessons and book reviews with the group; lectures from in-house experts on various historical as well as photographic and technological tools for teaching the Holocaust; a presentation from Daniel Gaede, the director of education at the Buchenwald concentration camp, on his perspectives on Holocaust education in Germany; a tour of the photo history and oral history archives; a lecture by scholar David Crowe on the plight of non-Jewish victims in the Holocaust; a demonstration by the collections archivists of the techniques used in acquiring, storing, refurbishing, and rotating the historical artifacts in the permanent exhibit; testimonies from survivors; and open-ended discussions on pedagogical issues and instructional questions.

Following the summer program, fellows are required to create and implement an outreach project that will impact their sphere of influence. In the spring of the following year they return for a follow-up program at the USHMM to assess their various efforts and to continue their study of the Holocaust with museum staff and noted speakers.

My outreach project involved formulating a database of schools in Camden County, New Jersey, that reflected the current status of Holocaust education in my area of the state. I contacted every school in the county by questionnaire, and by collating names of teachers who taught the Holocaust, grade level taught, subject in which taught, length of unit, title of class, length of class, approximate number of students per class, and materials utilized, my objective was to create a resource for all teachers in my county to help facilitate the mandate for Holocaust and genocide education.

My Involvement with the National Consortium of Yad Vashem Graduates

As a member of a National Consortium of Yad Vashem Graduates headed by Dr. Karen Shawn, I meet annually with colleagues to discuss the latest in Holocaust pedagogy and to work hand in hand with representatives from Yad Vashem and the Ghetto Fighters'

Museum at Lohamei Haghettaot on preparing educational materials to be used in American classrooms.

The uniqueness of the consortium on Holocaust education lies in its departure from the usual workshop or conference format that requires attendees to assume the role of passive listeners. In this consortium all are active, hands-on participants. Each member must prepare and submit, in advance, proposals for a specific issue of concern in teaching the Holocaust, including a presentation of the problem to be discussed, the supporting materials, the questions for a work session, and an activity. It is a dream to join colleagues to remember our time of study in Jerusalem and the Galilee, to share our years of experience in learning and teaching, and to be afforded the opportunity to pick the brains of leading Holocaust educators and to critique works in progress as we discuss the pedagogical and philosophical issues raised by the teaching of the Holocaust.

Over the years, some of the original participants' proposals on which we collaborated in individual groups have been brought to fruition. One of the most notable of these is Susan Shear's *No Way Out: Letters, Laws, and Lessons of the Holocaust.* Susan, a member of the second generation, described her project in her initial proposal in the following way:

What began as my attempt at saving a few old family letters in a dusty box in my mother's basement developed into an extensive project that has taken several years to complete. In the beginning the goal was simply to preserve the story of my family's attempts at emigrating from Germany. But with the discovery of hundreds of letters and documents, the project grew into a collection of approximately 500 pieces of correspondence written to or by members of my family between 1938–1942. While working on this collection, I realized that the letters provided an invaluable resource for students and teachers. Using the letters together with Nazi laws, I developed an interactive workshop and, more recently, a unit for teachers. I am looking for help in the development, publication, and distribution of this unit.

Six years later, at the most recent meeting of the consortium, Susan, a drama teacher from Colorado, staged a Reader's Theater adaptation of her highly polished and now published teacher's guide, using consortium members as actors and audience. A "behind-the-scenes" look at the process Susan used to complete her work was presented in another session as well as the opportunity to discuss the philosophy and practicalities of designing and presenting our own Reader's Theater performances.

The impact of witnessing Susan's tribute to her family come to life in dramatic form was a highly emotional and personal one for the consortium members who had brainstormed with her. It also powerfully underscored the opportunities for interdisciplinary methods of teaching the Holocaust.

RECOGNITION

In 1996–1997 I was selected as my county's Teacher of the Year, as a finalist for New Jersey Teacher of the Year, and my students and I were filmed for a segment of the local television show *Classroom Close Up New Jersey*. In 1999 I was recognized as the New Jersey Council for the Humanities Distinguished Humanities Teacher and, once again, my classroom and I were featured in a *Hadassah Magazine* article on Holocaust education entitled "Letter from New Jersey." These acknowledgments were bestowed largely in recognition of my contributions to Holocaust education in the state, positions that afforded me a broader forum from which to exert what I viewed as my responsibility to address the imperative of Holocaust education for young people and to disseminate concrete suggestions on how such education could be most effectively implemented.

Earning a Master of Arts Degree in Holocaust and Genocide Studies

Incredibly, I found the time to enroll in the Richard Stockton College of New Jersey's Master of Arts in Holocaust and Genocide Studies program, the first degree of its kind in the nation. In the fall of 2000 I became the third graduate of this program.

The unique master of arts degree, under the direction of Dr. Marcia Sachs Littell, offered students of the Holocaust the opportunity to pursue study of topics that included the history of the Holocaust; the history of genocide; theology, philosophy and ethics of the Holocaust; the Holocaust and the American Experience; Holocaust and genocide education; the Holocaust and contemporary genocides; the psychology of genocide; Jewish history and culture in Eastern Europe; the literature of the Holocaust; the Holocaust in film; and a study seminar to the sites with the permanent faculty of the Richard Stockton College, as well as studying with such luminaries in the field as Franklin Littell, Carol Rittner, Dan Bar-On, Henry Huttenbach, Judith E. Doneson, and Michael Berenbaum. Working with bona fide experts on a day-to-day basis in seminar (as opposed to a one-shot lecture) was a stimulating and enlightening experience.

Central to the program was the contribution of Franklin H. Littell. Often referred to as "the father of Holocaust studies in America," his publication *The Crucifixion of the Jews: The Failure of Christians to Understand the Jewish Experience* was the pioneering book in the field, encouraging a generation of younger Christian theologians to examine the meaning of the Holocaust, antisemitism, the survival of the Jewish people, and a restored Israel.

In a course taught by Professor Littell on the history of genocide, he used the Holocaust as a standard to assess the mass slaughter of peoples in past ages and then to direct major study toward contemporary genocides. By taking us through a mechanism of his own design for assessing the failure of a legitimate government, he clearly presented the necessity, in the historical wake of the Holocaust and other genocides, of using an early warning system to identify and inhibit the growth and action of potentially genocidal movements.

Most stunning was the tale he shared of his personal encounter with Adolf Hitler. In the summer of 1939, the young Franklin Littell was visiting Germany with a church group. The son of the family with whom Littell was staying in Nuremberg took him to a stadium that was a political shrine for the Nazi party. Part of the adventure was climbing the outside of the stadium to "sneak in." Once inside, light from huge spotlights reflected off of bayonets, part of the "cathedral of light" created by Albert Speer, Hitler's architect during the Third Reich. The stadium was packed with hundreds of thousands of Germans. On the floor of the arena danced little girls in pastel; from their center rose the evil enemy, a Siegfried-like depiction of the Jew, to be slain by the *Volk*. All lights were extinguished. Spotlights were then dramatically directed to a podium behind which stood Hitler. The audience responded by jumping to their feet and frenziedly shouting "*Sieg Heil!*" Franklin was overwhelmed and appalled by what he called the "magnetism of the mob." He left, feeling unclean.

Shortly thereafter while discussing the political situation with other members of the trip, their Nazi guide interjected, "Will Roosevelt make war?" to which Franklin riposted, "Will Hitler make war?" The guide responded, waving to the buildings they were passing, "Oh no, we have too much to do; the *Führer* won't make war." Based on the terrifying spectacle he had witnessed at the Nazi rally, Franklin Littell, 22-years-old, countered, "There will be war in six weeks." World War II started three weeks later.

A RETURN TO EUROPE AND THE CONTINUATION OF
MY WORK IN THE FIELD OF HOLOCAUST EDUCATION

During the summer of 2000 I felt myself inexplicably drawn back to Eastern Europe for another tour of the sites. My non-Holocaust friends were appalled; for years their standing joke had been that "normal" people take a vacation to Aruba or Cancun—and Becky goes to Auschwitz. My encounter began this time with an exploration of Berlin and its World War II environs, including the Wannsee Conference House, where the decision for the "Final Solution to the Jewish Question" was announced. By its end, I had visited the remains of seven concentration and death camps in Germany (Sachsenhausen), Poland (Sobibor, Plaszow, Majdanek, Auschwitz), the Czech Republic (Terezin), and Austria (Mauthausen). Initially, my goal was not clear, but I felt the ineluctable need to see and know more. Mesmerized by seemingly endless train rides to the Nazi installations that were my destinations, I found myself responding to a common query of my students by charting mental graphs of comparisons between the characteristics of camps in different countries throughout the Reich and between death camps and concentration camps in general. Curiously, it was on such a train ride on a wet, blustery day in Austria that it became clear to me that despite the Nazi-defined nomenclature that meticulously categorized the hierarchy of the camps, despite their ostensible purposes and locations, these creations of Hitlerian ingenuity were more alike than different—ideologically, structurally, operationally, and in the relentless manufacture, by one method or another, of their ultimate product: dead Jews. I realized that during my initial visit to the camps some years earlier the assault on my sensibilities had been so great that I was rendered numb. Even though I "knew" the horrors that had occurred where I was standing, I was bereft of an adequate mechanism by which to process an understanding of the atrocity that it represented. This time my reaction was shockingly different: I was deeply, profoundly angry. Angry at the painstakingly chosen secret locations of death deep in the remotest forests of Poland; angry at the deviant efficiency that could dispatch a human being who had stepped off a train in the morning to ashes and flames by evening; angry at the site of a work camp set amidst bucolic, farmhouse-dotted hills in Austria where young men and boys, including my friend, William Zimmerspitz, were forced, in a state of near starvation, to repeatedly climb and descend the 186 stone steps carved into the quarry of Mauthausen carrying a load of granite rock on their backs; angry at the desperation that drove Dov Frieberg, long since bereft of dignity,

worldly goods, and family, to risk a bullet in the back by ventur-
ing an escape into the unknown from the Nazis who ran Sobibor;
angry at the dehumanizing and terrifying mental and physical torture visited upon my dear, kind friend, Leah Kalina, who, after
watching her family members led to the crematoria, collapsed on
a death march and awoke to life in a potato field; and angry at a
world where innocent people were condemned to humiliation, persecution, and death by the simple act of being born. Not unlike
the epiphany that consumed Helen Keller when, for the first time,
the painstaking labor of her teacher, Annie Sullivan, bore fruit and
liberated her brain with the conceptual meaning of the word
"water," the floodgates of my anger and awareness regarding the
true nature of Nazi ideology had been loosed not by the clinically
preserved buildings of the now-defunct Third Reich alone, but by
the written and oral testimonies of the survivors who bore first-
person witness to the atrocities perpetrated therein. Their stories—
those of Ruth, Dov, William, Hannah, Elie Wiesel, Leah, and yes,
Anne Frank—were the conduit that made the Holocaust real to me.
Their words had accompanied me on my journey; through their
words, I had seen and I had heard.

It is no exaggeration to say that my life has been, for a quarter
of a century, a waking/sleeping kaleidoscope of reading, teaching,
presenting, and studying about the Holocaust. From time to time,
I toy with the idea of taking a break from this work, of giving myself a reprieve both emotionally and physically, but my involvement
continues. How can one turn away when each day reports of a new
Rwanda or Kosovo emerge from some faraway country or a Matthew
Shepard-like hate crime (in which a young gay man was beaten
by two thugs, strung to a fence post in below-freezing weather, and
left to die) occurs in our own? In a perfect world, people do not
persecute and kill others as a response to difference, and respectful attitudes and value systems are instilled in children long before they climb on the bus for their first day of school; but sadly,
life does not always follow that script. I continue to teach the Holocaust because of its importance as a discrete historical event and
because I ardently believe that it is paramount for our young people
to cultivate an appreciation for and an understanding of the human
behaviors that incrementally led to this defining event in history.
I want to impart to my students the simple, yet powerful, lesson
my father taught me—to see good in others—even if the others look
different, profess different cultural creeds, or worship in a different way. While I observe my state and several other states embrace
Holocaust education at the dawn of the new millennium, I feel gratified that awareness is being directed to the value of teaching this

topic and gratified as well by my role as a "teacher of teachers," the culmination of a nascent dream that germinated in 1972 when an idealistic young woman from western Pennsylvania set foot into her first classroom with a Holocaust book in her hand.

REFERENCES

Anne Frank Remembered. (1995) 117 min., col., closed-captioned. Culver City, CA: Social Studies School Service. Videocassette.

Bitton-Jackson, Livia (1999). *I Have Lived a Thousand Years: Growing Up in the Holocaust.* New York: Simon and Schuster.

The Courage to Care. (1986) 28 min., col. and bw. Culver City, CA: Social Studies School Service. Videocassette.

Dafni, Reuven and Kleiman, Yehudit (Eds.) (1991). *Final Letters: From Victims of the Holocaust.* New York: Paragon House.

Delbo, Charlotte (1995). *Auschwitz and After.* New Haven, CT: Yale University Press.

Doneson, Judith E. (1999). "Holocaust Film Is Told in Language with Meaning." *The St. Louis Post-Dispatch,* February 7th, p. F4.

Hilberg, Raul (1985). *The Destruction of the European Jews.* New York: Holmes and Meier.

Isaacman, Clara (1984). *Clara's Story.* Philadelphia, PA: Jewish Publication Society of America.

Kitty Hart: A Return to Auschwitz. (1979). 82 min., col. Culver City, CA: Social Studies School Service. Videocassette.

Klein, Gerda Weissmann (1995). *All but My Life.* New York: Hill and Wang.

Krizkova, Marie Rut and Wilson, Paul (Eds.) (1995). *Vedem: We Are Children Just the Same, the Secret Magazine of the Boys of Terezin.* Philadelphia, PA: Jewish Publication Society of America.

Langer, Lawrence L. (1995). *Admitting the Holocaust.* New York: Oxford University Press.

———. (1991). *Holocaust Testimonies: The Ruins of Memory.* New Haven, CT: Yale University Press.

———. (1998). *Preempting the Holocaust.* New Haven, CT: Yale University Press.

———. (1982). *Versions of Survival.* Albany: State University of New York Press.

Leitner, Isabella (1978). *Isabella: From Auschwitz to Freedom* (including *Fragments of Isabella*). New York: Doubleday.

Littell, Franklin H. (1986). *The Crucifixion of the Jews: The Failure of Christians to Understand the Jewish Experience.* Macon, GA: Mercer University Press.

Meed, Vladka (1979). *On Both Sides of the Wall.* New York: Holocaust Publications.

Senesh, Hannah (1973). *Hannah Senesh: Her Life and Diary.* New York: Schocken.

Tec, Nechama (1982). *Dry Tears: The Story of A Lost Childhood*. New York: Oxford University Press.

Volavkova, Hana (Ed.) (1993). *I Never Saw Another Butterfly: Children's Drawings and Poems from Terezin Concentration Camp, 1942–1944*. New York: Schocken.

Wiesel, Elie (1969). *Night*. New York: Avon.

Yahil, Leni (1991). *The Holocaust: The Fate of European Jewry, 1932–1945*. New York: Oxford.

Chapter 2

~

Making Connections:
A Journey, A Destination

Elaine Culbertson

Popular culture tells us that we learn most of what is important by the time we leave kindergarten, and educational psychologists believe that our personalities are formed well before we ever enter school. If one's psyche can be determined even before one is born, then I was probably destined to teach about the Holocaust and to write about it long before I came into this world. Every step of the journey, whether taken by me or by those who bore me, has prepared me to do this work.

Yehoshua Sobol, an Israeli playwright, wrote that when we remember the past, we in fact imagine it, and when we imagine the future, we in fact remember it. Remembrance is actually imagination of the past. The present is the blink of the eye before remembrance becomes imagination. The present is the line at which imagination and remembrance touch and the point where they reverse positions.

I cannot remember a time when I did not know about the Holocaust, although that word did not come into my vocabulary until I was an adult. In my house we called it by a Yiddish word (*chum*) that roughly translates into "the disaster" or "the horror." It was a part of daily discussions, part of family meals, an accepted family event, that colored everything we did, everything we spoke about, and the way we approached everything in our lives. We did not even need to acknowledge that it sat as an uninvited guest at every family gathering and that most of the family decisions were predicated upon it, because it so permeated all that we were.

My parents are Holocaust survivors. My mother is the only survivor of her immediate family, and my father survived the war with
his brother, who has since passed away. My parents are concentration camp survivors who witnessed unbelievable horrors at an
impressionable age, and whose losses have haunted them all of
their lives. Though they married and came to America after the war,
raised a family, and established a successful business, not a day
has gone by that they have not thought about the events of the
war and that they have not mourned for their families and their
lost childhoods.

I know that my life has been indelibly marked by everything that
they went through. From the time of my birth I represented the
only family they had, and even my names are testament to their
need to connect and remember. I was named for my grandmothers
who never lived to see me. Though I bear the Hebrew names
Chavah (Eva) and Malkah (Mala), I was called Mamele (Little
Mother) by my mother, and my younger brother has always been
Tatele (Little Father). Whether this occurred because it was too
painful for my mother to call us by our given names, or because it
gave her comfort to call us "mother" and "father" I have never
understood, but the names persist until this day.

I was raised speaking Yiddish as my first language. Although I
was born in the States, my parents spoke Yiddish to me, and we
reserved English for the outside world. The mix of languages is even
more complex, since my parents spoke Polish to each other when
they wanted to keep things secret from me and my brother. I grew
up hearing Yiddish and responding as a child in Yiddish, and eventually as I grew older, and as school became an influence, in English. From early childhood, I was the "voice" of the family, the one
who spoke in unaccented English, who could be understood on the
telephone or at the doctor's office. I can remember being prompted
by my mother in Yiddish, translating into English for the benefit
of the listener, and then translating back into Yiddish for my parents. Many times the conversations were not ones in which a child
would ordinarily be included, but that seemed to be standard for
the events of my life. So much of what went on was about having
responsibility thrust upon me because of the events that had so
radically altered the normal chronology of childhood, both mine
and theirs.

I say this without malice, but with recognition of the differences
that my parents' experiences produced in my life. I know the value
of "getting" the native culture, whether that means the language
and its idioms, the social mores, or the cultural nuances. I know
what it means to have to explain to your parents that in America

things are done a certain way, and that it may not connect to their European sensibilities, but that is the way it is. How many hours were taken up in that debate I cannot count, and it still goes on to this day. All children of immigrant parents are aware of not fitting into their new environments, of not being like the others in their school class or neighborhood, but survivors' children are affected by more than just the cultural or language differences. Although much has been written about the second generation and our burden of being the heirs to such a ponderous legacy, those of us who lived it truly cannot escape from it. Whether we share our parents' overprotective natures in our dealings with our own children, their paranoia about the government and foreign affairs, their penchant for secrets, their resilience in the face of adversity, their need to provide for the future at the expense of the present, their depressive tendencies, or their lust for life, we are different than others of our generation, and more like each other as a result of our families' wartime experiences, no matter how disparate the circumstances of their lives before the war. It is uncanny how survivors' children can bond and understand each other instantly, even if we have been raised in cultures as different as Israel and the United States. I am always amazed at how easily I can connect with another child of a survivor, perhaps because of the unabated immediacy of our birthrights.

Much of my life has been about trying to make connections. I have tried to understand who I was without being able to know where I came from. The physical places in Poland were described to me, but they were never real, particularly because there was no visible proof and because much of the description was in the negative. My parents' comparisons of Brooklyn in the 1950s to a small town in Poland in the 1930s was all about differences, and much of this I chalked up to past and present and not how different Poland and America really were. But it was much more than the difference between small town and cosmopolitan life; it was also about being strangers in the big world of America and being filled with a longing for a place and a time to which they could never return, even if my parents were to go back to their native land. Having been forced to leave and having their families murdered had destroyed their ability to retrieve their pasts, and though they were fiercely proud to be Americans, their nostalgia for a lost life persisted. Nothing in America could equal what they had known, but neither one of them would allow anyone to say anything negative about America in their presence. The cherries here did not taste as sweet as the cherries in Poland, but America was and is the land of their golden opportunities. Americans could not appreciate what they had here; only those who had known the ravages of war could fully understand the richness of American life. In particular, my brother and I could never be grateful enough for the bounties, because we had been lucky enough never to know the deprivations. We were, to our parents, both blessed by our lives of relative ease and cursed by our ingratitude.

My appearance has always been a source of both comfort and memorial to my family. From my earliest days I can remember being told that I was the image of my mother's sister, the one who had died so tragically in Auschwitz. I had her eyes and her stature, and to my mother I was Fradel all over again, even when I was too young to understand the intricacies of envy, love, and subsequent loss that had marked their relationship. To my father, I retained the look of his mother, who had been murdered by the Nazis three days after giving birth to her sixth child in 1942. I believe that my grandmother was about 38 or 40 when she was killed. Her son, my father, was only 18. She remains in his mind a young woman, never aging, always a source of comfort to him as a child, and the most beautiful of the sisters in her family. When he talks about her, and when my mother talks about her family, they always speak as if the stories had just occurred in the near past, and not more than half a century ago.

The memories are the legacy that I have inherited. While others may have family mementos, I have stories about people but no faces to match them to, because the photos that might have linked me to their past were all destroyed. The only ones that survive are those that were sent to America by my grandmother before the war, when she was communicating with her two brothers who had ventured forth to the new world. When my mother came to America in 1949 after surviving the war, she was sponsored by those uncles whose last glimpse of her had been of a little girl in the early 1930s. They showed her the photographs they had received from their sister. In them, my grandmother is wearing a beautiful fur coat and a stylish hat. She is flanked by my mother at age five, and my aunt, age six. My grandmother looks just the way I remember my mother looking at the same age: the full face and figure, the beautiful eyes, the high cheekbones that seem to distinguish their European faces. The picture was meant to convey a sense of wealth and stability. My grandmother had married well; her husband was a good provider, and her children were beautiful. She wrote a little note in Yiddish to her brothers on the back wishing them a happy New Year. I never noticed the writing when I was a child; I was so mesmerized by the faces. They were my only proof that we had had some semblance of a normal family, that I had a grandmother even though I could not touch her. This had been a trauma for me at one point. In fact, I did not even know the word "grandmother" in English, since there had been no need to understand it in my household. It was only when my first little friend, Irene, had told me that we could not play together on a particular Sunday because her grandmother was coming over, that I questioned my mother about what the word meant. When she told me that it referred to her own mother, I asked where she was and what had she (my mother) done with her. My mother burst into tears, and I realized that I had uncovered another family secret, that once again we did not have something that everybody else had, or that we had the wrong thing. This was to be the metaphor for much of my life.

People ask me when I knew about "the destruction." It is not so much about a sense of realizing as much as it is a sense of accepting. From very early on I was scared of the tattoo my mother had received in Auschwitz. It was crudely done and ugly, and I knew that other people did not have such marks. My mother was alternately self-conscious and defiant about it, sometimes wearing long sleeves to hide it, and at other times almost unaware of it. When I asked her what it was, she told me it was her phone number. I was about three at the time, and I feared that the phone company would come to our house and tattoo me if I did not know our phone number. To this day, I can recite that phone number of so many years ago, a number that I committed to memory almost before I understood what numbers and symbols were. When I was a teenager, I wished my mother had had the number removed, as some of the survivors had done, because it reminded me of what she had gone through, and I wanted her to forget all that and move on with her life so that I could forget as well. In my twenties I realized how important it was for her to retain her number, and she often remarked to me that the numbers that had been forcibly placed upon her were her lucky numbers for life. When my son was three, he asked his grandmother what those numbers were on her arm. By this time I had told my mother about my childhood fears and she was able to answer that the numbers had been put on her arm by bad people long ago. That was enough of an answer to satisfy his curiosity, and he skipped away, unscathed I hope. The 25 years between the two incidents had given both my mother and me some distance and perspective on how much her answer had affected me.

MAKING SENSE OF THE PAST

In my late teens, when I read Viktor Frankl's *Man's Search for Meaning*, or as a young adult reading Terrence Des Pres's *The

Survivor or Primo Levi's *Survival in Auschwitz*, I wondered how my mother's life would have been different (and of course, how different my own would have been) if she had been an older, more educated person at the onset of the war. Would she have been able to theorize and intellectualize her suffering as Frankl had done, and would that have meant that I would have viewed the entire experience with a different perspective? Would she have suffered less because she would have already experienced the adolescent behaviors that would have caused her to become independent of her parents? Would having had a more normal childhood, one without a ghetto experience and the deprivation and death that marked her years before the time in the camps, provided her with a different set of coping skills? And would that have made all the difference for me? Reading Helen Epstein's *Children of the Holocaust* or Aaron Haas's *The Aftermath: Living with the Holocaust* gave me permission to acknowledge that life in a family such as ours was different from what my peers had experienced, and that the brutality and loss that had been my parents' experience could not help but color the lives of their children and grandchildren. The issue for me would be what good could come of it.

I always think that I know everything that happened to my mother and father until they tell me one more story and swear that they have told it to me before. Just recently I was walking with my mother and she started telling me about a time in Auschwitz when a transport pulled in and she witnessed a young woman in a bridal gown getting off the train. My mother had already been in Auschwitz for a long time, and she told me that many things ran through her mind. She was surprised that people were still getting married, that the world was going on with its regular business while she was interned in this hell. She also wondered about what that young woman must have felt as she descended into my mother's hell. Each time I think about the nonchalant way my mother related this story to me as we walked together, I am struck by the peculiarity of my reality. I have incorporated the knowledge of my mother's imprisonment, and her family's murder as baseline data, and those things no longer make me gasp. Stories like the bride in the railway car cause me to shake my head and wonder what it must have been like, and what I would be like if I were an eyewitness and not an auditor to these horrific events. They also make me wonder what I would be like if I had never heard about these things until they were mentioned at school or I was old enough to confront them on my own.

FROM THE PAST TO THE PRESENT:
MAKING CONNECTIONS

When I work with students or teachers on Holocaust-related material, I know that my experiences make my reactions different than theirs. A colleague once remarked that she was amazed I was able to tell the stories of my family without becoming visibly emotional. She believed that she would not be able to do work in this field if she were so closely connected. How could I explain to her what I was truly feeling; how upset I surely was, but that I was duty-bound to tell the stories; that I could not risk stopping and indulging my sorrow; that each time I told the stories I felt the presence of my grandparents, their approval at being remembered, their insistence that it was in the stories of individuals that the greatest truths were revealed. As a classroom teacher I knew that my students reacted most strongly to the stories about my family, to what had happened to one group with whom they could identify. As a teacher of teachers, I continued in that same way, always using personal illustrations, from my own family if they were applicable, or from the stories of the many other survivors who had been my extended family as I grew up. I never compared suffering, but I did compare lives. I asked students to think about what they were doing when they were 16, and then I told them what my mother and father had been doing at the same age. I told stories about the sacrifices that my grandparents made in order to keep their families alive and intact, and then I asked students to tell me what they would do in a similar situation. Making it real, making it human was what made them respond. It was never about a faceless "them" in another place, long ago. It was about real people who had connections to the world of here and now. I knew then as I know now that connections to real people are the most profound ones that students can make during the study of the Holocaust, and the ones that will affect their lives.

Several years ago a friend of mine who is a Holocaust scholar asked me to write a paper about my teaching. I refused, insisting that I was a practitioner and not a theorist, and that no one would listen to what I had to say. He persuaded me to write about my classroom. The paper was a great success, but he wanted to push me further. He told me that the stories I had told him about my parents' experiences were the real work that I should be doing. He urged me to write those down, to compile them into a teaching guide, because they had more validity than any theorizing about the Holocaust. He told me that my transmitting the lessons of the Holocaust was in the way I told those stories. Again I didn't believe

him, at least not right away. The more I work in this field, the more
I believe that he was right, that my work will be the transmission
of the stories I have shared, of my family's past and my own, and
of the stories that other survivors tell through testimonies, diaries,
and memoirs and of the connections that can be made to students'
own lives. Through those connections I hope to transmit a shared
sense of a lost past, and a morality and reverence for life.

One of the stories I tell is about my grandfather who jumped from
the train that was taking him and his two daughters to Auschwitz.
He disappeared that day and was never seen again. No information about his whereabouts ever came to my mother. When I was
a child I dreamed that my grandfather was still alive and that one
day I would meet him. As a teacher, I realized that this story was
about much more than one person trying to save his own life. It
was about the struggle that a father must have felt, whether to
remain with his daughters or attempt a return to his wife and
young children who had not been "eligible" for the transport that
bleak January morning in 1943. It was about the terror those girls
must have experienced, going to who knows where, but with their
father who then suddenly jumped from the train. It was about the
hope that must have lived within my mother that her father might
still be alive, a hope that probably sustained her through some very
dark times. All of this is about the indomitable human spirit that
will not give up even when death stares it in the face.

I tell about my mother's baby sister and how my grandparents
had the opportunity to give her to a Christian family to save her
life, how they could not bear to part with her, and so she died with
the rest of the family. That story is about last chances as much
as it is about the need for a family to stay together, the goodness
of people who offered to help at risk to themselves, and the incom-
prehensibility of a war machine that for the first time in history
targeted women and children.

I tell about the night my father, a boy of 18, left a bunker where
he and ten others were hidden, in search of food, and he stepped
on something in the darkness. A closer look revealed the body of a
dead woman, whose infant was desperately nursing at her breast.
At a very young age, my father had to make a decision that no one
should ever have to make, whether to take that living child back to
the bunker and endanger the lives of ten others, or to leave that child
where it was, surely condemning it to death. Who does one cry for?
The baby? My father? Or a world where that could happen?

These are some of my stories, a legacy that has marked my life's
journey. They have shaped my life and heart. They have not made
me hate others; they have helped me to understand that people

have the capacity for good as well as evil, and that what they choose to do is a direct result of what they have learned. I share these stories with students and with teachers. As much as I give away, my legacy does not diminish. It may enrich those who take a piece of it, but it has enriched me most of all.

USING THE PAST TO EDUCATE

I did not come to teaching the lessons of the Holocaust with a fully developed plan or even a deliberate motivation. In the first years of my teaching, I had only the materials that were available in the book room of an English department in an inner-city high school, Simon Gratz High School, in Philadelphia. Holocaust education was neither a priority nor even an issue for me or for the school. In fact, I had no intention of teaching about the Holocaust or making a personal connection to it in front of my students if the subject ever arose. In the second or third year of my teaching, when some boys in my class used the phrase "jew somebody down" in a conversation I overheard, I realized that I had to confront them or risk going home that day knowing that I had let the teachable moment pass. Asking them to explain what they had said only brought blank stares. They could not understand that I had taken offense at the phrase, especially since they did not believe that I was a Jew. Their disbelief was based on the perception that I did not look Jewish (have a big nose) or even act that way (stingy, selfish, domineering). These African American teens in the early 1970s were adherents to some of the same propaganda that Adolf Hitler had so successfully disseminated in Germany in the 1930s. Challenging them about their stereotypes was the beginning of a long and complicated journey that has led me to do some of the most rewarding work of my career. But the start was not particularly auspicious.

Visiting the book room, I found only about ten copies of *The Diary of Anne Frank*, most of which were torn and had missing pages. This was before the era of copy machines in the schools, so I found myself typing passages from the book onto ditto masters and distributing them to my students to stimulate a class discussion. The problem was that they did not know the context of World War II and could barely identify anything about that era except the name of Hitler and the shape of a swastika. Most of the history texts did include accounts of the war, but not of the actions that we term the Holocaust. There was no mention of the special treatment reserved for the Jews or any of Hitler's other enemies. The text of Anne Frank's diary was not about the Holocaust in the strictest sense, and my students could not see what was so terrible about having to hide for a year in a place that was warm and dry, and that allowed you to remain with your family. Remember that these were students from the ghettos of North Philly and you will understand that deprivation is subjective, and prejudice is an everyday occurrence. They found it interesting that someone that was white was the victim of other whites, but they did not understand how there might be any connection to their lives. The fact that the diary did not make mention of Anne's subsequent death was a problem as well, since students did not know what happened to her until I explained it to them. Somehow, the feelings of connection, empathy, anger, and indignation that the diary had evoked in me as a young teen did not spill forth from them. Where could I begin?

At that time, the history department was in possession of two films that might be used for Holocaust education. One was an animated short entitled *The Hangman*, which was loosely based on the poem of the same name by Maurice Ogden. The film's premise was that allowing evil to be perpetrated on others while you stood idly by would eventually bring you into the hands of the same evil as its victims. Students enjoyed it, laughed at its clever animation, and did not make the connection with anything more profound than the fact that, as they would say, "what goes around comes around." The second film was deeper and darker. It was called *Night and Fog*. I showed that film one semester more times than I can count, so much so that I could recite some of the script by heart. Some students found it disturbing, while others seemed completely unmoved. It was a cold and uninvolving film, one that allowed them to disconnect in the same way that the Anne Frank diary had done. I could hear their words in my head: "Who cares? That was then, this is now! Jews in this country are rich and powerful. Nothing like that will ever happen again. It didn't happen to anyone I know." That's when it struck me that I would have to make this information more real, less easily dismissed. The only way I could think of to do that was to use the stories of people with whom I had connected, and hope my students might connect and break their detachment. I began to search for survivors who would be willing to come into my class and tell about what they had experienced during the war. I did not bring my own parents, at first, because I was not sure how I would handle that situation, what it would be like if the students were not completely sympathetic to my parents' story, or what I would feel as a teacher with my own parents in my classroom. That reluctance eventually passed, and I found that some of the most moving experiences for my students came when my mother was the guest speaker. Their ability to hear a survivor, to talk with her, and to have known her daughter as their teacher gave them a direct connection to the events of the Holocaust. When we talked about loss, it was no longer the loss of six million, but the loss of a particular family, whose names we could name, whose faces we could imagine because we could look at the one remaining face.

There were times when my mother's visits to the classroom were as revealing for me as they were educational for my students. When I was teaching in an all-African American junior/senior high school in North Philadelphia, my mother spoke to my classes at the end of our Holocaust unit. The students arranged the chairs in the classroom into a large circle, and we agreed that my mother would speak twice that day, to about 40 students at a time, so the room was crowded. A teacher in the building who was our media chair decided that the speech and subsequent question-and-answer period should be taped. I agreed and my mother consented. The students prepared their questions ahead of time. During the testimony, my mother read some of the pieces she had written right after the war, and some that had been written many years later. She detailed the last days at Birkenau and the death march out of the camp. She read to them about her return to her hometown in a fruitless search for her father, and how she had been threatened by her Polish neighbors, who feared that she had come home to retrieve her family's possessions. The students were spellbound, but the most dramatic moment came in the question-and-answer period when one of the students asked if my mother would show her number to them. As she rolled up her sleeve, the entire group stood up and walked over to her. One student reached out to touch my mother's arm, and the video camera managed to capture the encounter between the teenager from the ghetto and my mother, for whom the word ghetto had an entirely different meaning.

At a different school, my mother told the story of her sister's death in Auschwitz. The two of them had been assigned to a labor detail in a quarry. On a particularly cold and snowy day, my mother's sister Fradel had been given the task of bringing in the soup kettle for the prisoners' meal. The kettle was suspended on a wooden support that had wheels on the bottom. Several girls were to roll the kettle to the appointed spot and help dole out the broth. Wearing wooden clogs on the icy stone, the girls lost their footing and the kettle overturned. My mother had always told the story up to that point, and I assumed that the girls had been scalded to death, but that was not the case. As they lay writhing in pain from the burns, the SS man shot each of the girls in the head, in front of the rest of the command. He spoke these words, "So beautiful, and so young," as he pulled the trigger. My mother had to carry her sister's body back to the barracks at the end of the day's work, so that the number who had left in the morning equaled the number that returned in the evening, dead or alive.

I gasped in horror as the story ended. My students could see that I was upset, but they did not learn the truth until the next day. Driving my mother home after the testimony, I asked her about what she had said. I assumed that she had made a mistake, or that someone else's story had been incorporated into hers, but she told me that it had happened as she had told it that day, and that she had assumed I knew the truth. In school the next day, I spent some time talking with my class about what had happened. I know that my students will never forget that day, nor will I.

In fact, years later, sitting in a restaurant I was approached by a handsome young man who was in his twenties. He asked me if I recognized him, and I did. He had been in my senior English class the day that my mother spoke. He told me that after high school he had enlisted in the navy, and that he had been around the world several times. He explained to me that his quarters on a ship were quite small, and that storage was always a problem. It seemed that many of his shipmates found it odd that an African American would be obsessed with reading about the Holocaust, always squirreling books away in his tiny cargo space, and shopping for books while on leave in cities around the globe. That was as a result of our studies and the day that my mother had come to our class, he said, and he told me that it had changed his life from being "me-directed" to being concerned about the welfare of others. He made it a point to share his books with others on his ship, and I am proud to think that my mother's testimony and my teaching may have touched the lives of many whom I will never know.

In Philadelphia, we have had an active survivor community with whom I have been involved since childhood. My parents' membership in the Association of Jewish Holocaust Survivors provided a wide circle of friends as I was growing up, but more importantly, it connected me to the Memorial Committee for the Six Million Martyrs. This group was composed of survivors, clergy of many denominations, professionals in the Jewish federation in Philadelphia, and educators from the public and parochial schools and local colleges. In the 1960s, the group was responsible for the erection of a monument to the six million martyrs in the center of Philadelphia. The monument was designed by a famous sculptor and was quite an expensive undertaking. At the time, the organization made the decision to support the public monument, rather than funding a library or study center for the Holocaust. I was a child during this time and knew only that we had to go to the monument on *Yom Hashoah*, and that when relatives came to town one of the destinations was always the monument. When I joined the committee as an adult and I learned of this large outlay of money I was incensed that the monument, which goes largely unnoticed from one year to the next, had taken precedence over a place of learning. But the survivors who had spearheaded the project felt the need for public recognition of the Holocaust in the 1960s, and they did what seemed right. Every year, they sponsored a citywide commemoration on *Yom Hashoah* that was attended by survivors as well as thousands from the Jewish and non-Jewish community. The Memorial Committee worked on the program all year long, bringing in a prominent guest speaker each year, and attempting to highlight different aspects of the Holocaust during each presentation. When I was asked to join the committee, because of my work in my own classroom and my connection to the Association of Survivors, I tried to initiate projects that would involve more young people in the program. We added younger speakers, found ways to bring school children in as participants, and tried to broaden the appeal of the event. Though I know the monument has great meaning for some, I regret that the money was spent in memorial and not on education. There are too many stones and not enough opportunities for study and dialogue, even to this day.

FIRST STEPS TO CITYWIDE INVOLVEMENT

During this time, my husband and I were involved with the writing of the first public school curriculum on the Holocaust, produced in Philadelphia in the mid-1970s. When I look back on that document today, I am amazed at all we did right and everything we did wrong. The curriculum was historically based, but it made many attempts to be topical by referencing contemporary events. It engaged in a kind of comparative exercise that I do not believe is necessary or even productive, where other events are likened to the Holocaust and students are asked to engage in a compare/contrast of tragedies that have befallen other ethnic or religious groups. At the time, it seemed like a way of being inclusive of everyone's miseries, but I see it now as a futile attempt to rank one tragedy against another. I believe we have evolved beyond that methodology now, but it certainly was groundbreaking then. What it successfully accomplished was the distribution to many teachers of a board of education-sanctioned guide with appropriately researched information and documentation, including a list of resource speakers.

This sent a signal to Philadelphia teachers and many of their counterparts in other school districts that Holocaust education was an acceptable activity.

At the same time that the guide was being produced, the Jewish Community Relations Council in Philadelphia began sponsoring a one-day-a-year forum called the Youth Symposium on the Holocaust. It was an opportunity for teens from many schools to view a film, hear a speaker, and meet with a survivor. Teachers from Philadelphia and the suburbs brought their students to a central location for the day. During the first years of the activity, my husband was the chairman of the event and I was involved because I brought students from my high school classes. Later I began to run workshops with the teachers who attended, while their students were watching the film or listening to the guest speaker. I offered strategies and ideas for making Holocaust education a more engaging activity, and I started developing bibliographies of diaries and memoirs that were just starting to be available in paperback. I also began working with survivors to help them in telling their stories more effectively and more succinctly. I was able to offer them tips on shortening their presentations and zeroing in on those pivotal moments that students would find most interesting.

MEETING AND STUDYING WITH VLADKA MEED

In 1988, I met someone who has had an indelible influence on my career and my life. That person was Vladka Meed, a heroine of the Warsaw Ghetto resistance, and a force behind the establishment of the United States Holocaust Memorial Museum (USHMM), with her husband Benjamin Meed. I was attending a gathering of teachers who had gone to Israel to study about the Holocaust and Jewish resistance with a program that Mrs. Meed had conceived of and helped to find funding. My husband had been among the first group of teachers selected to go on this trip to Israel in 1985 because of his involvement in Holocaust education, and the gathering in Washington, D.C. was an attempt to keep his group and the ones that followed connected. It also provided the teachers a chance to see the site for the proposed national Holocaust museum on the Mall in Washington. The group at that time was still small enough that I had the chance to talk with Vladka and Ben, and both of them encouraged me to apply for the program that summer. When I was accepted, I knew that I was embarking on a whole new part of my involvement. I had never had any formal training; all of my studies had been on my own, motivated by a personal

desire for information, or because my students were asking questions that I could not answer. Now I would be studying the Holocaust with 44 other teachers, hearing lectures from prominent
scholars, immersed in the topic all day for three and a half weeks.

To say that the experience changed my life is an understatement.
I had been to Israel once before as a teenager to visit family, and I
had visited Yad Vashem (the Israeli authority for the remembrance
of and education about the Holocaust; it is composed of a museum,
a memorial, an archive, and a center for the dissemination of Holocaust materials to be used for research and education) then as
a matter of course. Now, we would be studying there for a full week,
as well as spending time at Kibbutz Lohamei HaGhettaot (the
Ghetto Fighters' House) in the Galilee. I reread Vladka's book, *On
Both Sides of the Wall*, with new purpose. I also reread Raul
Hilberg's *The Destruction of the European Jews*; Nora Levin's *The
Holocaust*; and Lucy Dawidowicz's *The War Against the Jews, 1933–
1945*. I was overprepared and frightened to spend so much time
with the subject, but I was eager for the opportunity to connect
with teachers from all over the country who were engaging in the
work and who would, in some cases, become lifelong friends.

The weeks on the program were emotionally draining and I remember feeling that if anyone ever mentioned the topic of the Holocaust to me again, I would probably run in terror. To speak about
this topic all day long, at every meal, during each coffee break, as
we walked together in the evenings, on our time off on the Jewish
Shabbat, was more than the total immersion that I had imagined.
The dichotomy between the scholarly presentations by Holocaust
academics and those of survivors who were the experts because
of life experiences was brought home to me more and more. I was
convinced that the testimonies of survivors, whether in the form
of diaries, memoirs, or the spoken word, were the most dynamic
and teachable components of the experience.

My relationship with Vladka became one of mother and daughter. She enjoyed speaking in Yiddish with me, and there were many
evenings when we walked to the sea in Nahariya and talked about
the future of Holocaust education in the United States. I was honored to be with her, to incorporate her stories into my repertoire
of materials, and, in particular, to feel that she trusted me to deliver the important message of the truth about Jewish resistance
during the war. Her inspirational commitment to portraying Jews
as responsive and proactive during the Holocaust years was the
driving force behind all of our studies. We learned that resistance
did not have to be physical in order to be respected and that the
pervasive notion that Jews had gone like sheep to the slaughter

was not only inaccurate but a slander to all those who had done anything they could to sustain human life.

I still treasure a photo I took of a plaque on the wall of the Ghetto Fighters' House whose text reads:

> To smuggle a loaf of bread was to resist
> To teach in secret was to resist
> To cry out warning and shatter illusions was to resist
> To rescue a Torah scroll was to resist
> To forge documents was to resist
> To smuggle people across borders was to resist
> To chronicle events and conceal the records was to resist
> To hold out a helping hand to the needy was to resist
> To contact those under siege and smuggle weapons was to resist
> To fight with weapons in streets, mountains, and forests was to resist
> To rebel in death camps was to resist
> To rise up in ghettos, among the crumbling walls, in the most desperate revolt, was to resist

Those words became a sort of mantra for me in my teaching, especially in guiding me to find testimonies of how the daily lives of individuals were heroic. I returned from the summer seminar and became a different teacher, one who was no longer trying to justify the need for Holocaust education on the grounds that it might make students understand and have compassion, but one who believed that students would be empowered in their lives if they could think about the choices they were faced with, and make decisions based on the collective responsibility of each individual for the rest of mankind.

PENNSYLVANIA HOLOCAUST EDUCATION TASK FORCE

My work in the Philadelphia area brought me in contact with a group of public and parochial school educators and laypeople who were forming what eventually became the Pennsylvania Holocaust Education Task Force. Many of them, including my husband, were responsible for the development of *The Holocaust: A Guide for Pennsylvania Teachers*, which was published jointly by the Pennsylvania Department of Education and Millersville University. Our first work was the dissemination of the guide, and from there we structured an annual summer teachers' workshop at Shippensburg University. We were successful in securing public and private funds to ensure that Holocaust education might be a part of every Pennsylvania child's education. We have implemented professional development programs all over the state. In addition, we have provided classroom libraries of Holocaust materials and speakers for classrooms and schoolwide assemblies. We have paid for class trips to the USHMM, funding for teachers studying here and abroad, production of several videotapes of survivors, and sponsorship of speakers and conferences throughout the state. We also have initiated an annual award for students who have exhibited exemplary behavior as a direct result of their Holocaust studies, and for individuals who have contributed either monetarily or legislatively to the reality of Holocaust education in our state. From a small group of dedicated individuals, a movement of great magnitude has developed, and I am proud to serve as the chair of this organization that has touched the lives of so many schoolchildren.

FACING HISTORY AND OURSELVES

In 1993, I was invited to attend a summer session of Facing History and Ourselves, a nationally recognized program that uses Holocaust materials as a paradigm case in their tolerance education program. Though I had seen Facing History materials and had even used some of their testimonies in my classroom, I had not experienced the full training. I was overwhelmed by their resources, both texts and videos, their access to outstanding speakers, and the dedication of their highly trained staff. Their perspective on the Holocaust was perfectly in tune with my own. They saw the need to connect the lessons of the Holocaust with the lives that students lead today. With a thoroughly developed curriculum that is both interdisciplinary and easily differentiated for varying levels of student ability and maturity, they have provided a comprehensive program that can be adapted to the needs of a particular classroom or school. Their use of survivor testimony, art, and primary documents gave the lessons a hands-on approach that allowed students to investigate the Holocaust as a "case study," giving them an opportunity to draw conclusions about then and now.

I was delighted to be asked to become a member of their national teacher corps. In Philadelphia, we were able to purchase classroom sets of their student resource text, and they were kind enough to provide us with their videos and access to their regional training.

An activity that Facing History suggested was one that I found provided my students with a powerful vehicle for expressing their feelings at the end of our Holocaust unit. Students were asked to create a Holocaust memorial with modeling clay. My students took this one step further and created a gallery of memorials that became an exhibit in one of the hallways of the school. They put together a program of music and readings, and they were the docents for their own gallery of memorials. I remember the pride and satisfaction I felt that day, as my students took over and became the creators and owners of this knowledge.

WORKING WITH VLADKA MEED

In the fall of 1994, Vladka Meed called me one evening and asked me if I would consider accompanying the 1995 summer seminar group to Poland and Israel. I remember that I was home alone that night; my husband was away at a conference and my son had already gone off to his freshman year in college. I put down the receiver and stood dumbstruck in the kitchen. I had no one to verify what had just happened, and I sincerely believed that it had been a hallucination, that I had imagined the entire event, phone call and all, especially by the next morning. The opportunity was so extraordinary for me, both as an educator and as a daughter of survivors, that I could not believe the offer had been made. It was true, though, and in the summer of 1995 I made the first of five trips to Poland and Israel as the curriculum and workshop coordinator for the seminar.

That first visit to Poland was one of the most difficult experiences of my life. This was the forbidden place, the place that my parents would not even consider going back to visit, and I was terrified of what I would find and how it would affect me. Even landing at the airport was unsettling, as I faced a large group of Poles who had come to greet their relatives, completely oblivious to our group of 45 American teachers. Each day in Poland made me want to leave, but the day at Auschwitz-Birkenau was the most harrowing of all.

The night before we left the United States, my mother had told me to look for Block Nine in Birkenau. That was the place where she had spent the longest part of her internment, and she wanted me to see it. I don't know if I ever found her Block Nine, but the time I spent alone in one of the remaining buildings was cathartic and illuminating. I had brought memorial candles with me to light for my family members, and I lit them at different places around the camp, one at the bombed crematorium, one at the small gas chamber in Auschwitz. When we arrived in Birkenau, I counted off to the ninth building of a row of barracks that faced the electrified fence. This was the building that my mother had told me about, one where she could see the fence every day, the one where she had shared a bunk with her sister and another inmate or two for most of the two and a half years she had been there. I was not sure if this was my mother's Block Nine, because there were many views from many destroyed buildings that could have been the one she had told me about, but it really didn't matter. The candle I kindled in "Block Nine" was the one that caused me to break down and cry. I sat on the ground and thought about my sixteen-year-old mother and the miracle of her survival. I understood more about her in those few moments than in all the years that had gone before. I also understood more about myself in those five days in Poland than I ever had, and I vowed that I would continue my Holocaust work no matter where my career took me. I put a small piece of wood from the barracks into my backpack, promising to give it to my mother upon my return, along with the picture of the memorial candle sitting on the floor of the barracks. When the pictures were developed, there was evidence of all kinds of lights coming through the rafters and causing a kind of veil to hang over the room that was not visible to me at the time. When I offered the pictures and the wood to her, she told me to keep them, and I still touch the wood before I have a speaking engagement, as a kind of talisman that keeps me connected.

On that first trip to Poland with the Teachers' Summer Seminar, I wanted to see as much as I could of the old world that had not been completely destroyed during the war or by the Communist-era rebuilding. I was trying to connect with the past that I had never been able to visualize in a satisfying way, a past that had eluded me because I was never certain that the photos I had seen of Polish Jews in shtetls, in Hasidic garb, were in any way connected to the life that my family had lived. I knew much about the towns in which my parents had spent their youth, but I had no strong mental picture to go along with the stories I had been told.

The Warsaw of 1995 was bleak and uninviting. The concrete buildings stretched for blocks on end. The city seemed to be all one color, a monolithic gray that was made even more so by the gloomy weather we encountered unexpectedly in July. The rain matched my mood. It was a cloudy place in more ways than one.

We spent only five days in Poland, literally running from one site to another. A day at Auschwitz, another at Majdanek, a day in the old town of Warsaw, and then finally the Sabbath came, and we joined Ben Meed on a walk to the synagogue. Though the visit was optional, most of the teachers came along, women dressed in long skirts and modest blouses, men in ties and jackets, a change from the traveling gear we had been wearing for the last four days. The synagogue was filled with Americans who were visiting Poland, some young teens who were on a "heritage tour," some older retired folks who were visiting the "homeland" they had never known. We separated into two groups, men going onto the main floor, led by Ben, while the women went up to the balcony with me.

Most of the teachers on the seminar are non-Jews, and for many this was their first time in a synagogue. They were excited and curious, and I spent some time explaining the practices of the Sabbath service to them. It was uncanny how familiar the prayer book and the melodies were, though I had never felt as far away from home as I did that morning. As the service went on, the Jewish women who were interspersed through the balcony watched the men praying; sometimes they joined in, sometimes they talked among themselves. The steady murmur of prayer began to have an effect on me, and I could feel my tensions easing and my fear departing.

I looked down at the men on the main floor. Some of them were engaged in prayer; some were talking to each other. Ben was explaining the activities to the male teachers. From inside the synagogue, the light of the day was untouched by clouds. The windows, some stained glass, others just smoked glass, transformed the sunlight into a pearly haze. I watched as a young man, clearly a prosperous American Jew, rocked back and forth to the ancient melodies. Near him, an elderly man with a long beard and a tattered suit pulled his prayer shawl over his head, secluding himself in the privacy of his moment with his God. He rocked with the same rhythm as the young man, though the two probably did not notice each other. In another section, a middle-aged man in shirt sleeves with a tattooed number clearly visible on his arm was rocking to the same beat. In the balcony, the women who were able to read the Hebrew left their conversations and began to rock. My eyes went from the old to the young, the survivor to the next generation, the women to the men, and a feeling of complete connection flooded my being. I realized that I was rocking as well, as were the women who stood in the row with me, teachers from all over the United States, all of whom were touched by the moment of community that the religious service had provided. For many of them, and for me, it was one of the highlights of the trip.

When we returned to the hotel, we tried to explain to the others what we had experienced, but words did not convey the moment. I know we had experienced a special event together, a blending of the past and the present, a reaffirmation of the spirit, a recognition of the power of faith and the awe one feels when something beyond our explanatory powers takes place. How can one teach this? I only hope those who were present that day use it as a way of making sense of the connectedness of all people and that it somehow touches every student that they come into contact with, whether it is in their teaching of the lessons of the Holocaust or in some other subject or class.

For the next five years I would accompany Vladka and Ben Meed and the teachers to Poland and Israel. My job was to make the connections between the sites and the speakers and the teachers' own classrooms, helping them to determine how they might best convey the large amount of information they were receiving in the seminar to their students back home in the States. Those years were the most productive in terms of my Holocaust work. Every year I would put together materials, presentations, artifacts, and film clips that I thought would stimulate teacher discussion and synthesize the scholarly world with the real world of middle and high school classrooms. I produced an annotated bibliography of books that I felt would help teachers in choosing materials for their classrooms, materials that would emphasize the life of the ordinary individual and not of the perpetrator, materials that would honor the memory of those who had been killed by telling their stories with compassion, emphasizing the dignity of the life before, during, and after the Holocaust. (Those books I find most powerful and/or informative are listed at the end of this essay.) I helped to develop a strong network of fellow teachers who were committed to teaching the lessons of the Holocaust and who shared news, book reviews, ideas, and plans daily through e-mail. As the summer seminar has progressed from 1985, more than 600 teachers from all over the United States have been involved, and their teaching has been instrumental in the dissemination of some of my beliefs about Holocaust education. The teachers who have had the opportunity to travel with Vladka and Ben are indeed fortunate. The time in Poland is seen through the eyes of someone who lived there, who had a wonderful childhood, but whose life was shattered by the events of the war. Vladka's testimonies, given each year at different points during the seminar, but culminating with the details of her mother's capture and Vladka's inability to save her own family after having saved so many others, is as fresh and heartbreaking for me as the first time I heard it. The tears in her eyes are visible 55 years after the event, and the true heartbreak she felt at her helplessness is palpable in the seminar room. No one who sees this tiny lady can imagine that she was the heroine of so many dangerous escapades, but anyone who has ever spent any time with her will know that her indomitable spirit is every bit as strong today as it was in 1943. It is this same determination that has infused the seminar with its particular blend of personal and intellectual history. Every other year, the seminar holds an alumni conference in Washington, D.C., with the USHMM as its partner. At these conferences, the network of teachers is revitalized and strengthened, as we are treated to extraordinary speakers, who are both witnesses and scholars. Past speakers have included Elie Wiesel, Deborah Lipstadt, Jan Karski, Gerda Weissman Klein, Aharon Applefeld, Lawrence Langer, Michael Marrus, Yehuda Bauer, Nechama Tec, Isabella Leitner, Raul Hilberg, Deborah Dwork, Yaffa Eliach, Christopher Browning, Daniel Goldhagen, Henry Feingold, Eva Fogelman, Samuel and Pearl Oliner, Martin Gilbert, Michael Berenbaum, Robert Jay Lifton, Philip Hallie, Richard Rubinstein, and many others. The conference provides us with thought-provoking speeches and affords us a chance to establish a dialogue between the well-known authority and the classroom teacher. This mix of scholar and practitioner has been one of the hallmarks of this program. Not the least important part of these conferences is the opportunity to share our success with each other. The tips gleaned from my colleagues have been a vital part of my continuing education, since I sincerely believe there is no problem one teacher is confronting that another teacher has not already solved.

BECOMING A MANDEL SCHOLAR

In 1996 the USHMM honored me by selecting me as one of its first Mandel Scholars. This program, which brings together teachers from all over the United States who have demonstrated a level of expertise and commitment to teaching the lessons of the Holocaust, was endowed by a philanthropic family from Ohio. They saw the need to provide advanced education for teachers that would directly link them to the resources of the museum, and that would require them to structure projects in their local communities to further Holocaust education. My time at the initial seminar at the USHMM provided valuable contacts with many museum professionals, and afforded me the chance to study along with some of the most experienced Holocaust educators in the United States. My subsequent project allowed 42 Pennsylvania teachers to visit the USHMM for a special seminar designed expressly for us by the museum's educational outreach department. That contact was the first time some of the teachers had been to the museum; it established a connection with museum professionals that continues to this day, allowing those teachers and many others with whom they have shared in Pennsylvania to continue accessing the resources at the museum. For me, the museum has been a visible reminder of this country's commitment to prevent anything like the Holocaust from occurring again. The location, the prominence, the quality of its exhibits, publications, programs, and staff, and the popularity it enjoys are affirmations of the importance that teaching the lessons of the Holocaust has in our society. The museum provides the average American with a chance to confront the Holocaust on many different levels. One can walk through it briskly and get an overview; or one can linger in particular areas for a more in-depth study. Those who learn best from the stories of others can spend time listening to the survivors' testimonies that are so prominent in the last exhibit. The children's tiles project can connect even the youngest visitor, and the archives and research center can provide the sort of information a scholar might desire. On my first visit to the museum, with a busload of survivors from Philadelphia that included my mother and father, I found myself unable to leave the boxcar located in the permanent exhibit. The stories of my mother and my grandfather swirled around me, and the tangible evidence of the reality was almost more than I could bear. So this is what it had been like! Even the visit to Auschwitz and my first look at the bunk beds had not been as difficult as standing in the boxcar. Perhaps it was because it was here in America, that my bus that would take me home was waiting outside, that my mother and father had already walked through and gone on to the next exhibit, but I don't think I have ever left that boxcar. The journey continues; the destination is always up ahead.

BOOKS I HAVE FOUND TO BE PARTICULARLY POWERFUL AND/OR INFORMATIVE

Ayer, Eleanor (1995). *Parallel Journeys*. New York: Atheneum.

Berenbaum, Michael (1993). *The World Must Know: The History of the Holocaust as Told in the United States Holocaust Memorial Museum*. Boston, MA: Little Brown and Company.

Fluek, Toby K. (1990). *Memories of My Life in a Polish Village*. New York: Knopf.

Friedman, Carl (1994). *Nightfather*. New York: Persea.

Friedman, Ina (1990). *The Other Victims: First Stories of Non-Jews Persecuted by the Nazis*. New York: Houghton Mifflin.

Grossman, Mendel (1970). *With a Camera in the Ghetto*. Galilee, Israel: Ghetto Fighter's House.

Isaacson, Judith (1990). *Seed of Sarah*. Urbana: University of Illinois Press.

Klein, Gerda (1995). *All But My Life*. New York: Hill and Wang.

Korczak, Janusz (1978). *Ghetto Diary*: New York: Holocaust Library.

Leitner, Isabella (1978). *Fragments of Isabella*. New York: Dell.

Lewin, Rhoda (1990). *Witnesses to the Holocaust*. Boston, MA: Twayne.

Marks, Jane (1993). *The Hidden Children*. New York: Fawcett.
Meed, Vladka (1979). *On Both Sides of the Wall*. New York: Schocken.
Nomberg-Przytyk, Sara (1985). *Auschwitz: True Tales from a Grotesque Land*. Chapel Hill: University of North Carolina Press.
Orlev, Uri (1992). *The Island on Bird Street*. Boston, MA: Houghton-Mifflin.
Richter, Hans Peter (1987). *Friedrich*. New York: Puffin.
Rittner, Carol (1986). *The Courage to Care: Rescuers of Jews during the Holocaust*. New York: New York University Press.
Sender, Ruth Minsky (1986). *The Cage*. New York: Bantam.
Tatelbaum, Itzhak (1985). *Through Our Eyes: Children Witness the Holocaust*. Jerusalem: I.B.T. Press.
Tec, Nechama (1982). *Dry Tears*. New York: Oxford University Press.
Vos, Ida (1991). *Hide and Seek*. Boston, MA: Houghton-Mifflin.
Wiesel, Elie (1960). *Night*. New York: Bantam.

REFERENCES

Dawidowicz, Lucy (1975). *The War against the Jews, 1933–1945*. New York: Jewish Publication Society.
Des Pres, Terrence (1976). *The Survivor*. New York: Oxford University Press.
Epstein, Helen (1979). *Children of the Holocaust*. New York: Putnam.
Frankl, Viktor (1963). *Man's Search for Meaning*. New York: Washington Square Press.
Haas, Aaron (1995). *The Aftermath: Living with the Holocaust*. New York: Cambridge Press.
Hilberg, Raul (1961). *The Destruction of the European Jews*. New York: Quadrangle Books.
Levi, Primo (1960). *Survival in Auschwitz*. New York: Orion.
Levin, Nora (1973). *The Holocaust*. New York: Schocken.
Meed, Vladka (1979). *On Both Sides of the Wall*. New York: Holocaust Library.

Chapter 3

∿

Just the Facts

Steve Cohen

I don't remember ever hearing the word "Holocaust" until after I graduated from college. I knew all about Nazis or, rather, I thought that I did. Growing up in the borough of Queens in New York City in the 1950s, the Nazis were on our minds a great deal. Whether Hitler was alive in South America or whether he had really killed himself in his bunker (whatever a bunker was) was a subject of great debate on the way to the Jamaica Jewish Center for classes after "regular school" at P.S. 117. Our Hebrew school principal had numbers on his arm, and we knew what that meant. Mass murder wasn't something that we studied or discussed in class; it was something that he had luckily escaped, and something we whispered about.

I remember sneaking looks at the *World Book Encyclopedia* to read about Hitler and making sure that nobody caught me doing it. There was a fascination and a fear and a perpetual series of questions, but it was nothing that was spoken about in school except as a fact. It had happened.

It was, after all, the 1950s, and it was time for us, as Jewish kids whose fathers (and some mothers) were first-generation college graduates, to be real Americans. We were the people whom Superman was protecting every night on WPIX-TV. "Truth, justice, and the American way" were our values and those that stood for the Free World. By the 1960s, however, some of those ideals began to look tarnished. "Racial" hatred had not disappeared after the war, and, in fact, we saw evidence of it in the South as we watched the television news. The Soviets had taken the place of the Nazis as

our enemy, and the Red Chinese were none too good either. We
were, of course, as the Bob Dylan song soon made clear, the people
"With God on Our Side." Dylan was cynical, and he made things
more complicated. He even made us reconsider what had happened
less than a generation ago in Europe. We knew that he was Jewish,
and in that song, he sarcastically indicated that the Germans had
murdered six million in the gas chambers, but that now the
Germans, too, had God on their side. How had that happened?

Even if explanations were not forthcoming, the atmosphere in my
environment was filled with hints of the depths of the issue. I grew
up knowing German Jews who had fled to the United States, some
before 1939 and others later. They were friends of my parents and
lived in our neighborhood. Sam and Laura were important people
in my life. The parents of two girls who played with my sister while
my brother and I played ball, Sam and Laura were a constant presence at our house and we at theirs. I heard stories about how Sam
had skied out of Germany with papers hidden in his wooden skis.
Wherever we went with them, Sam was always meeting someone
he recognized from Berlin. While it wasn't always clear that either
they remembered him or they had even been in Berlin back then,
I was later astounded to find out how small the Jewish population in Germany was. Sam must have known all of them, and those
that hadn't died must have all been in New York! His stories, and
he could tell great ones, were about people, not politics. He told
me more about Alger Hiss (innocent, said Sam, because Hiss had
told him so when they had met at a dentist's office) than Adolf
Hitler.

Martin's story was different. A scientist who worked for Sperry
out on Long Island, Martin's wife and child had been murdered by
the Nazis. He had escaped and survived. He became an additional
member of our family because he had no other. An old childhood
image of Hitler searching for Martin has stayed with me for over
40 years. That was exactly the way I saw it—Hitler searching a
room, a house, the woods, and the zoo for Martin. Martin loved
animals and science, going to the zoo, and making home movies.
I never dared to ask him what had happened. How could I ask?
What would I say?

Those who knew weren't saying very much either. History was
important at the Passover Seder (the retelling of the Exodus tale,
an ancient book read in chorus at the Passover feast, the Seder),
which was our major religious ritual, but when Art, Sam and
Laura's friend, read a prayer about the six million at the Seder we
attended at his house, I was amazed. That wasn't in my Haggadah!

The mention of the six million by Art, which was clearly important having been mentioned during the Seder, and the fact that I
loved to read, resulted in my paging through William Shirer's best-
seller, *The Rise and Fall of the Third Reich: A History of Nazi Germany* (1960), to try to learn more about the murder of the six
million. Shirer's book was a big one in my education about the
Holocaust. The murder of six million Jews wasn't just one man's
vendetta. There were more things to know than I knew.

While school didn't explain the murder of the Jews and mainstream culture didn't usually do more than mention it, Mel Brooks
and Woody Allen referred to it all the time and in funny ways. In
his *2000-Year-Old Man* and other albums, shticks on television, and
memorably in *The Producers*, Brooks often referred to Nazis and
their horrors. He did so through comedy that some may not have
found funny, but to me it was uproarious and exactly true. I can
still recite part of his bit on the "Peruvian Indian." The title character, of course, was a Nazi in hiding. Many of Brooks's characters
were obsessed with what had happened to the Jews of Europe.
Nazis were also showing up in Allen's routines and short stories
as well. Some of his later stories, purportedly the memoirs of Nazi
underlings, seemed as memorable to me as the real ones I have
subsequently read.

So, for me growing up, the Nazis were figures to curse. The exact details weren't talked about, but their deed was clear. They had
murdered six million Jews. No lengthy or deep explanations were
even necessary—they were antisemites, and they acted on it. Hitler
was a modern-day Haman. Nazis showed up in all kinds of movies,
war games, and even sitcoms. (Colonel Klink and Sergeant Schultz
of *Hogan's Heroes* weren't competent enough to be war criminals,
but they were on the side of evil.) They were the perfect enemies.
They were even useful for consumer decisions. We weren't going
to buy any German cars!

History courses in high school didn't answer the big questions
(or many small ones either). Memorizing facts took the place of
thinking about those facts. What had happened to Jews during
Hitler's rule? What had led to those unexplored events? Why then?
Why there? If the question wasn't going to be on the Regents exam,
there was no sense in wasting time on it. The approach was vin-
tage Joe Friday in *Dragnet*, "Just the facts, ma'am."

At Williams College, where I majored in history, I did learn some
stuff. At the almost monthly Sunday morning bagel-eating meetings of the college's Jewish association, professors would often give
a talk on an issue of interest, usually antisemitism. I often thought

of those as the "why they hate us" brunches. I can't really remember the answers, but the fact that there was actually something to discuss was quite enlightening.

I took a significant religion course during our winter study term in January 1972. The course, taught by the visiting college chaplain, dealt with whether God could exist after Auschwitz. It was the only religion class I ever took, and it was quite powerful and intriguing. I don't remember why I registered to take it or even whether it was my first choice. It was the first in-class reading I had done on the mass murder of the Jews, and we read André Schwarz-Bart's novel, *The Last of the Just* (1960), and Richard Rubenstein's *After Auschwitz* (1966). Both books were provocative and challenging.

Schwarz-Bart opened the questions of righteousness and evil in the world. He forced one to question whether good triumphed over evil. Rubenstein's description of his own religious odyssey was fascinating to me. Could one still believe in God after Auschwitz? Did religion have a role to play in society or had the historical events of the twentieth century made it irrelevant? He took these questions seriously. That forced us to do the same. It affected how and whether and what we believed. Those were not questions merely for High Holiday services but for what one did with and in one's life.

The other relevant college experience was hearing Robert G.L. Waite (1977), who was writing his psychobiography of Hitler, *The Psychopathic God*, give a memorable lecture. While much of the talk centered on whether or not one of Hitler's testicles was undescended, Waite's lecture, in fact, was the only regularly scheduled academic presentation that occurred during the student strike, which followed the "incursion" into Cambodia in May 1970. That speech was, for me, a continuation of my interest in these issues, but it didn't really push me to focus on Nazism in my coursework. After all, there was a war in Southeast Asia to stop, and a great deal about the world to learn.

BECOMING A TEACHER

Entering graduate school as a comparative history major in the fall of 1973 would, in retrospect, have seemed to be a fortuitous time to look for answers to these questions about Nazi Germany. While other departments at Brandeis University were actively thinking about these issues, that was less true of the history department. I studied a bit with Rudolph Binion, who, like Waite, was also writing a psychobiography of Hitler, but hearing two psychohistorians arrive at very different analyses of the same person convinced me that that was not the road for me to follow. The book that really opened my eyes to thinking about the Holocaust while I was in graduate school was Robert Paxton's *Vichy France: Old Guard and New Order, 1940–1944* (1975). It was important to me in two ways. It reminded me that I liked reading history, an enthusiasm that graduate education was doing its best to defeat, and it pushed me to begin to read more systematically on this topic. I had seen *The Sorrow and the Pity* in a New York City movie theater just before reading Paxton's book, and it had also made me realize that there was much more to this study than just Hitler.

I left graduate school to teach high school in 1976, putting my doctoral research on a corner of my desk until I finished it with one great surge of energy four years later. I had the good luck to teach high school history at the Cambridge School in Weston, Massachusetts, with colleagues who encouraged teachers to think seriously about what they wanted to teach, why they wanted to teach that, and how they should do it. Teachers also had to answer the related questions of what the students would get from this course, why they should study it, and how they could best encounter the material. All of these questions excited me about teaching and still remain the criteria I ask myself before planning a new course.

I began teaching seniors and sophomores. The latter took a modern European history course that looked at the ancien régime and went through the middle of the nineteenth century. The seniors had their choice of a number of courses under the rubric of culture and politics. Many of these courses were interdisciplinary, and the combining of history books with novels and poetry and the use of the arts in the classroom helped the classes come alive. In courses on twentieth-century Europe that we taught for seniors, we provided students with much more than a traditional textbook version of the world. I didn't want students to think that history was just past politics, and I made the case that literature and the arts were essential components, not extras, to studying the past.

Soon after I had started teaching about the Holocaust, George Mosse, a noted Holocaust historian who taught at the University of Wisconsin at Madison, came to Boston and gave a series of different talks at various colleges and universities in the area. I went to all that I could and was captivated by his scope of learning and his range of expertise and his evident joy in trying to explain difficult topics. Mosse's ability to explain the intellectual climate of the era and the ways in which ideas turned into policies was particularly striking. He actually came up to me after one of the talks and

asked if I was following him. I told him that I was just doing what
any good teacher would do—stealing everything that I could!

Over the course of the years, various books proved influential in
my understanding of the Holocaust. More specifically, Karl
Schleunes's *The Twisted Road to Auschwitz* (1970) was one of the
most important books for me. It compelled me to think about
Nazism as I would think about other political forces. The Nazis, too,
were individuals who worked within external constraints, but
wanted their views to prevail. The notion that the Nazis had to do
more than terrorize, but sought also to win friends and influence
people, deeply changed my initial understanding of the events of
the 1930s and 1940s.

In very similar ways, Christopher R. Browning's works have also
reminded me of the importance of never forgetting that we have to
explain the actions and ideas of real people in real situations who
made real decisions. These have become the markers for me in
teaching.

At about the same time as my contact with George Mosse, I realized that many of my students didn't know what had happened
to the Jews of Europe during the twentieth century, and I felt a
responsibility to talk about what was now widely referred to as the
Holocaust. Today it is truly astonishing to realize how few resources
were available two decades ago, and, indeed, how little I knew! I
used *Night and Fog* in that course and was both impressed and
worried by my students' reactions. Alain Resnais's documentary
intersperses footage from World War II with views of Auschwitz a
decade after the war. It is almost poetic and elusive in its subtitles.
The word "Jew" never appears in the film, but the footage is all
about what had happened in a certain time and in a certain place
and asks the question whether it could happen again and whether
it already has.

Nobody ever spoke after they saw it. The silence in the class was
always complete. It was often as if nobody were breathing. I concluded that meant they had watched it carefully, and the film had
hit them hard. I wanted that to happen. But I worried whether the
film was too much. Had it been so powerful that it had moved from
the realm of history to something else? Was that good? Wasn't the
Holocaust a historic event that needed to be studied as other events
were?

I have not used *Night and Fog* in many years. I found it harder
and harder to use as I learned more about the Holocaust and
changed the way I taught about it. That was also true as other films
became available. I think, however, much of the difference was in
me. The horror that is in *Night and Fog* just became unrelenting

after I started viewing it with a parent's eyes. I had always seen the horror before and intellectually understood it. I thought that I had felt it before as well, but after my kids were born, the utter devastation of what it must have been like for a parent, not to be able to protect your child, just took over every other emotion. I am far more reluctant to show films to my classes than I used to be. I will show a brief clip much more often than a full-length film. They can watch films at home. In class, I want them thinking, and I want to be able to probe and challenge their assumptions, and encourage them to explain what they mean. Oftentimes teachers say that they won't use some film because of its effect on kids. Many times it is because of its effect on us.

FACING HISTORY AND OURSELVES

One evening during the spring of 1979 I attended a presentation by Bill Parsons, an old friend of mine who was teaching eighth grade at the Lincoln School in Brookline, Massachusetts, and Margot Strom, who was teaching at the Runkle School in Brookline, on a curriculum they had developed entitled Facing History and Ourselves. I was impressed and excited. The animated film, *The Hangman*, was the single most exciting piece that sold me on using the curriculum. Its question was one about individual responsibility, and how hard it was to stand up and be counted.

I had been asked to teach the ninth grade in the fall of 1979, and my department head, Trumbull Smith, agreed with me that the Facing History material might be a great place to begin. It was.

Starting the course with the questions of identity and the definitions of prejudice, discrimination, and stereotyping were the perfect vehicles to get kids talking and to learn who they were just as they were beginning a new school and their high school careers. It also reminded me that the content had to connect to kids. It wasn't that students had to study only things that they had experienced or material that was part of their background, but that whatever was worth studying had to raise questions that students cared about. Looking at the Holocaust, those questions were legion. I used the original spiral-bound copies of the Facing History curriculum that year and added Elie Wiesel's *Night*, his memoir about being engulfed in the Holocaust, as well.

The guest speakers who came to class made the course take on an urgency that was transmitted to the ninth graders. Father Robert Bullock, a parish priest at Our Lady of Sorrows in Sharon, Massachusetts, came in to talk about Christianity and anti-semitism, and he did that in part. But, as an outstanding teacher, he actually began by talking about something he had heard in the hallway before class that made stereotyping come alive. He made the connection between the issues that he was talking about historically and those that our students saw around them every day. The students had been discussing the group they disliked the most—preppies! Father Bullock probed the class and asked why they disliked preppies. When he heard their list of complaints, he asked whether all preppies they knew fit this list. As he questioned them further, realizations began to appear on their faces and in their comments. They had created an in-group and an out-group. They had been studying stereotyping, and they had been experiencing it as well. The groups were different, the time was different, the place was different, but the mechanism of separation was astoundingly similar.

Another guest, Elizabeth Dopazo, spoke about her membership in the Hitler Youth movement and the decisions that she had to make in the complicated and frightening situation in which she found herself. One student, when I told him who was coming the next day, didn't want to meet her or hear her, and was angry that I insisted he come and listen.

Elizabeth's story complicated his picture of the era. The Nazis had killed her father and arrested her mother as Jehovah's Witnesses, and made her life and that of her brother and grandparents miserable. She had joined the Hitler Youth and had even enjoyed it, but she had never adopted its ideology. For my student, history became real that day. It was no longer cut-and-dried and inevitable. It contained nuances and demanded attention. Judgment was not easy; context mattered.

Herb Koplow, a survivor whose daughter was a student in the school but not in that class, agreed to speak, and his daughter came to listen. She had never heard his whole story, and the class sat in respect and openmouthed concentration as he haltingly told us what he could. My memory focuses on the six cups of water he lined up in front of him when he began speaking and the number of times I left the room to refill them. He spoke not of one killing center but of numerous labor camps and of an empire of murder. The way he spoke, as well as what he told us, remained indelible.

USING FACTS

At the high school, college, graduate school, and adult education levels, I have continued teaching about the Holocaust for the past 23 years. When I first began, a teacher had to start by explaining what the Holocaust was. Twenty-six years later, it is something that many people feel they have heard too much about. In the spring of 1999, on a National Public Radio station talk show in Boston, a caller complained to the editor of the *Boston Globe* that the paper carried too many stories on the Holocaust. This was 54 years after the end of World War II, said the caller, and enough was enough.

Quantity and quality, however, are not synonymous. Although much has been said about the Holocaust, I am not sure that the most important questions have continued to be placed in front of our students. That Nazis were bad is easy to get across. But the real challenge is to think about how the "bad guys" were able to do what they did. The Nazi era raises serious questions about democracy and humanity. That history is made by real people who make real decisions must remain in the forefront of our teaching. Explaining how the Nazis came to power, gained popularity, and won so many admirers is the heart of the issue.

For the last two decades I have spoken in middle and high school classrooms for the national organization Facing History and Ourselves. Most of the time I talk about the meaning and results of World War I. Eighty-five years after its beginning, that war remains alive. I try to get students to think about how Humpty-Dumpty fell apart, and how the winners of the war tried to put him together again. Students might not have to memorize exact details from the battle of Verdun, but they surely need to know what battles like that meant. It was that war that changed the world forever.

I have, as I have taught about the Holocaust, found myself pushed to continue reading about the 50 years before Hitler came to power. Starting with the end of World War I is too late. Focusing just on Europe also limits our perspective. I have realized that the global history of the era is something that is often neglected. The teacher's major dilemma—the need to specialize in understanding every aspect of one event and yet realizing that the event needs to be contextualized for it to be understandable for students or general readers—is one that I struggle with as I teach about the Holocaust.

I have become more and more convinced that it is critical to challenge our students to think about the context of events. Facts are our stepping stones to understanding, but lists of facts or three causes of this and five results of that are not using facts in helpful ways. For some, critical thinking has become a mantra; for others, a symbol of trendy education-speak. What it really is, however, is a warning to us that the material we teach matters and matters deeply. We must present our students with the difficult questions of the past in all their complexity and push and prod and inspire our students to struggle for explanations. Facts help us do that, but as Thomas C. Holt (1990) noted in his piece on teaching history, "Thinking Historically: Narrative, Imagination, and Understanding," "The facts will not simply speak for themselves" (p. 5).

When I started teaching I thought I knew some things. Now, after reading extensively, writing a little, teaching a lot, and trying to understand, I see more and more what I don't know. It doesn't stop me from carrying on with all of these activities, but it is, nevertheless, a critical realization. I think that it is easier to make great pronouncements than it is to prove little details. It is, however, in the details that real life lies.

So, in order to excite my students about history and to help them realize the importance of the past, I want to help them to use details to understand the complexity of the world. I am less interested in their ability to diagram the flowchart of power in the Nazi state than I am in their understanding of the complexities of life under the Third Reich. What happens to real people in real situations? What decisions do they make? Why do they make them? How do you know? I am looking for students who can use information to analyze situations, and those are the questions I pose to my students.

With a greater amount of time spent in reading and in trying to understand what happened under the rule of Adolf Hitler, I have found myself moving further and further away from asking my students solely "objective" questions about the era. I have never given a multiple-choice test in my career, and I think it is because anything I put in that form immediately trivializes it. I love information and details, but I think that for my students, information is only worth knowing if it is usable.

Whether I am teaching tenth graders and graduate students as I do in the fall, or whether it is undergraduates and interested adults in the spring, the more I learn, the richer the course that I can provide. But that doesn't mean I believe students have to memorize these details for a test. Instead, they need to be able to refer to information in order to try to explain how something occurred and why we need to think about it.

I also think that we as teachers must be very careful. Sometimes, when we deal with something as difficult as this era, we become preachy. We want students to see the connections between eras, and we lead them to see things in a certain way. They have learned that Nazis are bad; therefore, showing students excerpts from *Mein Kampf* and excerpts from the speeches of David Duke is not, I think, getting them to think critically. It is, instead, allowing them to give answers that we want to hear. But we aren't challenging them to analyze and say why Duke's remarks should give thoughtful people pause and cause for concern. We must push our students to do the hard thinking, not to make the comparisons for them.

With much of my teaching focused these days on prospective social studies and history teachers who will be getting their Master of Arts in Teaching (MAT) degrees at Tufts University, I have tried to emphasize the global connections. All of my students will be teaching in more diverse settings than I did starting out two and a half decades ago. In order to enable students to think about the meaning of the Holocaust, it is critical that we teach them about what the world was like in the nineteenth and early twentieth centuries. They need to think about what the New Imperialism did to Africans and Asians, what World War I meant to countries and peoples all around the world, and how the Treaty of Versailles impacted upon winners and losers alike. Questions like these, I have found, have helped teachers to see the Holocaust as not just the culminating act of a madman, but as a series of events that need to be explained, thought about, and taught. Hitler didn't invent racism; the assumption that there exists a hierarchy of peoples on the basis of their culture and civilization was not limited to German thinkers. These categorizations of people were not a feature of society unique to Nazi Germany. Realizing this makes the importance of teaching about the Holocaust even greater.

While the particular setting of the Holocaust is essential to understand what happened, at the same time, I am not comfortable with the idea that the Holocaust has been so different from all other examples of man-made human tragedy. It is essential to confront all of them, I think, not because we can evaluate one as being the "worst" of all time, but because, on the contrary, there are always similarities and patterns to recognize. "Ethnic cleansing" in Bosnia, autogenocide in Cambodia, and the 1994 genocide in Rwanda are not different types of events. These are all unique but ones that share a similar pattern, which for all of our sakes, we had better learn to prevent. I have never been mesmerized by the "unique" versus "universal" debate. All historical events are unique, and all have universal aspects as well. Studies of these events must be undertaken in depth.

Studying the Holocaust, then, has forced me to think comparatively. I do not think that the Holocaust is an event that is anything but human. I often wish that it were not so, but I am afraid that it is. What that means is that people in power set up a situation in which it was possible for perpetrators to murder victims while others stood by, averted their eyes, or avoided knowing. That is not a pleasant conclusion, and it is one that I would rather not have drawn.

It is also no more unique to the Holocaust than it is to a great many other events. I recently taught a course on war crimes and reconciliation. The Holocaust, not surprisingly, was a major focus of our study. But so were Kosovo, Rwanda, and South Africa. Again, these cases are each unique, but they all demand answers to similar questions. The answers often infuriate us, but we must strive to build societies in which we won't have to ask these same things again and again.

I have also always feared the *Eyewitness News* sorts of investigations—the "How did you feel about the hurricane that killed your family?" approach. Neither the Holocaust nor the genocide in Rwanda was a "natural" disaster. People carried it out, and all of us have to work together to understand how such things have happened and continue to happen.

Many years ago, I worked in a summer camp. After the 1967 war between Israel and many of its neighbors, one of the directors hung a poster that said Never Again. It was clear from the context what that meant. Never Again rings in our ears, and the noise is giving us headaches. Every history teacher can recite, or at least paraphrase, George Santayana's dictum about the cost of forgetting history. In the wake of the recent mass murders in Europe and Africa, in the light of the truth commissions in South Africa, Guatemala, Argentina, and Chile, and in the shadow of the possible trial of General Pinochet, we can see that events related to those that occurred under the Nazis have happened again and again, and we know a great deal about them.

LOOKING BACK, LOOKING AHEAD

I hope that I have helped my students understand that history is not finished. It is only dead in classrooms in which issues have been decided. Few issues are. The questions are alive and up for grabs. Learning is important for that reason. As I heard someone argue once, "It's not the things you don't know that hurt you. It's the things you do know, that ain't so."

Scholars have taught us a great deal about the Holocaust, and they will undoubtedly continue to do so. This is laudable and important. What we must do as teachers is to take this knowledge and help students use it. The Holocaust is not sacred history with little relevance to today. It is, rather, incredibly relevant to so many things today. The links are critical.

They are also dangerous. One has to be very cautious about making these essential comparisons. What makes the case study approach so important is that it means teachers and students will know details about many things. Simple comparisons, such as hate can bring about murder, may well be true but they don't challenge us beyond mere platitudes. Comparisons are worthwhile only when students have looked at something in a serious and detailed way. Holocaust scholars, like secondary teachers, need to learn about events outside their specialties to help others raise questions and initiate collaborative efforts that don't merely separate all of us into investigators of singular horrors but help us learn from each other about how to prevent them.

Superman linked "Truth, justice and the American way" for me when I was growing up. Truth and justice, however, can be at odds. As teachers, I think that we must seek the truth and hope that from there justice may follow. Education, as tenuous a chord as it is, does remain one way to fight against the repetition of the horrors that have been so powerfully exhibited in the past century. Getting our students to think through issues, especially confusing and difficult ones, is our job. Facts are the pieces of the puzzle, but we must help them to use those facts. The context, the meaning, and what they hint at for the next week, next month, next year, and next millennium are at the core of our mission. We surely haven't succeeded yet, but we don't dare stop trying.

REFERENCES

Binion, Rudolph (1976). *Hitler among the Germans*. New York: Elsevier.

Browning, Christopher R. (1992). *Ordinary Men: Reserve Police Battalion 101 and the Final Solution in Poland*. New York: HarperCollins.

———. (1992). *The Path to Genocide: Essays on Launching the Final Solution*. New York: Cambridge University Press.

Holt, Thomas C. (1990). "Thinking Historically: Narrative, Imagination, and Understanding." New York: College Entrance Examination Board.

Paxton, Robert (1975). *Vichy France: Old Guard and New Order, 1940-1944*. New York: Columbia University Press.

Rubenstein, Richard (1966). *After Auschwitz*. Indianapolis, IN: Bobbs-Merrill.

Schleunes, Karl A. (1970). *The Twisted Road to Auschwitz*. Urbana, IL: University of Illinois Press.

Schwarz-Bart, André (1960). *The Last of the Just*. New York: Atheneum.

Shirer, William (1960). *The Rise and Fall of the Third Reich: A History of Nazi Germany*. Greenwich, CT: Fawcett.

Waite, Robert G.L. (1977). *The Psychopathic God: Adolf Hitler*. New York: Basic Books.

Chapter 4

~

An Unlikely Journey: A Gentile's Path to Teaching the Holocaust

Carol Danks

FORMATIVE YEARS

I was born into a middle-class, Southern Baptist family on April 10, 1945, and for a long time I had no idea that the month of my birth coincided with the liberation of prisoners in numerous concentration/labor camps in Europe: Buchenwald, Ohrdruf, Bergen-Belsen, Ravensbruck, Sachsenhausen, Dachau, Westerbork. However, the fact is that the day after my parents were celebrating my arrival on earth, hundreds of prisoners at Buchenwald were celebrating the American forces' arrival in their hell. I often think about my birth into a safe, nurturing environment at the very time the terrifying, destructive environment of the camps was ending. Why was I fortunate to be where I was, when I was?

My years through high school were spent in a small town in the middle of Illinois, literally surrounded by cornfields. Entirely white and virtually entirely Christian, Effingham was about half Protestant and half Catholic, with the Catholics split between the Irish and German churches. I remember always wondering why each parish had its own elementary school but the Irish Catholic kids went to the public high school rather than to the German Catholic high school. The apparent divisions even within the Catholic Church seemed odd to me. I grew up with Protestant friends whose parents refused to allow them to date Catholics, a refusal, which, of course, meant that a number of my friends dated them surreptitiously. While I primarily dated a Methodist (who ultimately became my husband), I also dated a Catholic and the one Jewish boy in town. Never once did I hear my parents condemn or speak disparagingly about Catholics or Jews. However, the majority of these small-town Christian folks clearly did not accept minorities. No African American families live in the town to this day, and growing up, I remember realizing that only rarely did I see them even stop for gas, much less go into a restaurant. I learned later that Effingham, a town on the migration route from New Orleans and Memphis to Chicago, was known by African Americans to be a place to move through quickly. When my late mother-in-law sold her house there in 1990, my husband and I learned that the deed had a codicil attached (now illegal) stating that the house could not be sold to a business or to "Negroes." When college choirs sang at the Baptist Church, African American students stayed with the minister. Only one Jewish family lived in town, the owners of the local junkyard as it was then called. This family, with a son my age, were neighbors and friends of my parents, and my first experience with any Jewish observance was going to the son's Bar Mitzvah in a town over an hour away. Effingham certainly could not raise a *minyan* and did not have a synagogue. I remember hearing sly comments from my friends and even some friends of my parents about "all the money" the family had and how "pushy" the son was. These were my first direct encounters with antisemitism.

While Christianity has done more than its share of promoting and teaching antisemitism, I have no memories of any such comments or teachings in the Southern Baptist Church my family attended. The evils of dancing and dating non-Baptists received more focus in the sermons than the "evils" of Jews. All non-Christians, not just Jews, were seen as lost souls desperately in need of the church's proselytizing and saving. Through organized classes and youth groups, I received a very solid grounding in the Bible, something I now greatly appreciate as a literature teacher. However, I was troubled as a teenager by the strong emotional, rather than logical, rational basis for the religion. A skeptic early on, I left the Baptist Church when I entered college; but I was indelibly marked by the intolerant attitudes I observed. I knew I did not want to ever be like that.

My mother, especially, provided a strong role model for me as I realized that she had little or no time for gossip, something which can be a kind of national pastime in small towns. Her tolerance for others and the quiet dignity with which she bore the hardships of her early life made a deep impression on me.

None of this early life may sound as if it would be fertile ground for sowing the seeds of my compulsion to study and teach about the Holocaust. And yet the experiences of seeing Christians perceive huge divisions between themselves; of seeing Christians refuse to open their restaurant or motel doors, much less the real estate market, to African Americans; of seeing and hearing disparaging remarks toward a classmate simply because he was Jewish all sensitized me to prejudice. I could not understand how such attitudes could exist in a community that proudly bore the mantle of Christianity, a religion that teaches among other things, "do unto others as you would have them do unto you." But at the core of my personal life were parents who provided role models for me that acceptance of, but not necessarily agreement with, others was better than intolerance.

AN AWAKENING IN POLAND

My various courses at three distinguished universities — the University of Chicago, Rutgers University, and Kent State University — never once mentioned the Holocaust. It was not until January 1978 when my husband Joe was named a visiting psychology professor at Warsaw University and we packed ourselves and our two young sons off to that then-Eastern bloc, communist country, that the real seeds of my Holocaust education were sown. Warsaw at that time was a dreary city dominated by the Palace of Culture, or Stalin's Wedding Cake, as the locals preferred cynically to call it. A few horse-drawn carts filled with coal and other commodities shared the streets with small cars and big buses and trams.

During our six months there, we saw oranges and bananas only three times; learned how to get veal through the black market; met warm, gracious people; and saw war memorials decorated with fresh flowers on what seemed like every street corner. Encountering these memorials made me begin to think about the events of World War II and the impact they had had on Poland. I learned about the total destruction of the city by the Nazis while the Soviets watched from the eastern side of the Vistula River. While visiting friends in Kraków, we saw a small stone commemorating the roundup and murder of neighborhood citizens by the Nazis. I saw the memorial to the Warsaw Ghetto Uprising; the small granite stone memorializing Mila 18 where the final stand of the Jewish ghetto fighters occurred; the tiny plaque on the property of a gas station indicating that this was the *Umschlagplatz*, or railway sidings, where thousands of Jews from the Warsaw ghetto were deported to their deaths in Treblinka. We visited Auschwitz with its rather sterile, yet powerful preservation of the buildings and open spaces where Nazi power rendered individual dignity and freedom dispensable. Birkenau at the time was very unkempt — and somehow more real than Auschwitz. Tall grasses surrounded the dilapidated barracks, which looked as if nothing but nature had been there since liberation. The smell of filth invaded our nostrils as we walked into the dirt-covered rooms. The sight of slatted, wooden bunks asserted that prisoners once had been there. No snack shops or souvenir stands were anywhere to be seen. Our walk along the overgrown railroad tracks from the entrance building to the crematoria remains vivid in my mind. How could such places have existed?

We visited Majdanek one bleak late winter day with a Polish friend and were shown around by a Gentile who had barely escaped being caught in one of the Nazis' periodic, unannounced street roundups in Lublin. During these acts of indiscriminate harassment, the authorities cordoned off streets and rounded up innocent people as a means of instilling terror within the population. Whether Jew or Gentile, whether guilty of underground activities or innocent of such activity, an individual caught in one of these police acts of terror was subjected to beatings, interrogation, and/or imprisonment prior to release or deportation or death. The smell of creosote, used to preserve all of the wooden buildings, still fills my nostrils, and the sight of barrack after barrack crammed from floor to ceiling with the shoes that were not good enough for the Nazis to send back to Germany still fills my eyes. An enormous mound of small, gray bits of human ash under a specially constructed roof emphasized that this had been not only a place of massive incarceration and theft, but also of massive death. All of these sights and experiences were beginning to push the Nazis' wars against both the Poles and the Jews into my consciousness.

Only a few days after our arrival in Warsaw, a friend's husband brought us two true gifts: a bottle of Bulgarian ketchup (we were told that for months shopkeepers had said *nie ma* or have none) and Polish lessons. As he was going through the basic pronunciation of letters, we reached one of the letters not found in English: a *z* with a dot above it. To exemplify the sound of this letter, he said, "*zhe*, like in *zyd*." The curl of his mouth and the edge of his tone made it apparent that whatever "*zyd*" was, it was something he despised. His pronunciation of the word for "Jew" made it sound dirty and told me more about him than I wanted to know.

Another experience was much more positive. The woman with whom my husband did research was approaching her teenage years at the beginning of World War II. The only child of fairly affluent, Gentile parents, she had a nanny and private lessons and a seemingly charmed life. Soon after the war began, her father became very active in the underground, and the dreaded heavy knock on the door in the middle of the night came in early 1940. Her father was taken away by the Gestapo and murdered soon thereafter at the local police station. Her mother was imprisoned in the Ravensbruck concentration camp for the duration of the war. Our friend, who had been hidden during the Gestapo's actions, was taken in by an aunt and uncle on the east side of the Vistula River in Warsaw. In my sheltered life in the United States, I had never encountered anyone whose life was so directly impacted by war. Our friend said her mother had received every package that had been sent to her at Ravensbruck because she was not Jewish and because the family followed the German postal rules precisely. The required stamps and signatures meant that her mother received the monthly treasure of clothing and food. Then she commented that that was the only way her mother was able to survive and that her mother shared some of the goods with other prisoners, including Jews who were never allowed to receive packages. I remember being stunned by the realization that whether or not a woman in Ravensbruck received a package of essential items depended on two things: following the postal rules and not being Jewish. The first requirement made some sense to me; the second made no sense at all.

EARLY EFFORTS AT TEACHING THE HOLOCAUST

On our return to the States, I began reading general books about World War II, but was quickly drawn to information about treatment of the Jews. Looking back on my upbringing and my experiences in Poland, I am not really surprised. I was drawn to the experiences of a people who were victimized by prejudice to the point of genocide solely because of who they were. I was incensed at the unfairness of it all and nearly ignorant of how such events could actually occur.

I also returned to the classroom in the fall of 1979, having taken a seven-year "sabbatical" to be at home with our sons while they were little. As I worked with ninth-grade students in Akron, Ohio, whose biggest concerns seemed to be that they were "starved" by lunchtime and that they did not always have the "right" label in their clothes, I decided that introducing them to the Holocaust was one way to sensitize them through historical and literary examples to the needs of others and to the dangers of inaction whenever they saw or experienced discrimination and intolerance. Very little was being done with Holocaust education at that time, especially in secondary schools. No library had a shelf filled with curricula; educational journal articles were not addressing the issues;

bookstores did not have an entire section devoted to "Holocaust." But I knew that I had to create a unit in my ninth-grade English classes that would focus on the literature of the Holocaust. And so I began.

Because I wanted to have as much time as possible to establish rapport with my students, I planned the unit for the spring. I had read Terrence Des Pres's *The Survivor: An Anatomy of Life in the Death Camps* (1976) and *Out of the Whirlwind*, a collection of Holocaust literature edited by Albert H. Friedlander (1976). I remember feeling as if I were treading on hallowed ground as I tried to conceptualize how to broach this subject with my students. How could I, a Gentile born and raised in the United States, have the audacity to present information and confront issues about the Holocaust with my public school, mostly Gentile students? How dare I help them raise questions for which I had no idea of the answers! And yet, something about the events and individuals plus something within me pushed me forward.

While I read and thought, I felt I needed more direction from someone who knew much more about the subject than I did. A mutual friend suggested that I call Esther Hexter, who worked with library resources at the Akron Jewish Community Center. The phone call began a professional and personal relationship that has proven invaluable in my work. Esther affirmed my direction and reading and inspired me with the confidence to continue. In the ensuing 15 or more years, she unselfishly provided ideas, resources, and support as I have grown in both my knowledge and my teaching skills concerning the Holocaust. She provided connections with the area's Holocaust survivors and early on paved the way for having these invaluable individuals speak with my students.

In addition to the early guidance of Esther, I was fortunate to have supportive administrators. My attitude toward activities in my classes is that it is easier to ask for forgiveness than for permission. A major role of an administrator, I believe, is to provide support for teachers but then stay out of their way. Unfortunately, many teachers with the courage to confront the Holocaust with their students find they have to confront administrators who fear the inclusion of such units. Perhaps my administrators were influenced by the university atmosphere in Kent, the home of Kent State University, or by the positive parental attitudes in the district, or by their faith in my professionalism. Whatever the reasons, none of them ever said one negative comment about the Literature of the Holocaust unit; in fact, they shared with me complimentary remarks from parents. This administrative respect and support are two more reasons why my work continued. My energies could be focused on my work with students and not be sapped by having to fight the local authorities.

If someone had asked me that first year why I was teaching this unit, I would have replied, "Because I have to; it's probably more for me than the students." Never in my wildest dreams did I imagine the ripple effect that four-week unit would create. The first year I taught the Holocaust literature unit, I remember some students in other classes asking me, "Why don't we get to study about the Holocaust?" Then other ninth-grade English teachers indicated they were interested in including a similar unit, so the second year we held sessions in which I provided information and guidance for them. During those sessions I often felt as if it were the "blind leading the blind," but together we forged ahead learning the history and literature. That year, all ninth-grade students studied the Holocaust. Our faculty shared ideas and materials and stories, and found an overwhelmingly positive response from the students. A few years later when we were revising curricula in the department, there was no question in anyone's mind that the Literature of the Holocaust unit was a required part of the curriculum for all ninth graders. This "bottom up" support and development seems to me the most effective way to incorporate Holocaust studies in the secondary curriculum. Mandated Holocaust studies do not ensure a consistently well-taught unit; in fact, they may do more damage than not teaching about the Holocaust at all if the teacher lacks the knowledge and/or skills to deal with this difficult material. Because I felt, rightly or wrongly, that to test students over the material would be somehow sacrilegious, I decided to have them write reactions to their reading and viewing experiences. This early implementation of reader-response strategies later influenced me to implement a workshop approach in all of my classes. Elie Wiesel's *Night* (1982) became the linchpin in the unit, coupled with selections from a variety of other sources, including primary source documents, poems, diary entries, and short stories. Students read, wrote personal responses, studied vocabulary, and wrote creative responses. I distinctly remember the first time I sat down to read their writing for an assignment, which simply stated: "Write a creative piece—poem, short story—in response to something you have experienced during the unit." Having worked with ninth graders, I had seen the level of their thinking and writing and was absolutely unprepared for the depth and quality of their work on this assignment. As I read their poetry, I was stunned by the power of their connections with what we had studied and moved by the depth of their emotional reactions to their new knowledge. Their writing

showed me the power of Holocaust studies when students establish some connection with the people and events of that time. As
a result of their creative work, we published a class book entitled
Reflections on the Holocaust: Man's Inhumanity to Man, writings by
class members that became one of the major events for each succeeding class. Copies of the books still are distributed everywhere,
from the local library to the United States Holocaust Memorial
Museum.

Students are moved by *Night* and the poems from Hana
Volavkova's *I Never Saw Another Butterfly* (1993); outraged by
Varian Fry's "The Massacre of the Jews," a *New Republic* article
from December 1942, detailing atrocities being perpetrated against
the Jews; and uplifted to learn about the actions of Righteous Gentiles. However, nothing affects them so powerfully, I discovered, as
hearing in person from people who were there, be they survivors,
Righteous Gentiles, or liberators. The first speaker we brought to
Roosevelt High School in Kent, Ohio, was Rabbi Abraham Feffer,
a survivor who now resided in Akron, Ohio. My sense of anxiety is
still palpable as I think about my concerns: Would the students
behave themselves? Would we be able to hear the speaker, who I
had been forewarned spoke in a soft voice? Would the students be
patient and try to understand his accent? The noisy, hyperactive
ninth graders entered the auditorium and settled down, somewhat.
As Rabbi Feffer began his story in his quiet, accented voice, the
atmosphere in that room changed. We were all transported back
to a time and place beyond our imaginations but that were clearly
part of the speaker's reality. I had never seen my rambunctious
students so attentive or so respectful and their ensuing questions
indicated that they had been fully engaged by what they had heard.
Since then, students at our school have been privileged to meet
and hear the stories of local survivors and liberators as well as
survivors who live beyond our state, survivors such as Robert Clary
and Gerda Weissman Klein, Righteous Gentile Irene Opdyke, and
liberator Leon Bass. At those moments when my own energy begins to lag and I wonder if I want to keep on with this work, I simply think of these dedicated individuals and realize how foolish I
was to even consider quitting. When I recall the students' reactions
to hearing these extraordinary people, I know the work is worthwhile.

Recently, Gerda and Kurt Klein spoke at our school. Gerda survived the Holocaust and Kurt, who later became her husband, was
a U.S. soldier who helped to liberate Buchenwald. As had occurred
with Bass's talk, students cut other classes to attend. Unfortunately, teachers are somewhat used to students cutting class to

have fun, but these students were cutting a class so they could attend a lecture! Gerda Klein's quiet dignity and genuine acceptance of others touches all who hear her, and that certainly was the case with our students and faculty. The squirming and muted talking, which pervade most assemblies of adolescents, were noticeably absent when Gerda spoke. As students of many races enveloped this beautiful, 70-plus-year-old woman after the talk, it was clear that breaches so often created by age, race, and religion had been closed, at least for the moment. Perhaps my most vivid memory about the Kleins' visit directly involved not Gerda, but Kurt. After Gerda's speech, he talked to about 40 students, half freshmen and half seniors, in my classroom. In this intimate setting, he described his first image of Gerda, a kind of stick figure at the gate in Buchenwald, and his almost immediate recognition of her inner beauty. Then he read one of the love letters he had written her later in their courtship. As this quiet man read his words of love, admiration, and devotion to this woman so long ago, there was not a dry eye in the room. Suddenly, in the presence of this man and the special relationship his words portrayed, gender and age differences dissolved as we all responded to expressions of deep-seated, genuine acceptance of another.

As I taught the Literature of the Holocaust unit over a 15-year period (1981–1996) to ninth graders, I always approached it with trepidation. More specifically, watching their reactions and growth during the unit always made me feel as if I were stripping their childhood away from them, opening their eyes to things that perhaps it would be better if they had not seen. However, I felt that they needed to see and know these events because they are a part, albeit an ugly one, of what it means to be a part of humanity. Over the years many, many students, both during and long after their year with me, have said that the unit that impacted them the most was the Holocaust unit. I must admit that a few parents expressed concerns because their children's newfound knowledge upset them. I always responded that my intention was never to upset any students but rather to open their eyes, minds, and hearts. I commented that we were fortunate our children were learning about these atrocious acts through books and films rather than in person as so many other young people had. Conversely, many parents have said that they were so glad that their child "got" to study about the Holocaust because it was such an important thing for them to know. I often think about why that is the case. On the surface, I am asking them to study one subject many of them despise, namely history, and another subject many say they do not like, namely English. Why, then, does learning about this genocidal event affect them so deeply? There are many reasons, but one is the intrinsically compelling nature of the situation: How could one civilized people try to destroy another civilized people in Europe in the twentieth century? Many of the readings focus on young people, and my students have connected with them in deeper ways than even I had imagined they would.

I have found and believe that to teach Holocaust literature in a powerful and pedagogically sound manner one must know and understand the history of the time as well as the literature created both during and after the events. Students must be guided through the chronology of the gradual tightening of the Nazi noose around the necks of Jews and other "undesirables." Because the literature of the Holocaust is riveted in these historical events, teachers must help students understand the impact of these events on humans and how those events and reactions are transformed into literature. Having students read nonfiction accounts can provide them with direct personal experiences about the impact of events. Poetry, with its transformative power, can crystallize experiences and observations and focus thinking on many levels. I shied away from teaching fiction of the Holocaust for a number of years, because I did not want to give my students any opportunity to say that the Holocaust itself was fiction. However, I now believe that fiction can be a powerful means of sensitizing students *if the historical information is accurate, if the narrator is authentic, and if the piece is clearly identified as fiction.* Literary truths are as important as historical ones. Both are rooted in facts, but the literary ones are presented through the transforming lens of the author's imagination while the historical ones are presented through the analytical lens of the author's reasoning. Students need to be led to understand this distinction.

In addition to reading various texts, students must write and be given the opportunity to speak. They need to write in response to what they read so they can process the emotions the material churns up, so they can analyze causes and effects, and so they can try to find levels of understanding in the literature. They need to have ample time to discuss what they read because in so doing, they can clarify ideas and emotions. For all of these things to occur in the classroom, the teacher must be careful not to try and focus on too many pieces of literature. "Less is more" is a key motto for me as I work with students, meaning it is most important to choose a few solid works of literature and spend time truly helping students make those pieces their own.

Reflecting back on my efforts, I would say that my primary goals in teaching about the Holocaust have been to (1) educate myself and others about the historical events that led to this genocide and about the literature that has risen from these events, and (2) sensitize myself and others about the need for compassionate acts toward others and the strength to speak out when hurtful, hateful acts are discovered.

Educating myself has resulted in my becoming a student of the history. Among the historians who have influenced me the most, Martin Gilbert's *The Holocaust: A History of the Jews of Europe During the Second World War* (1985) has been key in my understanding of the myriad players in this genocidal saga. David S. Wyman's *The Abandonment of the Jews: America and the Holocaust: 1941–1945* (1984) forced me to address the complicity of the United States and has helped me answer questions raised by my students about these issues. On a more individual and frightening level, Christopher Browning's *Ordinary Men: Reserve Battalion 101 and the Final Solution in Poland* (1992) made me aware of how easy it is to cross the line to become a perpetrator. His findings, too, have been extremely helpful as my students question how and why individual citizens behaved as they did.

One individual in particular, Lawrence L. Langer, has had the most profound impact on my thinking about Holocaust literature. His insights on the creative process and the Holocaust have both broadened and deepened my own knowledge and understanding. Two of his volumes have especially spurred my thinking: *Versions of Survival: The Holocaust and the Human Spirit* (1982) and *Admitting the Holocaust: Collected Essays* (1995). The former book helped me understand the role that language itself plays as we try to write or talk about experiences of atrocity. More specifically, that using our words and images to deal with victims' and survivors' experiences creates yet a third reality and thus we need to be ever cognizant of that fact. Further, it was impressed upon me that the voice of Auschwitz and the voice of civilization are not the same and to try and find hope or redemptive elements in the Holocaust is futile. *Admitting the Holocaust* insightfully addresses a number of authors and writings about the Holocaust and helps me better understand, especially, the complexities of "transforming" human experience with atrocity into a literary experience that posits no simple answers.

When I began this work with students, I think I believed the now ubiquitous George Santayana quote, "Those who do not know history are bound to repeat it." However, it is now evident that those who do know history also repeat it. Simply knowing the history is not enough. I now believe that to teach young people about the Holocaust in the hope that they, individually, will be able to prevent

future genocides is naive. Had my Ohio students been young people
during World War II, there is nothing they alone could have done
to stop Hitler. Today, they, by themselves, could do nothing to stop
the Hutu-Tutsi violence; they could not force Milosevic to end
ethnic cleansing in Kosovo. To pretend that they could is to create
a sham, and young people see through shams very quickly. On the
other hand, as individuals they can be informed intellectually,
emotionally, and ethically about such issues and cooperate with
others in speaking out against genocidal acts. The teacher's job is
to provide students not only with opportunities to learn the facts
of history, but also with options to act responsibly whenever and
wherever deprivation of human rights and genocide appear later.
I believe that perpetrators of genocide will not be moved to stop
their aggressions by one voice, but they may be moved by the voices
of many.

To study the Holocaust and experience literary responses to it
should, I believe, make us more sensitive to the impact of intolerance, to the insidious nature of any hatred when we allow it to seep
into the pores of ourselves and society. Thus, we begin the unit
with a week of focusing on issues of general intolerance, of asking
students and teacher alike to seriously examine their own attitudes — as uncomfortable as that may be. With these moments of
introspection as a groundwork, students then can move on to begin to see what unleashed intolerance and hatred can create. The
example of unbridled prejudice and intolerance, such as the
Holocaust, definitely makes a powerful impact on the students. By
studying various nonfiction works as well as chronologies of the
Holocaust period, which delineate the gradual implementation of
laws and regulations aimed at removing Jewish rights, they learn
that the Holocaust did not occur overnight. In turn, this engen-
ders wonder about what would have happened if the early out-
breaks of intolerance had been stopped. And therein lies the major
reason I now teach about the Holocaust. What if the early acts of
intolerance had been stopped, vote by vote or person by person?

Gradually, during the course of study, my students talk about
being more aware of ethnic jokes and sometimes gathering the
courage to speak out against them, of no longer going along with
the ugly comments other students make about the mentally and
physically challenged students who share our hallways and caf-
eteria. They talk about being more aware of genocides around the
world. They begin to realize that the end of tolerance and genocide
in the world begins with the individual and that genocide occurs,
in part, because some individuals band together to act upon intolerances and hatred while other individuals stand by in silence

to do nothing. Thus, our individual acts are supremely important. Any unit of study that makes students more aware of and sensitive to these issues and, perhaps, gives them the courage both to speak out against injustices and to behave in positive ways is a success. The Literature of the Holocaust unit does that.

DEEPENING ACADEMIC AND PROFESSIONAL INVOLVEMENT

Our family spent the 1984–1985 academic year at Stanford University where Joe was a visiting faculty member. I secured professional leave from my teaching job and embarked on an exhilarating, stimulating year of auditing courses. At Stanford Dr. John Felstiner offered a Literature of the Holocaust course, which I took, and this course helped me organize and refine my ideas as I encountered new literature and revisited old in a haven away from my daily teaching responsibilities. I remember much discussion about the poetry of Paul Celan, and I can still hear Felstiner reading "Todesfuge" in English and then German, and feeling in my gut the power of that poem.

The course syllabus included *This Way for the Gas, Ladies and Gentlemen* (1983), a book of short stories by Tadeusz Borowski, a Gentile survivor of Auschwitz who was previously unknown to me. To this day I have an indelible memory of the opening of his short story "The People Who Walked On" as it describes the excellent location for a soccer field at Auschwitz, near where people were gassed to death. The sense of normalcy of the violence and death in the camps shocked me and forced me to consider the way humans cope with situations that seem impossible. Another window opened for me when Felstiner's wife Mary, a professor at San Francisco State University, came to class to show slides of the paintings of Charlotte Salomon, a woman who used art as a coping mechanism during the Holocaust. Seeing this artistic work, done during times of such danger and stress, and hearing the story of Salomon's life moved my thinking about resistance to a new level as I better understood resistance outside the context of violence.

Because of the difficulty of Celan's poetry and the awful power of Borowski's work, I tended not to include them in my work with ninth graders. But artists' works have become important for me in helping students to begin to understand the complex meaning of resistance during the Holocaust. They begin to understand that the art work by the young people in Terezin or by Salomon or by any artists were ways to enhance and perhaps extend life, and that in itself was resistance to Nazi goals.

In 1986, then-Governor Richard Celeste of Ohio convened a group of educators, clergy, liberators, survivors, and other interested parties in Columbus to form the Ohio Council on Holocaust Education. The council's purpose was to provide information, resource materials, suggested pedagogical strategies, and exposure to the Holocaust for the public, private, and parochial schools in the State of Ohio. Because of my Holocaust work in the secondary classroom I was asked to serve on this council; this appointment ultimately had a major impact on my professional life, as over the next two years we analyzed the problems and needs regarding Holocaust education in the state.

I was appointed to the Materials and Curriculum Committee, whose charge was to produce teaching materials for dissemination to schools throughout Ohio. The subcommittee was chaired by Leatrice Rabinsky, a woman whom I had admired from a distance because of her early groundbreaking work in Holocaust education. She began teaching classes in Holocaust literature at Cleveland Heights High School, Ohio, in the 1970s and was widely respected for her expertise, energy, and skills. Much to my great good fortune, Leatrice asked me to join her in coediting the curriculum that the committee was charged to produce. I agreed, and an extraordinary professional and personal relationship was born.

Leatrice and I might be seen as a bit of an odd couple, as she is a devout Orthodox Jew and rabbi's granddaughter, and I a Gentile from the Christian tradition. But our passions for literature, justice, and teaching about the Holocaust bound us together quickly. She seemed to know detail upon detail about the Holocaust; she seemed to know virtually every Holocaust survivor in the Cleveland area; she seemed to be ready to work 25 hours a day. I felt as if I were sitting at the feet of a giant. While I learned many things about the Holocaust from Leatrice, perhaps the most important things she taught me concerned Orthodox Judaism. I remember clearly the first time it really sunk into me that she would not, for religious reasons, eat food which I had prepared in my kitchen. At first I was almost offended because when I visited in her home, she fed me as if I were a queen. But in our ensuing discussion, I came to understand the source of her beliefs, to respect her right to hold them, and to embrace her as a friend in spite of this difference between us. This experience made me think seriously about how we teach tolerance. I did not view myself as intolerant and yet in the fact of my own ignorance about Orthodox religious dietary beliefs, I found myself creating a barrier between us. Civil, direct discussion and explanations removed that barrier; and I became more sensitized to the importance of helping students find ways to talk through differences.

Over the next couple of years, Leatrice and I gathered teaching materials from middle and secondary teachers from around Ohio. We were determined to create and include curricular materials that had been tested in real classrooms and had proven successful. Thanks to the cooperation and generosity of teachers from throughout the state, we published *The Holocaust: Prejudice Unleashed* in 1989. One major goal for the Ohio curriculum was to provide both history and English teachers with accurate materials and field-tested teaching strategies in a format that would enable them to tailor the materials to their own classes. Thus, we used a chronological approach and included primary source historical documents, short explanatory essays, and literary selections. Every secondary school in Ohio was sent a copy of the curriculum. Summer teachers' workshops were instituted and a cadre of educated teachers was created. In 1994, Leatrice and I revised the curriculum and a second edition was published. Leatrice has been a professional role model and wonderful friend to me since our first collaboration; her wisdom, tolerance, expertise, and generosity are exceptional.

After being appointed to the Ohio Council on Holocaust Education, I became even more involved in working to expand Holocaust education in the state. This volunteer council of energetic and dedicated educators and others committed to Holocaust education coordinates numerous summer workshops for teachers and outreach programs. My participation in the council's workshops has only strengthened my belief that grassroots work with teachers *and* grassroots implementation of the curriculum is the way to create long-lasting positive effects. No one is well served by programs that make an initial bright flame but then fizzle out shortly thereafter. And no one is well served by forcing educators to deal with challenging and sensitive material when they have no desire to do so. However, when teachers voluntarily spend an intensive week studying the Holocaust and ways to teach about it, when they are personally engaged with the material and issues and emotions, then they are more likely to be well prepared to engage their students. *That* becomes a solid foundation for the continuance of Holocaust education.

The Impact of Vladka Meed on My Teaching about the Holocaust

Another step in my development as a Holocaust educator occurred in July 1987 when I participated in a study program in Israel run by Vladka Meed with the support of the American

Gathering of Holocaust Survivors and the American Federation of
Teachers. This was an early trip in a now-established study program during which we spent three weeks in Israel, two at Kibbutz
Lochamei Hagettaot (Ghetto Fighters' House) in northern Israel and
one in Jerusalem, studying Jewish resistance.

Vladka is an amazing woman, a survivor of the Warsaw ghetto
who served underground as a courier smuggling both children
and weapons. Although she was older than anyone else on the
trip, she seemed to have more energy than any of us, pushing us
almost to exhaustion with seminar sessions and side trips. Whenever anyone complained about needing a break, she would reply,
"But there is so much to learn." And learn I did. To say that the
experience was life changing might be a bit of hyperbole, but it
certainly had a tremendous impact on my development in Holocaust studies.

A typical question from my students at that time was, "Why didn't
the Jews fight back?" In their youthful naiveté and assurance, they
would state what they would have done had they been in that situation. The study program not only provided me with more information, but it also complicated my thinking about resistance
issues. To be on the kibbutz, which was founded in April 1949 in
memory of the Jewish fighters and their families, made some of the
history come alive. I will never forget Reuven Dafne, a short, grand-
fatherly figure, calmly describing what it was like to parachute
behind enemy lines into Hungary with Hannah Senesh, a young
Palestinian Jew and poet. It was to Dafne that she gave her now
famous poem "Blessed Is the Match" just before she was captured
by the Nazis. As he recounted the beauty and strength of Hannah
and then the tortures she endured because she was unwilling to
name her accomplices, I realized even more how important it is to
share these examples with young people. Here was a woman barely
older than my students who accepted the challenges and risks of
resisting the Nazis through both the nonviolence of poetic words
and the violence of guns. Did she stop Hitler? No, but she did act
against evil and now provides a role model for all of us. Being
among people who knew Zivia Lubetkin and Yitzhak Zuckerman,
each a noted Jewish resistance fighter in Poland who managed to
escape to Palestine, made the risks and realities of armed and spiritual resistance almost palpable.

Spending time in the museums on the kibbutz and at Yad
Vashem, the national museum and memorial to the Holocaust in
Jerusalem, deepened my knowledge and understanding of what
occurred during the Holocaust and increased my awe that anyone
could have resisted at all. The idea of spiritual resistance through

poetry, song, and clandestine activities was something that I had not thought much about until this trip. Now that, too, changed. The scope and depth of the presentations and experiences not only increased my storehouse of information but more importantly deepened my own understanding of what it meant to resist the Nazis.

Through the forceful personalities of Vladka Meed and her husband Ben, a Polish Jew who survived on the Aryan side, teachers who participate in the summer seminar join a kind of fraternity where old contacts are maintained and new ones created. Working throughout the school year in isolated classrooms, teaching challenging emotional material to students with their own personal challenges, teachers need all of the help they can get. To be known as one of "Vladka's people" creates a bond of support among all of us who were privileged to be part of the seminars. That sort of support has helped me continue my work in Holocaust education.

Furthering My Education about the Holocaust in Greece

Thanks to my husband's academic work in psycholinguistics, my Holocaust education received another boost in 1993 when we spent six months in Thessaloníki (formerly Salonika), Greece, on a faculty exchange program. This vibrant, beautiful city perched on the hills by the bay had a population that was nearly 50 percent Jewish until 1927, when a massive exchange of populations occurred between Turkey and Greece. Speaking Ladino, a Hispanic language that borrowed words from Hebrew, Turkish, and Greek, rather than Greek, the Jews ran the port and numerous small businesses. By the autumn of 1940, the 50,000 Salonikan Jews still used Ladino and remained quite separate from the rest of the population. Then life changed completely with the April 1941 Nazi invasion. Between March 15 and the middle of May 1943, over 42,000 Jews were deported to Auschwitz where nearly all perished; and by August, Salonika was purged of Jews. In 1993 only about 1,000 Jews remained in the population of 1 million.

Few remnants of a previously vibrant Jewish life are visible in the city. Every time we went to the campus of Aristotle University, I was reminded of the Holocaust because the university is built on the site of the former Jewish cemetery. One section of a nearby wall incorporates Jewish tombstones. One small synagogue remains, but I was told that it is very hard to gather a *minyan*. A rebuilt Jewish cemetery with a large, impressive Holocaust memorial sits on the outskirts of the city, but few people at the university seemed to know it existed. An occasional building is graced with some

Hebrew or a Star of David, the only noticeable evidence of a once-thriving culture.

In the midst of this bustling contemporary city sits the small, crowded, vibrant Molho Bookstore, owned by a Jewish family who decided to return to Thessaloníki after the war. The grand dame of this store is the lovely, gracious, multilingual Mrs. Molho, whom I befriended. Sitting with her among shelves of books or in the little coffee shop next door, I received a first-person education in the impact of the Holocaust on this family. Over our visits together she told me in her lightly accented English that because they sold books, their store was one of the first to be seized and closed by the Nazis. Her husband managed to escape the city and was hidden on one of the eastern islands while through some family connections she fled to Spain. Thus, they both escaped the dreaded roundups and ultimate deportation.

During one of our conversations, when she was describing how much more active the intellectual life had been in Athens than Salonika, I remember asking her why they had returned. She hesitated a moment and then responded that they came back simply because they had been able to reclaim their bookstore. Life has continued for this highly educated family, but this wise woman's eyes and quiet demeanor suggest that there are many stories still untold. However, through her willingness to share as much as she did, I have a deeper understanding of the Holocaust's devastating impact on both communities and individuals and of the strength and courage of those who endured.

When I learned that the Jews of Salonika and Ioannina, a city in the northwest section of Greece, had been virtually wiped out by the Nazis but most of those in Athens had survived, my questions increased about means of survival—and destruction. How could the circumstances and outcomes have been so different for Jews in the same country? The answers are myriad and complicated. Salonika was controlled by the Germans, while the Italians initially controlled the areas around both Ioannina and Athens. The German takeover of Ioannina in April 1943 left the Jews of that city in peril. The Jews of Salonika and Ioannina had lived segregated from the rest of the population while the Jews of Athens lived totally assimilated among their non-Jewish neighbors. Salonika and Ioannina were led by rabbis who tried to save their people through appeasement of the Nazis while Athens' leader actively pleaded for and aided in escapes. The non-Jews of Salonika and Ioannina stood by while hazings, roundups, and deportations occurred, but the non-Jews of Athens were more willing to risk helping their assimilated Jewish neighbors. Having the opportunity to live in Greece heightened my awareness of the complexities concerning the Holocaust and made me even more cognizant of the necessity of helping my students understand those complexities.

THE WORK CONTINUES

In February 1994 I was appointed by the National Council of Teachers of English (NCTE) to be chair of its newly created Committee on Teaching about Genocide and Intolerance. The committee was charged "to develop and submit for publication materials on the literature of genocide and intolerance; to include in the materials components such as compilations of resources (for example, bibliographies, visual media, lists of agencies and associations) and materials on how to teach pertinent literary works." I vividly remember reading that directive for the first time and saying to myself, "This is an impossible task; it is too broad, covers too much territory." The original resolution submitted by eight NCTE members had focused only on teaching about the Holocaust, but the NCTE Executive Committee had expanded the scope to include a variety of issues relating to intolerance and genocide.

The resulting 18-member committee met for the first time at the November 1994 convention in Orlando. We discussed a myriad of topics and were acutely aware of the political aspect of our task. By the very nature of our work we were adamantly saying that the English classroom should be a place where social, as well as literary, issues are confronted. The English classroom should not be a place where only the aesthetics of language and language production are studied; it should be a dynamic situation in which literary conflicts and themes connect with our students' lives. We met face-to-face only once a year at the NCTE convention and yet managed to conceptualize three books that addressed a broad array of issues along the spectrum of intolerance to genocide for use by teachers at the high school, middle school, and elementary levels: *Teaching for a Tolerant World, Grades 9-12* (1999); *Teaching for a Tolerant World, Grades 6-8* (2000); and *Teaching for a Tolerant World, Grades K-5* (1999).

The most recent major step in my Holocaust education journey occurred when I was selected as a 1997-1998 Mandel Fellow by the United States Holocaust Memorial Museum. For a week in August 1997 we were immersed in the museum's exhibits and archives and consumed with discussions and presentations on why, how, and what to teach about the Holocaust. Of the invited speakers, Robert Skloot's discussion of teaching the Holocaust through theater impacted me the most. His in-depth comments about one

play in particular—Harold and Edith Lieberman's *Throne of Straw*—
coupled with his insightful thoughts on ethical questions related
to the Holocaust extended my learning and made a direct impact
on my teaching. The play raises questions about independence and
complicity in the behavior of Chaim Rumkowski, head of the
Judenrat, or Jewish Council, in the Lodz ghetto in Poland. Skloot's
thoughtful comments about the terribly complicated nature of decision making in the face of impossible choices, namely satisfying
the Nazis and simultaneously saving the Lodz Jews, moved me to
have my Advanced Placement seniors study the aforementioned
play. Combining historical and fictional figures, the play exempli-
fies the dilemma Rumkowski faced and provided a framework for
my students and myself to learn more Holocaust history and contemplate important ethical questions.

Another meaningful and practical part of the week included being introduced to and given time in the research areas of the museum, including the library, photo archives, and oral history
archives. As a typical secondary teacher faced with five classes a
day five days a week, I have too little time for research and reflection. Having ready access to the museum's incredibly moving and
educational permanent exhibits made it possible to revisit and
linger over displays, to feel in my bones a multitude of emotions,
ranging from the hate-filled atmosphere created by the Nazi propaganda, to the positive atmosphere created by the lists of Righteous Gentiles, to the heart-wrenching feelings created by the
stories of the survivors.

In 1997 I stopped teaching ninth graders, and thus am not inti-
mately involved each year with an intensive encounter of students
with the Holocaust. While I incorporate shorter works into my senior Advanced Placement English course and continue to write and
make presentations on teaching about the Holocaust, the Mandel
program has been invaluable for me. It has provided a rich network
of fellow Holocaust educators and important outreach opportunities that help serve as a clearinghouse for a variety of professional
meetings and activities.

A few years ago at a faculty holiday luncheon, a woman with
whom I had taught for many years began telling me about a recent conversation she had had with a Jewish student in one of her
classes. Knowing virtually nothing about Judaism and Jewish traditions, she was interested in what he and his family did at the
holidays. After she finished describing what the young man had
told her, she looked at me and asked, "How do you and your family celebrate?" Taken aback, I answered, "Well, we have a Christmas tree, give presents, go the Christmas Eve services, and. . . ."

Her face took on a bit of color as she asked in a voice of incredulity, "But aren't you Jewish?" When I asked her why she thought I was Jewish, she said, "Because you make such good chopped chicken livers and you teach about the Holocaust." The stereotypes inherent in her assumption are obvious, but I took them as a compliment. As a young girl growing up in a small town awash in religious and racial intolerances, I never dreamed that I would do either one.

REFERENCES

Borowski, Tadeusz (1983). *This Way for the Gas, Ladies and Gentlemen.* New York: Penguin Books.

Browning, Christopher (1992). *Ordinary Men: Reserve Battalion 101 and the Final Solution in Poland.* New York: HarperCollins.

Danks, Carol, and Rabinsky, Leatrice (Eds.) (1999). *Teaching for a Tolerant World, Grades 9–12.* Urbana, IL: National Council of Teachers of English.

Des Pres, Terrence (1976). *The Survivor: An Anatomy of Life in the Death Camps.* New York: Oxford University Press.

Friedlander, Albert H. (Ed.) (1976). *Out of the Whirlwind: A Reader of Holocaust Literature.* New York: Schocken Books.

Fry, Varian (1942). "The Massacres of the Jews." *The New Republic* December 21, 107(25): 815–819.

Gilbert, Martin (1985). *The Holocaust: A History of the Jews of Europe during the Second World War.* New York: Holt, Rinehart and Winston.

Langer, Lawrence L. (1995). *Admitting the Holocaust: Collected Essays.* New York: Oxford University Press.

———. (1982). *Versions of Survival: The Holocaust and the Human Spirit.* Albany: State University of New York Press.

———. (Ed.) (1995). *Art from the Ashes: A Holocaust Anthology.* New York: Oxford University Press.

Robertson, Judith (Ed.) (1999). *Teaching for a Tolerant World, Grades K–5.* Urbana, IL: National Council of Teachers of English.

Rudnitsky, Rose (Ed.) (2000). *Teaching for a Tolerant World, Grades 6–8.* Urbana, IL: National Council of Teachers of English.

Skloot, Robert (Ed.) (1982). "Throne of Straw," by Harold Lieberman and Edith Lieberman. In Skloot's *The Theatre of the Holocaust*, vol. 1. Madison, WI: The University of Wisconsin Press, pp. 113–197.

Volavkova, Hana (Ed.) (1993). *I Never Saw Another Butterfly.* New York: Schocken Books.

Wiesel, Elie (1982). *Night.* New York: Bantam.

Wyman, David S. (1984). *The Abandonment of the Jews: America and the Holocaust, 1941–1945.* New York: Pantheon Books.

Chapter 5

~

From Silence to Service:
A Holocaust Educator's Journey

Harold Lass

SILENCE

I came to the study of the Holocaust late in my teaching career, 15 years late. There were two reasons for this, really, not the least of which was my parents' virtual total silence about events in the Old Country. The only sense of loss I remember experiencing as a child because of these events was the absence of grandparents and the presence of few aunts, uncles, and cousins. "They're all dead," I was told. "Hitler killed them," they said. That was the total extent of what they shared with me.

My parents had left Poland as teens and arrived in Toronto in the late twenties where they met and married—long before the doors to European escape routes were slammed shut and the death camps "opened for business." Both of my parents had been sponsored by a relative already here. It was assumed life would be better for them in Canada. That assumption proved to be prophetic.

I was born in 1943 in Toronto, just before Elie Wiesel (a survivor of the Holocaust, a noted novelist and essayist, and a Nobel Prize recipient for peace) was enslaved in Auschwitz-Birkenau, and just after General Stroop quelled the Warsaw Ghetto Uprising and announced, "The Warsaw Ghetto is no more." The youngest of three children, I attended a yeshiva for two years, took lessons from a rabbi to prepare me for my Bar Mitzvah, and attended an Orthodox synagogue with my father, usually only on the High Holidays. Still, not a single word to me from anyone in the Jewish community about the massacres in Europe. So, when I married and began my high school teaching career in 1965, it was not surprising that the events of the Holocaust were far removed from my mind. Over and above that, my first English teaching position was in the small town of Fort Erie. There were only two other Jewish households in the community, and I felt, for whatever reason, that I should keep a low "Jewish" profile. Tellingly, one day after my wife Diana and I had just returned from services for Rosh Hashanah at a Reform temple in Buffalo, a school trustee who saw me in town that afternoon on a school day reported me to the principal, accusing me of taking off an illegal day. He had never heard of Rosh Hashanah. After teaching English for two years in Fort Erie, I was hired by a large Toronto public high school to teach English and history. Not until 13 years later were the events of the Holocaust to enter my life and my career.

I said there were two reasons for my late encounter with the history of the Holocaust. The silence of my parents and the Jewish community, no doubt, played their part; but more importantly, it was the absence of even the mention of the word "Holocaust" or "Jew" in Canada's public high school curricula in the 1950s and 1960s. When we studied World War II, the texts seemed to obscure, even negate the murder of millions of Jews. In 1979, that rigidity was about to change, and I would, by checking off a box on a conference evaluation form, help initiate that change.

THE COMMITTEE

In October 1979, I attended a local one-day Holocaust conference for educators. There had never before been one for Toronto teachers. Two of the conference organizers, Alan Bardikoff (who was working on his doctorate in psychology at the time and later became a therapist) and Rabbi Mark Shapiro, opened the day with a film (*Holocaust*) and a brief explanation about the importance of teaching the Holocaust in the public schools. We eventually broke into smaller seminar groups to speak with a survivor. The survivor's experiences were remarkably vivid. On the death march from Auschwitz, in the dead of winter, emaciated, wearing only threadbare cotton prisoner's rags and wooden clogs, he ran for miles on threat of death. He said he was so exhausted, he slept while he ran. He wept when he told us that he now wears a heavy sheepskin coat in the winter but still feels chilled. His story had a profound effect on me. I had never met a survivor until then and as he conveyed his firsthand ordeal, I found myself wondering how he ever survived such a nightmarish experience. It was then that I realized that the events of the Holocaust carried such a powerful message that they had to become part of the public schools' curricula. To make students aware of the process by which this man had been enslaved, demeaned, and brutalized might alert them should the process begin again with any group of people as the target. So, on the conference evaluation form, I placed a check mark beside the statement, "I would like to become a member of the Holocaust Remembrance Committee." The rest, as they say, is history.

Prior to the creation of this committee, awareness of the Holocaust in Toronto's public schools didn't exist. Consequently, we had to devise a strategy to interest board administrators, teachers, and students in the value of Holocaust studies. Since Toronto prided itself on its cultural diversity and the Toronto Board of Education was committed to fighting racism in any form, we decided to contact those administrators on the board whose responsibility it was to formulate and implement antiracist policies and programs for Toronto schools. As a result, Alan Bardikoff convinced two board administrators that because the Holocaust was this century's most thoroughly documented racist act, the study of the Holocaust history and literature would alert Toronto high school students to the brutal realities of racism unchecked.

The Toronto Board agreed to host a series of three evening lectures in the spring of 1981 by noted Holocaust educators and scholars for the purpose of convincing Toronto Board members of the importance of addressing this history in Toronto's public schools. Margot Stern Strom of Facing History and Ourselves, a noted Holocaust education organization based in the United States; Professor Michael Marrus, a highly respected historian and author of *The Holocaust in History*; and Dr. Gunther Plaut, senior rabbi of Holy Blossom Temple, were our invited speakers. The response to the lecture series was encouraging in that we had managed to get the board's attention. The teachers were next.

THE SEMINARS

From the outset, Alan and I realized that to enable teachers to teach this complex history they would need solid understanding of the history as well as sound classroom strategies. Another key concern we knew we must address was: How do you get through all this without drowning in despair? We decided, therefore, to establish an annual seminar on teaching the Holocaust to be held each fall, so that if teachers wanted to explore the Holocaust with their students that school year, they would have already attended the seminar. We focused on a seminar theme (like "Rescue and Rescuers") and not only invited a high-profile author like Yaffa

Eliach, survivor and author of *Hasidic Tales of the Holocaust*, to deliver the keynote address and to conduct seminars, but also provided teaching strategy sessions for history and English teachers. Among the many issues we agreed to address were the importance of avoiding simple answers to complex questions, stereotypes of the victims and perpetrators, and "survival" games and other forms of role-playing. We also furnished sample course outlines and appropriate classroom activities. To this day, subsequent sessions of this well-attended seminar continues to provide current research and teaching strategies to high school teachers.

I also decided at this time to introduce a senior literature course on the Holocaust in my department at Northern Secondary School. I asked one of my colleagues, Barb Walther, to join me because she had read a great deal of fiction and nonfiction Holocaust literature, had exceptional analytical abilities, and was sensitive to the needs of her students. She accepted, and we developed a course in which the content consisted of a variety of memoirs (for example, *Night* by Wiesel, *Fragments of Isabella* by Isabella Leitner, *None of Us Will Return* by Charlotte Delbo), poetry (for example, "The Hangman" by Maurice Ogden and "Babi Yar" by Yevgeny Yevtushenko), documentaries ("Genocide," an episode of the British Broadcast Corporation's *The World at War* television series), short stories, and encounters with Holocaust survivors. The success of that course, which was the most popular English elective in the school, led to the introduction of a one-semester literature course on the Holocaust at Northern in grade 11 where it remains to this day. (It is worth noting that Barb went on to write a curriculum, along with Frank Bialystok, a historian and a noted Holocaust educator in Canada, for the Toronto Board. They adopted an interdisciplinary approach, and the curriculum is still available and still used.) The upshot of these efforts was that the introduction of Holocaust studies in a Toronto public school had taken root. Now it was time to reach a wider audience.

While the annual seminar on teaching the Holocaust attracted many teachers from different school boards, the power to include Holocaust studies in any English or history school curriculum was vested in the individual department head at a school. It was necessary, therefore, that Alan and I speak to the various associations of English and history. Toronto's was our first.

Now in the many years I've been involved in bringing Holocaust studies to educators, only once did I encounter resistance from a teacher that, I felt, stemmed from antisemitic sentiment. That said, I must add here that teachers and department heads did raise serious legitimate concerns about the material. That was anticipated. They felt that teachers would need specialized training to help them deal with the sensitive questions posed by their students, the possibility of the presence of deniers in the classroom, the feelings of desperation or hopelessness the material might engender, and so on. On the other hand, the individual who expressed antisemitism was an English department head in a high school located in a very affluent area of Toronto, and his objection seemed unreasonable. I felt certain there was an ulterior motive to it. More specifically, the department head insisted we would offend students whose family origins were German by teaching about the Holocaust. But it was quickly pointed out by me and others at the meeting that World War II had been taught in history classes for years. And history clearly saw Germany and Japan as aggressors. No one seemed concerned about the "feelings" of Canadian students of German and Japanese origin in those classes. It was further pointed out that teachers in his own department taught novels that clearly identified certain countries, like South Africa and its apartheid system, as criminal regimes, yet no one was concerned about the feelings of students who were from South Africa and whose parents still had strong economic and political ties to the white pro-apartheid government. Besides, Alan and I were careful to emphasize, the study of the Holocaust was not intended to point fingers, but to present a side of human nature that we should take steps to avoid in the future, if possible. The department head persisted in saying that he couldn't understand how studying about what happened to Jews could have to do with English literature. There was silence in the room. That his intentions were spurious was driven home to me a number of years later when we met at a conference. The Israeli incursion into Lebanon was under way at the time. He made the effort to find me during a coffee break and announced that the new Nazis had finally invaded Lebanon.

Ultimately, our presentations to department heads in Toronto and other boards gradually began to generate minicourses dealing with the Holocaust in a variety of schools. It was then that we also set about to reach our largest audience. In 1980 the committee established an annual seminar on the Holocaust for students.

From 1980 to the present, this seminar has been so heavily subscribed (over 600 students register each May), that we are forced to turn many away for lack of physical space and personnel. We have thought about running the seminar day twice, but our limited resources would make this difficult. Like the teachers' seminar, we began the day in plenary with a film. One year it was *Now You Are Free*—a documentary about U.S. soldiers who entered the Buchenwald concentration camp—and this was followed by a keynote speaker, Dr. Leon Bass, an African American who appeared in the film. He was one of the U.S. soldiers who was present when the GIs "liberated" Buchenwald. Bass held the 600-plus students rapt as he told them that as a young African American, he believed that he and other black Americans were the only minority group who were suffering discrimination at the hands of those with power—that is until he entered Buchenwald. The army, and life in general, hadn't prepared him for what he witnessed—the walking dead, the Jewish survivors who were barely clinging to life in the camp. It was then he realized racism could target anyone, that hatred had caused the suffering of these survivors just as surely as though their skin had been black. Following a question-and-answer period after the keynote address, students were divided into small groups for a discussion led by facilitators around Holocaust-related issues. Then, after lunch, the students had a session with a survivor. One of the survivors, Gerda Frieberg, was repeatedly asked about punishment she endured in the camp. She told of the time she and the other women prisoners debated whether or not they should fast on Yom Kippur (the Jewish Day of Atonement). They decided to fast as a sign of spirit and defiance. So, that morning, after the meager "breakfast" was issued, the food remained untouched as they were marched off to slave labor in the nearby town. The commandant said nothing. The next morning, the women prisoners were desperate to end the fast. When they lined up for roll call, the commandant informed them that since they were not hungry yesterday, they were most likely not hungry today. The women, who were all close to starvation, went 48 hours without food. Privately, Gerda told me that she never related to the students any of the beatings she suffered, like the time her sewing machine jammed at a uniform factory where she was a slave, and she was beaten, nearly to the point of unconsciousness, because she was accused of sabotage. So well known has this seminar become that we have busloads of students arriving from out of town.

Eventually we introduced a separate seminar for seventh and eighth grade students. The question of age appropriateness has always been one with which the committee has struggled over the years: "At what age do you begin to deal in a formal way in the classroom with the Holocaust and related issues?" I can remember speaking to a group of adults once when the question of age appropriateness was raised. I mentioned that I had compiled an annotated bibliography of books about the Holocaust specially written for elementary school children. The parents wouldn't let me leave until I had taken every one of their addresses and promised to mail them the bibliography. Clearly, many parents want their kids to know about what happened but don't know how or when to tell them. My experience has been that grade six is the earliest I would introduce the literature and history of the Holocaust, and then only by using books that have been written specifically for that age group. Any earlier than that requires a maturity that many children wouldn't yet possess.

WORKS THAT HAVE INFLUENCED MY EFFORTS IN HOLOCAUST EDUCATION

At this point I should note that numerous texts have influenced my thinking, curriculum development, and teaching on the Holocaust. Among the scholarly works that have most influenced me are *The War against the Jews, 1933–1945* by Lucy Dawidowicz and *The Holocaust in History* by Michael Marrus. In my mind, for a thorough historical description of the events leading up to and including the Holocaust, there is no finer book than *The War against the Jews*. Dawidowicz writes in lucid prose that sheds light on the working of the Nazis and the thinking that motivated their murderous acts.

Of all the historical accounts written about the Holocaust, I found Marrus's book to be the most valuable. He not only discusses the major events of the Holocaust in detail, but also places them in context. It is his belief that the "Final Solution" was not initially part of the German plans, but rather evolved over a period of time as conditions changed. The behavior and responses of individuals and governments can be better understood by examining the conditions and the circumstances under which decisions were made.

While it was important to read scholarly texts in order to know the history of the Holocaust, it wasn't until I encountered the images and symbols in Holocaust memoirs and literature that I was able to see and feel the events that I will never understand. Among the many books that have profoundly affected and influenced me as a teacher are Wiesel's *Night* and Charlotte Delbo's *None of Us Will Return*. Both authors make use of a key symbol or image, which made the works memorable—and teachable.

A peculiar type of imagery that emerges in a number of Holocaust stories pictures the victims as consisting of disembodied parts— the mouth, stomach, feet—never the heart or the brain, the seat of emotion or reason. The parts of the body can thus be observed, not felt, like a limb that has fallen asleep. This image of the parts of the body as wooden appendages devoid of any sensations culminates in Delbo's account of "Alice's Leg." The women prisoners discover Alice's wooden leg lying behind Block 25, the morgue, where they piled up the corpses removed from sick bay:

Lying in the snow, Alice's leg is alive and sentient. It must have detached itself from the dead Alice. We used to go just to see if it was still there and each time it was intolerable. Alice abandoned, dying in the snow. Alice whom we could not approach because weakness held us rooted to the spot. Alice dying alone and calling to no one. Alice had been dead for several weeks while her artificial leg continued to lie on the snow. (Delbo, 1968, p. 47)

Other works that have also had a profound impact on me are *None Is Too Many: Canada and the Jews of Europe, 1933–1948* by Irving Abella and Harold Troper, and *Shielding the Flame: An Intimate Conversation with Dr. Marek Edelman, the Last Surviving Leader of the Warsaw Ghetto Uprising* by Hanna Krall. Abella and Troper's book caused a sensation when it was first released in Canada. In fact, it was the primary reason Canada opened its doors to the Vietnamese "boat people." The book revealed Canada's shameful, antisemitic immigration policy during the Holocaust. Canada, in fact, admitted the fewest number of Jews of any country to which the Jews turned for asylum. An antisemitic government official named Frederick Charles Blair, who was director of the Immigration Branch of the Department of Mines and Resources, slammed the door shut. When asked how many Jews should be allowed to enter Canada, his response was "None is too many." The book disclosed that he wasn't alone in his views. Indeed, it made it clear to students that any democratic country can commit gross moral sins.

Krall's was one of the first postwar books published in Poland to deal with the Holocaust. Published in 1986 (and later translated into English), it was mainly a transcription of a series of interviews Krall had with Dr. Marek Edelman. The book revealed the bravery and ingenuity of the small group that struggled in the face of impossible odds. Details of the uprising, which were just historical facts to me, came alive as I learned of individual deeds, strategies, fears, and hopes. Edelman, for instance, would often show up at the departure platform where Jews were herded on the trains to travel to Treblinka (a death camp, where the Jews were gassed and burned on arrival) and, as a medical doctor, claim that individuals he pulled at random from the line were carriers of typhus and a danger to the authorities present. He single-handedly rescued many lives from certain death. Edelman said he was "shielding the flame" of human life from the capricious whims of a vindictive God.

YAD VASHEM: THE HOLOCAUST MARTYRS' AND HEROES' REMEMBRANCE AUTHORITY

I had heard of Yad Vashem, Israel's official Holocaust memorial and Holocaust research center in Jerusalem, and its three-week educators' course in the summer in Jerusalem from some committee members, but knew little about the program. My opportunity to attend came in 1982. It was my first trip to Israel. Remnants of my wife's family live in Israel (Diana, too, had lost all grandparents and most aunts and uncles and cousins in the Holocaust), and so I could finally meet her family and study and tour in Israel. The course was rigorous; over the three-week period it provided me with a wealth of information and insights. I was fortunate that some of the most noted names in the field of Holocaust research were my lecturers: Yehuda Bauer, George Mosse, and Yitzhak Arad, among others.

But one of the most interesting observations I made while there was the transformation in attitude that was occurring in Israeli society about the Holocaust and Holocaust survivors. For years, prior to 1982, native-born Israelis, especially the ones who had fought in the Six-Day War and the Yom Kippur War, felt a mixture of shame and anger toward the survivors. In many of their eyes, the victims had allowed themselves to be stripped of all their rights, ghettoized, and "led like sheep to the slaughter" without so much as firing a shot. Now, however, I saw that the educators at Yad Vashem took on the task of placing the survivors' experiences in context and in doing so they were actually working toward dispelling the mistaken impressions tied up with the "sheep to the slaughter" notion. Herein lies the major difference between the Toronto (and most Canadian Holocaust curricula) and the Israeli Holocaust curriculum. Whereas the Toronto curricula stressed the antiracist aspects of the Holocaust and from there universalized, the Israeli curriculum, produced for Israeli schools by Yad Vashem, focused on acts of resistance (like the Warsaw Ghetto Uprising, the escape from Sobibor, the destruction of crematorium IV in Birkenau), acts of heroism, and the creation of the State of Israel after the Holocaust. And so today, the attitude toward survivors has changed significantly. Today, in Israel, as in Canada, survivors are sought after to relate their experiences and are held in the highest esteem.

One of our first classroom discussions at Yad Vashem centered on the Holocaust as a unique versus a universal event. There were many reasons offered for both. We were informed that it was unique because the ultimate goal became to murder every Jew on the planet, and universal because there have been other attempted genocides. The term that should, perhaps, be used is "unprecedented." Woefully, mass murder has stalked human society long before the Holocaust, but never before with such ferocity, determination, cooperation, and coordination.

The one thing I've learned to avoid in the discussion of unique versus universal is what one American participant called "the victimization sweepstakes"—your 6 million is trivial compared to my 11 million. Such comparison of pain is absolutely pointless. And whether we see the Holocaust as unique, universal, unprecedented, or whatever, Yad Vashem—and all other educational organizations I've encountered—have always maintained that there are lessons to be learned from this darkest chapter of history.

That the study of the Holocaust can provide students with warning signposts along the road of racism has always been central to my motives for teaching about it in the classroom. Yet, today, even this area is being hotly debated. In *The Holocaust in American Life*, for example, author Peter Novick (1999) concludes that the Holocaust doesn't teach lessons at all and that a visit to any Holocaust museum won't make us better people. But I believe that a prepared and competent instructor who teaches about the Holocaust through history and literature can lead students to understand that "different" and "bad" are not synonymous, and that respect, not love, is "what the world needs now." Otherwise, I'd quit teaching the Holocaust.

One classroom incident in particular from the summer at Yad Vashem stands out in my mind. Not all the students who take the Yad Vashem course are Jewish. A number were Christian and one of them was a woman from the United States, who, with her husband, had become an Israeli citizen. She had been a welcomed participant and a significant contributor to the classroom discussions. Our last class of the summer was a course evaluation session during which we were encouraged to speak freely. This woman did. She began by relating why she took the course. As a Christian, she was ashamed of the murderous acts of many Christians during the Holocaust. By confronting the "sins" of the perpetrators and bystanders, she hoped she would come to some understanding as to why Christians behaved the way they did, dissipate whatever anger she felt toward the church, and atone. But then, in tears, she went on to share her experiences as an Israeli citizen. She claimed that with all the efforts she and her husband had made—learning Hebrew, leaving behind a comfortable life in the States, immersing themselves in Israeli culture, studying the Holocaust to expiate the misdeeds of Christians—they were still treated as outsiders.

She felt that because she was Christian she would never be accepted by Israeli Jews. She simply didn't know what more she could do. The silence in the room was followed by hugs from various participants for the woman who had spoken. I was feeling ill at ease because I had heard similar stories (that is, about being treated as an outsider by Israelis) from other people as well—*only* they were Jewish. It is tough to adopt a new homeland and often it may take many generations before the fit seems comfortable for all concerned. But I couldn't help thinking that there was a time and place where "outsiders" had lived for many generations, had made significant contributions to their adopted home, and were ultimately turned against, turned away, and mass murdered. Fully laden with new curricula, teaching strategies, and history, I headed home where the next major development in Holocaust education for Toronto and its surroundings was about to occur.

HOLOCAUST EDUCATION AND MEMORIAL CENTRE

In 1985, the decision was made to create a Holocaust Memorial Centre for Toronto. Priority was given to the educational component. The centre was to be not only a place of commemoration, but also of learning. And so Alan Bardikoff and I, because of our involvement in the public schools, were asked to join a small committee that included Nathan Leipciger, chair and survivor; Gerda Frieberg, survivor; and William Glied and Rookie Green Goldstein, both members of the Holocaust Remembrance Committee, to determine what the educational component should be and how it should be displayed. The matter of choosing a name for the centre arose quickly. "The Holocaust Memorial Centre" was favored by most, but I insisted that the word "education" appear. Eventually, we chose the name "Holocaust Education and Memorial Centre."

We also decided to produce a comprehensive booklet containing text and photos outlining in detail the history of the Holocaust and the roots of antisemitism for distribution to educators and visitors to the centre. Besides the display of a number of artifacts from the period, the focus of the centre would be a multimedia presentation projected on a large screen. A historian, Dr. Paula Draper, was to write the booklet and the multimedia dialogue. The result was an informative and deeply moving slide and music presentation called "From Out of the Depths" with original music composed by Srul Irving Glick, a well-known Canadian composer, and narration by the actor Lorne Greene. Over the years thousands of public school students, along with their teachers, have seen the production.

After years of use, a decision was made to digitize all images and sound and to computerize the entire presentation. It is now in an electronic format and can also be copied to discs. As more and more archives were opened across the globe and more documents were made available to historians, especially the documents released by the former Soviet Union, it became clear that "From Out of the Depths" contained inaccurate or incomplete information. Also, since Lorne Greene was no longer alive, the option of rerecording with him was lost to us. So, I suggested that those parts of the narration with inaccuracies and mispronunciations should be recorded with a woman's voice. Having a male and a female narrator, I argued, would improve the presentation because the presence of a woman's voice would remind students that both men and women had been victims. The program continues to be an active center for learning and dialogue, and I'm proud to have been a part of it.

HOLOCAUST AND HOPE

In July 1988 I was chosen to be one of the participants on a B'nai B'rith-sponsored journey called "Holocaust and Hope." It was a three-week tour of Germany, Poland, and Israel for 15 Holocaust educators from across Canada. During the trip I kept a travel diary. Below are some of the reactions I recorded at the time during the German and Polish legs of the trip.

Germany, July 15th: Munich is "unreal" — the Disneyland of the Rhine, of Bavaria. Built from the ashes to resemble what was there before the Third Reich, they have nicely cleansed the city and the collective conscience.

July 16th: The group met with Dr. Julie Wetzel, who researched Holocaust education in Germany. Depending on the political jurisdiction, what is taught varies. Interestingly, Holocaust literature is not taught. Julie introduced us to two students, and they both confirmed Julie's observation that the older the teacher, the less said or explained. What was most curious was that the criticisms, reluctance, and resistance to teaching the Holocaust in Germany are similar to those I've encountered occasionally in Toronto. (Why upset students with stories of brutality? These events happened long ago and are of little relevance today.)

Poland, July 18th: I had great feelings of apprehension about Warsaw. My mother spent some time here as a teenager. Poland was the country of profit and pain for my family. How would I feel? Tomorrow we begin our visits to the sites. After dinner, we had our usual group discussion. One of the participants raised the issue of Christian guilt over the Holocaust. This was hotly debated. There were only four Jewish educators on this trip and the four of us remained silent. One of the participants insisted that no Christians bore any responsibility for the Holocaust. Others were quick to point out that many Christians were willing participants in or by-standers of the murderous events. The participant categorically denied that these individuals were Christian. They may have called themselves Christians but by virtue of their acts, they were not Christians and therefore, no "true" Christians had anything to atone for. Semantics, as far as I'm concerned. I cautiously stepped into the fray. I related a story from Kurt Vonnegut's *Slaughterhouse-Five*. It was about a creature from outer space who rewrites the Gospels because they contain a flaw. What they are supposed to teach is that people should be merciful, but what they really teach is that before killing someone, make sure he isn't well connected. Because even though Jesus looked pretty ordinary, he was the "Son of the Most Powerful Being in the Universe." So when they cruci-fied him people realized they picked the wrong guy to lynch that time, which meant there were right people to lynch. In the "Gos-pel from Outer Space," the rewritten version, Jesus really is a no-body, a bum, and a pain in the neck to a lot of people. They figure it's OK to kill this guy because he's a nobody. And then, just be-fore the nobody dies, God speaks, saying he is adopting this bum as his son. From now on, He will punish anyone who torments a bum with no connections. The story drew some applause from the group. The point is we are responsible for our behavior, regardless of the circumstances. No amount of rationalizing (that "true" Chris-tians behaved morally) will wash.

July 19th: Today we toured what used to be the Warsaw ghetto — many monuments and virtually no Jews . . . After dinner, the group discussion dealt with "Holocaust," but we all wondered where was the "Hope" promised in this "Holocaust and Hope" trip? Some felt we were losing the "Hope." I asked them what they expected to find here. Of course there are only monuments to Jews. The Germans completed the task. Whatever was Jewish in Eastern Europe is now extinct, and only monuments mark their one-time existence. To-morrow, we go to Majdanek.

July 20th: This camp is different from Dachau in that Dachau was preserved by a people who want to forget and Majdanek was preserved by a people who will never forget. The site has not been "cleaned up" — on display: 800,000 victims' shoes (Majdanek was the central storehouse for possessions stolen from prisoners after their arrival to the death camps), thousands of caps, original build-ings, gas chambers intact, crematoria littered with human ash, a body room where corpses were once stacked, which now displayed human bones. After seeing this, I could understand why the Poles will never forget. Many Poles died here. Only one monument has been erected in the camp, a cupola over an enormous mound of human ash bulldozed from the surrounding fire pits. Inscribed on the face of the cupola, these words "Let our fate be a warning" (translated from the Polish). I felt I should weep, but I was so shocked by what I had seen this day, I could not.

July 24th: Waiting aboard the Russian jet for takeoff. Getting out of Poland was a bureaucratic fiasco — armed guards, multiple checks, long lines — and here we wait on the ramp for clearance to roll and on my lips, the words "Never again; I will never return to Poland." It was a vow I would fail to keep — and I would weep.

MARCH OF THE LIVING

Every two years (beginning in 1988), Jewish high school students from around the world gather at Auschwitz in Poland to walk the three kilometers from Auschwitz I to Auschwitz II (Birkenau), the same march tens of thousands of Jews made during the Holo- caust — the march of death. The "March of the Living" is one of life — an affirmation that Jews survived because, ultimately, the Holocaust failed to eradicate all Jews from the face of the earth, which was the intended Nazi "Final Solution." The teens complete the trip with a week in Israel.

I said, after the "Holocaust and Hope" journey, "I will never re- turn to Poland." But when I was invited to develop study material for the 1990 march for the Ontario participants, I was also invited to be a chaperon. So it was I found myself on a flight back to Po- land, and I must admit that when we landed in Warsaw my breath became labored. Poland was a coffin to me. Even so, this trip would eventually prove to be profoundly more emotional than the one I undertook with the 14 teachers in 1988.

We arrived in April to discover Poland in bloom. When we bused the kids to Auschwitz to tour both camps, many were confused. This was not the way it was supposed to be. Green leaves, flowers — in Auschwitz? It was then that I realized these kids knew Poland only from the black-and-white photos of the 1940s. Singing birds and nature in bloom were out of place. The camp should be som- ber, lifeless and colorless — like the existence endured by the pris- oners. After the tour was completed, one of the girls on my bus came to me and asked, "What's wrong? Why am I not crying?" I realized we had a problem. She and the others had been led to believe that crying was the only meaningful response here and the lush surroundings weren't helping any. The answer is, of course, that we all arrived in Poland with different agendas—some to record with pen or with camera, some to pray, some to mourn, and some to cry. There are many ways to experience this trip—no one is expecting any stock response. She, and the rest of us, however, were about to experience the "stock" response.

It occurred at Majdanek. After my last visit, I hoped never to see it again. And I figured if I felt this way, it was bound to be tough for the kids to get through. I told everyone we'd meet at the cupola (the one with the mound of human ash and the inscription "Let our fate be a warning") at the end of our visit, and there we would conduct a memorial service. My 17-year-old daughter, Jenny, was a participant on this march and while I gave her lots of breathing space during the trip, I asked her if she would walk the camp with me (more for my sake than hers, I suspect). It was cold and overcast. The wind hissed as it blew through the barbed wire. I remember we were silent most of the walk. What could we possibly say in the presence of what had transpired here? Eventually, we arrived at the cupola and about a third of the marchers were already there. I returned to the main camp to move others along gently because I was concerned that we not spend an inordinate amount of time by the mound of human ash. I returned to the mound. It was time for the commemoration. There were shouts. This was in such sharp contrast to the silence at the memorial—only the wind could be heard—that I was confused at first. The shouts continued. "These are my fucking people!" the voice screamed over and over. It was one of our male participants. I moved quickly to where he stood because he had a Polish male teenager by the neck and was choking him. Others were looking on in horror. The Polish teen was bent over backward on the retaining wall above the pit of human ash and appeared to be almost lifeless. I'm convinced that if I and several others hadn't intervened, he would have, at the least, been injured. We pulled our participant off his victim who then retreated and vanished in short order. I quickly made my way back to where Jenny stood and when I reached her, I could hear the sound of crying—a few of the kids at first, and then more and more. Then I put my head on my daughter's shoulder and began to weep convulsively. I couldn't stop. And between breaths, I kept repeating "I'm never coming here again." Someone said the mourner's Kaddish (the Jewish prayer for the dead) hurriedly and we moved the kids away from the memorial as quickly as we could.

In many ways, the incident was cathartic because, eventually, the Israeli flag, which had been brought along, was unfurled at the foot of the mound and many of the marchers formed a circle around it and chanted again and again, "Long live Israel." From despair to ecstasy, we felt it all. And what was the cause of the "incident" in the first place? Our male participant saw the Polish boy with a friend hanging onto the barbed wire at various times that afternoon, pretending to be electrocuted. But it wasn't until the boy threw a coin onto the mound of human ash that our participant, and finally the rest of us, lost it. . . . I haven't been back since.

RACISM TODAY: ECHOES OF THE HOLOCAUST

A participant in the 1990 "Holocaust and Hope" trip, Dr. Carole Ann Reed, who is currently the director of education for the Holocaust Education and Memorial Center in Toronto, was approached by a publisher to write a Holocaust curriculum for use in Canadian high schools. Because of Carole's heavy workload at the time, she approached me to take part in the project. The result was a curriculum we called *Racism Today: Echoes of the Holocaust*. Unfortunately, because of the publisher's limited funds, the curriculum remains unpublished.

Carole and I felt it was crucial that students recognize the Holocaust as the result of racist ideology and behavior. If they don't, the Holocaust may become nothing more than a "unique" page in history to them, with little relevance to events occurring around them every day. But if they can understand that the contemporary racist behaviors and beliefs described in our curriculum are some of those which resulted in the Holocaust just over 50 years ago, then they may understand the urgency of identifying and dismantling the racism we confront today. We intended our curriculum to help them see that connection by demonstrating how some of the major elements of racism created the events we know today as the Holocaust.

There is a large number of students who are unaware of racist manipulation and ideology, or who are uncertain about concepts and attitudes related to racism and about the racist nature of the Holocaust or even the events of the Holocaust itself. For them, this curriculum could serve as a clarification and focus for attitude changes and can spark a desire to become actively involved in antiracist activities. To believe otherwise relegates the role of antiracist education simply providing facts. Education is more than just a retelling of or exposure to facts. The story must be told accurately and in context, yes, but we must also try to learn from it. That is a moral imperative.

The structure of *Racism Today: Echoes of the Holocaust* is un-like most secondary school curricula and consists of a number of two-part "modules." The modules are designed to be flexible enough to allow a teacher to explore any number of them in any order with a class, depending upon the students' and teacher's needs. The unique aspect of these modules is the connection made in each to the Holocaust. While the first part of a module examines an as-pect of racism, the second demonstrates by discussion and docu-mentation how that aspect also fed the flames of the Holocaust. In each module the Holocaust illustrates, graphically, where the road of racism ultimately can lead us if left unchecked. On the one hand, the events of the Holocaust are unprecedented in their magnitude, ferocity, and complete lack of options for its main vic-tims—Jews, yet, on the other hand, universal in the ideology of in-tolerance that drove those events. It is on these universal elements that the Holocaust portion of each module is focused so that stu-dents can read the signposts, which point the way to eventual de-struction—the result of racist behavior.

PEDAGOGY

As for my own units on the Holocaust, I always present at the beginning of the unit a brief historical overview of the period us-ing overhead transparencies, including maps from Martin Gilbert's *Atlas of the Holocaust*. I do this for three reasons: to ensure that students will be able to read and discuss the material in some sort of context, to introduce many of the racist notions that fired the terrible events, and to dispel commonly held misconceptions. (Jews refused to leave Germany in the 1930s; Jews never rebelled; Poles were primarily responsible for the Holocaust; Poles never rescued anyone. . . .)

I also prepare myself by reviewing the guidelines for teaching the Holocaust that are provided by the United States Holocaust Me-morial Museum in its booklet, *Guidelines for Teaching about the Holocaust* by William S. Parsons and Samuel Totten (Washington, D.C.: The United States Holocaust Memorial Museum, 1993). Some of these guidelines are: avoid comparisons of pain (that is, avoid teaching that the victims of the Holocaust suffered more than any other group before or since); avoid simple answers to complex his-tory (just because it happened doesn't mean it was inevitable); avoid stereotypical descriptions (students should understand that not all Germans were Nazis, not all bystanders stood by inactive, not all Jews were observant or lived in small villages, not all nations turned their backs); and select appropriate learning activities and visuals.

On a different but related front, *I need to mention two films I never use: Charlie Grant's War* (about a Canadian who supposedly saved Jews during the Holocaust) and *Joseph Schulz* (about a German soldier who refuses to participate in an execution squad assigned to kill Jews in a village and is executed with the Jews). I avoid these two because both are works of fiction that were passed off as historical events.

We teach our Holocaust unit in grade 11 English classes at Northern. The core book we use is Elie Wiesel's memoir, *Night*. One writing assignment is a response journal. We divide *Night* into five sections and ask students to write a two-page response for each section. The writing is personal, so that it discloses as much about the reader as it does about the book. We also deal with *Night* as a powerful piece of writing through the images Wiesel uses. We ask the students to discuss the symbolic significance of certain images—like night, fire, food—and their effect on the reader. Some students who have never been avid readers, getting by on as little as they could during their high school career, have privately confessed to me that the only book they have read from cover to cover was *Night*.

Where We Are, Where We Are Going, What Is To Be Done

Once when Barb Walther, the teacher who taught the first Holocaust literature course for my department, and I made a presentation at a synagogue to a group of survivors, a woman survivor asked a question that seemed to be on the minds of most everyone there. She wanted to know if Barb and I thought the Holocaust "hype" would eventually cool to the point where nobody would ultimately care—or even worse—remember any more. I realized, immediately, that this whole thing called Holocaust education came down to one imperative—never forget, never again. That's all the victims wanted, that the sinister experiences to which they were subjected never be forgotten or visited upon some other hapless group of victims. Barb and I assured her that we would do our part to keep Holocaust education on the courses of study in the high schools of Ontario. All of us involved in Holocaust education in Toronto have ultimately done just that because the current Ontario government has mandated that the study of the Holocaust in literature and history be included in the new provincial English and history curriculum guidelines. That means all high school students in the province of Ontario will study the Holocaust in at least one year of their high school career. To assist us in continuing Holocaust education, Dr. Paula Draper, the Holocaust Centre's historian, undertook a sizable oral history project to record local survivor testimonies on videotape for future use in the classrooms. The result is an invaluable historical archive.

Because of Canada's multicultural makeup, I feel hopeful that antiracist education and Holocaust education will become priorities in Canadian schools. Though the Ontario Ministry of Education has mandated some Holocaust studies in the curriculum guidelines, this does not hold true for other provinces in Canada. What remains to be done is to include Holocaust studies in provincial curricula across Canada.

Service

There is criticism, however, about the pedagogical issues to which I and others have applied Holocaust education. That anyone can glean any possible lessons from this historical event, critics say—especially one so heinous as the Holocaust—is doubtful. The purpose of a historian is to gather the facts and interpret them, not look for moral lessons, they say. I would agree—that, indeed, is the task of the historian, but not the teacher. If the mere presentation of facts were all that were required of a teacher, a computer could probably do the job better. But if there is any point to teaching about the Holocaust, it is the educator's responsibility to help students to discuss the morality of the events. Does that mean we should sentimentalize the events of the Holocaust in order to teach lessons about "the triumph of the human spirit"? No. The facts are clear. There was very little "triumph of the spirit," very little decency and goodness. There was injustice; there was mass murder; there were few rescues and even fewer escapes, and who lived and died in the camps was primarily a matter of chance.

Events like the Holocaust don't happen suddenly; they are, in part, the result of a process of immoral decisions based on racist attitudes. What we can teach our children are the signposts along the road to mass murder. If they can see the destructive paths that have been embarked upon, they can change the direction. The Holocaust can teach us to see and change.

REFERENCES

Abella, Irving and Troper, Harold (1983). *None Is Too Many: Canada and the Jews of Europe, 1933-1948*. Toronto: Lester Publishing Limited.

Dawidowicz, Lucy (1981). *The War against the Jews, 1933–1945*. New York: Bantam Books.

Delbo, Charlotte (1968). *None of Us Will Return*. Boston, MA: Beacon Press.

Gilbert, Martin (1991). *Atlas of the Holocaust*. New York: Pergamon Press.

Krall, Hanna (1986). *Shielding the Flame: An Intimate Conversation with Dr. Marek Edelman, the Last Surviving Leader of the Warsaw Ghetto Uprising*. New York: Henry Holt and Company.

Marrus, Michael (1987). *The Holocaust in History*. Toronto: Lester and Orpen Dennys Limited.

Novick, Peter (1999). *The Holocaust in American Life*. Boston, MA: Houghton Mifflin Company.

Vonnegut, Kurt (1971). *Slaughterhouse-Five or The Children's Crusade*. New York: Dell.

Wiesel, Elie (1969). *Night*. New York: Avon Books.

Chapter 6

~

A Journey through Memory

Leatrice B. Rabinsky

MY FORMATIVE YEARS

I was in elementary school when I first learned that something very tragic was happening to the Jewish people in Europe. There were whisperings in our house, meetings at my grandfather's shul (synagogue) and then arrangements for the train trip to Ferndale, New York. My grandfather, Rabbi Dr. Shraga HaCohen Rosenberg, and my father, Sol Bergida, were leading a Cleveland delegation to meet with Rabbi Eliezer Silver, who was the national leader of the Agudath Israel. Our family had always been active in the "Agudah," a worldwide Orthodox movement devoted to religious observance, Torah education, and the welfare of our people. This time, an emergency national meeting was called to create a committee for rescuing the Jews of Europe. I remember the postcard from my father, "Papa and Rabbi Silver made inspiring speeches." The year was 1938.

Within the next two years, there were more frantic meetings, talks about going to the United States Congress, phone calls to arrange for affidavits and letters about a new group, the *Vaad Hatzalah* (Committee for Rescue). During this time we met some of the first refugees from Germany who had come to Cleveland. Sitting at my grandfather's dining room table, for example, Dr. Max Lowenthal told us how he had been awarded the Iron Cross during his service in the German army during World War I. He never could accept his dismissal from practicing in the hospital in Hamburg. Because they had no children, it was easier for them than for many others to arrange to leave Germany in 1936.

In junior high, I met students who had arrived from Germany with their parents, the Dannhausers, the Guggenheims, the Falcks, and later, the Kleebergs. They were the nucleus of a congregation of newly arrived German Jews, *Shaarey Tikvah* (Gates of Hope). The word "Holocaust" was not yet part of our vocabulary. We had yet to learn about what was happening in eastern Europe.

One cold Friday night, I went with my father to an *Oneg Shabbat* (Sabbath gathering) at our Young Israel Synagogue. Usually, our monthly *Oneg Shabbat* speakers were visiting rabbis, educators, or students home for the holidays. This meeting was different. I can still picture the hushed audience as our guest was introduced as, "*Amcha* from the *Churban*" (one of our people from the destruction). I did not understand Yiddish well, but I remember his words as he cried out, "*Rateveh unz!*" (Save us!) The year was 1943.

This was when we began to talk about ghettos, and deportation trains and the concentration camps. We had yet to meet survivors from the destruction in eastern Europe. We had never spoken at home of the killings in the concentration camps. Had my parents been aware of the extent of the destruction? I really don't know.

In our high school, however, the scene was different. There, we were galvanized to activity for the war effort—selling war stamps and defense bonds; writing to our alumni and many senior students who were serving in the army; taking first aid courses; learning about rationing of gas, sugar, coffee, and meat. Not once in any of our classes did we refer to or discuss about the traumatic happenings to the Jews and other victims of Nazi Germany. We had, though, an all-school assembly when the news hit like a bombshell that Joe, our popular football star senior who had enlisted at 18, was killed in Europe. We were in shock. This was someone we knew, our friend. The year was 1945.

In April 1945, President Franklin Delano Roosevelt died. Our classes were dismissed early after the principal spoke over the PA, "We mourn the death of our great president, FDR." In truth, he had been regarded as the savior of the immigrant generation of our parents. Knots of people gathered in front of apartments and houses. Cars pulled over. At home, my mother and aunts were holding their aprons to their faces and crying. It was a time of great sadness.

Just a few weeks later, on May 8, jubilation reigned: V-E Day, victory in Europe. Our boys would be coming home.

A year after the end of the war, our Young Israel Synagogue was alerted to the possibility of bringing the remnants of members' families to Cleveland. Our family was called to meet the surviving members of the Kleinman family. My sister and I were the same ages as Sylvie and Ruth (15 and 17, respectively), two of the seven survivors of the large Hungarian family of the Cleveland Kleinmans. We were all shy at first with the difficulty of language barriers. They didn't speak English and we didn't know Hungarian or Yiddish. We were told that they were all survivors of Auschwitz.

We were too shy or too embarrassed to question Ruth and Sylvie and their family members about Auschwitz. We were told by the Cleveland relatives that the parents of Ruth, Sylvie, their brother, Norman, and many other relatives had perished in Auschwitz. I do recall that Ruth developed a terrible cold the first winter in Cleveland. She told me in halting English that as a little girl, she was always dressed warmly, even having a rabbitskin fur coat and hat, and she always caught cold. But in Auschwitz, she had only a dress, no underwear and no coat, and she never had a cold.

Ruth, Sylvie, and Norman were apt students; so, in less than six months we all were able to converse in English. Our bonding led to lifelong friendships. Little did we realize how this relationship would inspire in me a passion and devotion to confronting and teaching about the Holocaust as a lifetime mission. The year was 1946.

Soon, we were all married, having been united in marriage by my grandfather, Rabbi Rosenberg. To this day, Ruth and her husband, Alex, recall my grandfather's admonition, *"Forgess nicht deine Abstammung."* (Don't forget where you came from.) Further, he cautioned them that in spite of their recent tragedies, the horrors and ordeals that they had suffered, they should hearken back to the glorious traditions of their parents and their families. Of course, all of our wedding ceremonies were conducted in *Hochdeutsch*, the high German of my grandfather's years in Austria-Hungary. The year was 1947.

Late that summer, a group of refugee boys, ages 17 to 19, came to Cleveland from the DP (displaced persons) camps in Europe. Temporarily placed in Bellefaire, the agency which had once been the Jewish Orphan Home, these boys were assigned to enter school or to be given opportunities for jobs in the community. As a young bride, I volunteered, through our Young Israel Synagogue, to help welcome the boys to the Jewish communal and social life in our city. The High Holidays were approaching, and I was asked to introduce the boys to families who would welcome them and host them for Rosh Hashanah, Yom Kippur, and Sukkot. This was how the Rabinsky family met Leon Shear, a bright, wiry, emotional 17-year-old who was born in Bendzin, Poland. He had endured more than five years in the Bendzin ghetto and in Auschwitz.

There was an immediate, loving relationship between Leon and my late mother-in-law, Esther Rabinsky. She, who had come after

World War I from Kaminetz-Litovsk in Poland, embraced Leon as another son. He spoke her dialect of Yiddish. He adored everything she cooked and baked—the *kishka*, the *chulent*, the gefilte fish— Jewish food that he hadn't seen or eaten since before his deportation. "*Azoi vi de Maman. . . .*" (Just like my mother used to make.)

Soon the floodgates opened. Leon had found a family whom he could trust and with whom he felt comfortable. By now, we had read and learned from survivors' sketchy accounts of their Holocaust years. Leon Shear was among the first to tell us in detail about his years in Auschwitz, working in the Canada Kommando (sorting belongings of arrivals), recognizing and not being able to acknowledge the arrival of his mother and sister at the concentration camp. Little did we know that within two and a half decades Leon would be one of the remarkable Holocaust speakers to my classes at Cleveland Heights High School.

Marriage, raising children, going to classes at the university, and then embarking on a graduate program consumed my energies for a number of years. Forming close friendships with many of the members of the Kol Israel Foundation (survivors of the Holocaust), I engaged in an intensive reading program to identify places that Ruth, Sylvie, Leon, Paul, Bertha, Jacob, and a host of other survivors had told me about. The survivors were my inspiration to pursue historical and firsthand accounts of the Holocaust years.

READING AND LEARNING ABOUT THE HOLOCAUST IN MORE DETAIL

Among the early books that I read voraciously were Arthur Morse's *While Six Million Died*, Nora Levin's *The Holocaust: The Destruction of European Jewry 1933–1945*, Lucy S. Dawidowicz's *The War Against the Jews*, Franklin H. Littell's *The Crucifixion of the Jews*, William Shirer's *The Rise and Fall of Hitler*, and Elie Wiesel's *Night*.

Morse's investigation into world apathy prior to and during the war reinforced my understanding of the desperate situation faced by those trying to escape Nazi tyranny. More specifically,*While Six Million Died* conveyed Morse's exhaustive study of such band-aid governmental efforts as the 1938 Evian Conference and the 1943 Bermuda Conference. Years later, I encouraged students to use this book to begin their research on the feeble attempts to help save the Jews of Germany.

As for Nora Levin's *The Holocaust: The Destruction of European Jewry 1933–1945*, it is an intellectual tour de force. In addition to meticulous care with data and chronology of events, Levin infused her book with emotional insights into life-threatening situations. Her account of the Warsaw Ghetto Uprising includes many riveting personal descriptions, such as Marek Edelman's description of the inferno. Country by country, Levin teaches about the German occupation, specific aspects of Jewish persecution and eventual deportation. Her book continues to be a major source of information for me.

Similarly, Lucy S. Dawidowicz's *The War Against the Jews* was my reference source in preparing to teach about the Holocaust. Dawidowicz delineates the chronology and escalation of the genocide period with intellectual integrity and clarity.

Franklin H. Littell's *The Crucifixion of the Jews* is a resource that delivers a forceful message of understanding in confronting the silence of church leaders during the Holocaust. Littell, a Christian theologian, is not hesitant in being explicit about evidence of Christian antisemitism. He challenges his church colleagues to be forthright in establishing communication between Christians and Jews.

Elie Wiesel's *Night* is paramount in survivor testimony concerning the horrors of Auschwitz, Buchenwald, and the agonies of a death march. Wiesel bears witness to the eclipse of humanity in that "other planet, Auschwitz." Perhaps because my own father grew up in the vicinity of Sighet (Austrian-Hungarian empire pre–World War I), I was riveted to Wiesel's description of his family, of the imposing of the ghetto in Sighet, of the deportations. Wiesel, like my father, had been a *yeshiva bochur* (a student in the religious academy). Wiesel's faith was challenged and tested by his sinister and terrifying experiences. My students, about the same age as Wiesel during his account in *Night*, speak frequently of the horrific burdens he shouldered during this stage of his life.

Following Wiesel's searing *Night*, I began to read more accounts by survivors and continued to immerse myself in personal Holocaust testimonies: Vladka Meed's *On Both Sides of the Wall*, Halina Birnbaum's *Hope Is the Last to Die*, Chaim A. Kaplan's *The Warsaw Diary of Chaim A. Kaplan*, Gerda Klein's *All But My Life*, Viktor E. Frankl's *Man's Search for Meaning*, and the powerful entries in *The Diary of Adam's Father* by Aryeh Klonymus and his wife, Malvina, concerning the fate of their child, Adam. In the latter book, the parents were discovered hiding near the farm and were murdered. Adam survived. Some years after the war, the relatives who had been designated to be contacted in the event of the deaths of Adam's parents came to claim the child. Adam refused to acknowledge that he was a Jew. He became violently angry. There was no reconciliation with the Jewish uncle. This, too, was a tragedy of the Holocaust.

In my mind, firsthand survivor accounts continue to be the most compelling resources in confronting the Holocaust. Levels of complexity emerge as survivors probe suppressed feelings and haunting experiences. For example, Vladka Meed, in her book *On Both Sides of the Wall*, describes the escalating horror in Warsaw after the establishment of the ghetto. The determination to resist drove her to incredible feats on behalf of her fellow Jews. Because of her fair complexion and light brown hair, she passed easily on the "Aryan" side of the ghetto wall. She found rooms and hiding places for orphaned children, obtained arms and materials for the final revolt, and helped smuggle Jews into Hungary. An emotional description of her return to Warsaw and the Jewish cemetery concludes Meed's insightful testimony.

I was also moved by Halina Birnbaum's *Hope Is the Last to Die*. She recapped the ordeals in Warsaw, Auschwitz, Treblinka, and Majdanek. Her brother, Marek, about whom she writes, is a retired physician in our city. It was a privilege welcoming Birnbaum to our home 25 years ago.

Stark lessons about the dismal life in the Warsaw ghetto were graphically described by Chaim A. Kaplan in his chronicle of events, *The Warsaw Diary of Chaim A. Kaplan*. Originally titled *Scroll of Agony*, Kaplan felt that his diary was his constant companion. We learn about daily events from the first day of the war, September 1, 1939, until August 4, 1944. Kaplan informs us about the struggle to maintain schools for the children; about chaotic orders given by a *Judenrat* leader, Czerniakow, whom he disliked; about diminishing physical strength of the inhabitants; about lack of food and coal for heat; about congestion in housing.

Gerda Klein's *All But My Life* proved to be one of the most engaging of the personal testimonies. We come to know her closeness with her family, their heartbreak at the "call-up" of her beloved brother, Arthur, the disruption of normalcy in their lives, the imposing of edicts and decrees. Poignant episodes reflect the loving care of her parents, such as her father's insistence about taking her heavy boots when she, too, was called up for labor camp. The boots proved essential to her survival. Klein's story is a legacy of goodness and compassion, her love and devotion to her friends, her devastation at the death of Ilse, her beloved friend whom she had met in the camps, and who had endured the trauma of the final death march with Gerda. Ilse died shortly before liberation.

At liberation, Gerda is emaciated and ill. She is rescued by an American soldier, Kurt Klein, who had been a refugee from Germany. Their growing love and eventual marriage provide a sense

of fulfillment. My students are always moved by their story. Over
the years, I've been privileged to meet and get to know Gerda, Kurt,
and her family, and have had her speak to my students on two different occasions.

ENTERING THE FIELD OF TEACHING AND MY INITIAL EFFORTS TO TEACH ABOUT THE HOLOCAUST

I followed the traditions of teaching inspired by members of my
family and was also influenced by some special English teachers.
My mother was a Judaic studies teacher, my grandfather was a
rabbi and teacher, and my father was a businessman and Talmud
teacher. Among my favorite teachers at school were my junior high
teacher, Virginia Lyle, and high school English teacher, the dynamic Sidney Vincent.

My first introduction to Holocaust studies took place during the
years 1965–1971 when I taught junior high school. Not part of the
regular curriculum, the historical background and survivors' stories and diaries were an integral part of a two-week unit that I
introduced to the grades 7–9 classes. I specifically brought in survivors who had been my students' ages during the Holocaust. Fearful of "breaking down," or embarrassed by a lack of fluency in
English, many survivors hesitated coming to school.

Tova Baron and Bertha Lautman were among the first speakers
to my junior high classes. Concentration camp life was a shock to
my students. They did relate, however, to Bertha's recounting of
her separation from her parents and her longing to see them just
one more time. Indeed, I remember the courage of Bertha Lautman,
who cried when she remembered her father placing his hands on
her head to bless her when she responded to the call-up to report
for a labor transport from Czechoslovakia in March 1942. What no
one knew then was that the transport's real destination was
Auschwitz.

I also vividly remember that when I introduced *The Diary of Anne
Frank*, my junior high students could not grasp the idea of having
to hide from the world. That was a big issue we discussed.

During these early years of teaching about the Holocaust, I was
fortunate to receive the manuscript of a book—*The Holocaust: A
History of Courage and Resistance*—by my friend, Bea Stadtler, to
use as source material for my students. Later, her book achieved
national acclaim.

To prepare myself for teaching about the Holocaust, I read the
books previously discussed and learned the stories of a great
number of local survivors. I also went to the bound journals of

newspaper and magazines in the library to see what the media had printed about the events leading up to and during the Holocaust period. I later introduced this as a special project for all of my Holocaust studies' classes. At this same time, I also began to attend conferences on the Holocaust.

SPECIAL YEARS: CONTINUING AND EXPANDING MY EFFORTS AT CLEVELAND HEIGHTS HIGH SCHOOL

After seven years of teaching seventh through ninth grade, I was promoted to Cleveland Heights High School. At Heights High the school administration and the board of education provided an opportunity for my Holocaust education activities when it offered teachers the option to write curricula and course guides for subjects of special interest. If enough students would elect the course, the subject would be part of the program offerings for the coming academic year. The year was 1973.

It was a perfect opportunity to focus on studies of the Holocaust. I recall sitting at the dining room table of our Tel Aviv apartment during a vacation visit to Israel, books and pamphlets piled high as I wrote the course of study, "Literature of the Holocaust," geared to senior students. Included in the semester-long, five-days-a-week program were books and sources that I have mentioned previously. Then, as now, I felt it was crucial for students to learn the chronology of events of the Holocaust. Topics for discussion and research included: the rise of Nazism; world apathy; deportation and ghettoization; moral dilemma of the *Judenrat*; concentration, labor, and death camps; the many forms of resistance; children of the Holocaust; Righteous Among the Nations; liberation; and aftermath—rebuilding lives. Developing the curriculum, I relied heavily on Morse's and Levin's works as well as many of the survivors' testimonies.

In the fall of the 1974–1975 school year, 28 students were enrolled in the first class. The course was offered each succeeding semester, and continues to this day, with enrollment sometimes reaching 35. Class members included Jewish and Christian students. It was moving and inspiring to have Second Generation students, whose parents were survivors of the Holocaust, taking the course. I recall Craig Spiegel saying,

My grandfather was an editor of a Jewish newspaper in Danzig. He was deported to Auschwitz and murdered there. My mother was fourteen when she was sent on the Kindertransport to London. My grandmother and aunts escaped Europe and were finally interned on Cyprus until the end of the war when they went to Israel. I have to learn more about what happened throughout the Holocaust years.

Craig's mother, Thea Spiegel, was one of the first survivors to give personal testimony to our class.

Each week another survivor came to meet with us. Rose Kaplovitz told how her family was shattered on the first day of the war when the occupying Germans forced her 16-year-old brother and her grandfather from their home. They were driven with other men to the edge of the cemetery where they had to dig a huge ditch. All were shot. Not a sound was heard in the classroom.

Hannah Rath spoke of her deportation from Germany to a ghetto. She was placed with other people in an apartment that had dishes with food in them on the table, obviously from other victims who had just been deported.

Susan Beer told of being in a political prison in Budapest together with Hannah Senesh. (A heroine of the Holocaust who had parachuted into Yugoslavia from Palestine to help in the rescue effort. Hannah was caught and subsequently executed.) How inspiring it was for the students when Susan related how Hannah shouted encouraging words from her cell and gave instructions for physical exercises to keep up the morale of the prisoners.

One of the child survivors, Paul Kupfer, cried as he related how difficult it was to be taken from his parents. He was fortunate, however, to be placed in a monastery where he was cared for until the end of the war.

Jacob Hennenberg's story was one of "miracles" as he conveyed how he lived through seven concentration and labor camps. After arrival at one of the camps, he told his friend, Arthur, that if he would receive the number 18 (which in Hebrew is *chai*, "life") he would be assured of survival. Arthur chided him and said, "How is that possible? There are more than 6,000 in this transport and you want 18!" After the turmoil of being registered and tattooed, the prisoners heard the commandant shout (in German), "From now on you have no names. In this place you are only numbers." Finally placed in their barracks, Jacob blurted out to Arthur, "You won't believe this, but I have number 18." The students were captivated as Jacob Hennenberg told of the miracle of his number, 64242, which, of course, adds up to 18.

Gita Frankel's experiences in the Lodz ghetto and Auschwitz and Shtuthof concentration camps were a saga of suffering and bereavement. She told of holding her starving 21-year-old brother, Yosef Leib, in her arms as he whispered, "If only I could have some milk and bread." After his death, Gita (age 18) and her mother received permission to bury her brother at the edge of the Lodz Jewish cemetery. Immediately after the war they placed a small stone *matzeva* (monument) on his grave. Gita somberly told the teenage students, "I was never your age."

I told my students many times, "These survivors are your true teachers. Listen carefully. Learn from them. We are privileged to be the generation to confront the Holocaust through the experiences of the survivors."

One of our first efforts to teach the community what we had learned about the Holocaust was our class's first Holocaust Outreach program held at the Jewish Community Center in January 1975. Chaired by student Louis Malcmacher, a Second Generation of Holocaust survivors, the event drew more than 300 parents, students, and friends. Featured in the program were two dynamic speakers, Father Robert Bonnell of St. Margaret Mary Parish and Rabbi Shubert Spero of the Young Israel Congregation. A history scholar and researcher, Father Bonnell spoke of his "awakening" at Yad Vashem, the world-renowned research center and memorial in Jerusalem for the six million Jewish victims of the Holocaust. He told how this tour introduced him to the tragedy and dimensions of the Holocaust, lessons he had never learned in all of his years of academic studies. Determined to be a spokesman for the idea of "Never again," Father Bonnell cautioned the audience, especially the young people, to "study, learn, remember and never stand idly by the suffering of others." Rabbi Spero spoke of two watershed events of contemporary times, the Holocaust and the creation of the State of Israel. "Had there been a homeland of refuge for the Jews, there would not have been a Holocaust," said Rabbi Spero. Completing the outreach event were recitations of original poetry by our students and songs of the Holocaust, such as "Ani Maamin" ("I Believe With Perfect Faith") and a partisan song, presented by the 160 members of Heights High Choir. The entire gathering joined in the singing of the spirited song of resistance (printed in the program booklet). This event was the first of hundreds of outreach programs by my students throughout the years—which continue through this very day—to universities, colleges, high schools, middle schools, churches, synagogues, and community groups.

The Genesis and Implementation of the Journey of Conscience Program

Soon after the success of our first outreach endeavor, the students suggested a spectacular and almost presumptuous idea.

Louis Malcmacher was the first to approach me. I recall how he was resolute and unwavering as he said, "Mrs. Rabinsky, I have no grandparents. They were all murdered in the concentration camps. Everyone has a cemetery to visit the graves and to say 'Kaddish' (memorial prayer) for their family members. We have been studying about the Holocaust for months. Why don't we take a field trip to Poland to see the places that we have studied. It will be a memorial journey for my grandparents and for all of the families of the survivors." "Field trip to Poland!" I exclaimed. "I can't even get a chartered bus to take us to the theater downtown!" Ronnie Kaplovitz and Craig Spiegel joined in the request. They, too, had never known their grandparents. Soon, the entire group of students were a chorus of, "We can do it. You always said that there is nothing beyond our reach if we are really determined to achieve a goal." And that is how the "Journeys of Conscience" began to the sites of the Holocaust in Europe and to Israel, Land of Rebirth. The year was 1975.

My colleague, Gert Mann, who had switched careers from dramatic arts to teaching and was now student teaching at Heights, joined with me in planning this unique pilgrimage. At first, no one believed that we would embark on such a venture, taking students to the sites of the concentration camps in Poland. Perhaps because of the innovative idea of confronting the Holocaust by actually visiting the places of trauma, involving both students and a survivor, the Jewish Community Federation subvented the journey. Students paid a minimum price for the two-week pilgrimage. We were very fortunate to have Bertha Lautman, an Auschwitz survivor, who came to know the students through her visits to class, accompany us as mentor and guide. She had always told the students, "At liberation, I had said that someday I would walk through the gates of Auschwitz as a free woman."

We left Cleveland on December 17, 1975, for a living experience that would impact our lives forever—18 pilgrims on the Journey of Conscience. This is what Gert Mann and I wrote in the foreword to our book, *Journey of Conscience: Young People Respond to the Holocaust* (Cleveland, OH: William Collins Publisher, 1979):

Bertha Lautman was the only one on the journey who actually lived through the Holocaust. The two teachers were fortunate to have been teenagers in America during this time. Several of the students had lost grandparents, aunts, uncles and cousins in the ghettos and concentration camps. Thus, each of us brought a different perspective to this journey—whether it was a historical investigation, a search for ancestral roots, or a religious conviction. We joined as a family, praying with the remnants in Prague, staring in disbelief at the bleakness that once was Lidice, crying together at the memorial in Auschwitz, rejoicing with Antek Zuckerman (second in command during the Warsaw Ghetto uprising) at the rebirth in Israel, and sharing our hope for tomorrow at the Anne Frank House in Amsterdam. (p. 4)

A wonderful dimension of our journey was the odyssey from Warsaw via Geneva and Zurich to Tel Aviv and then to Bethlehem on December 24. We arrived at Manger Square, a promise I had made to the parents of our Christian students, at 11:45 P.M. It was in time to hear the glorious chorale of voices from student groups representing countries throughout the world. We also saw the life-size projection of the midnight service on a huge wall of one of the buildings. Only VIP government representatives were permitted to enter the Church of the Nativity. Thoroughly exhausted, but bonded in friendship, our journey group returned to our Jerusalem hostel at 2:30 A.M.

The following morning we traveled together to the Western Wall, the remaining wall of the Second Temple, almost two thousand years old. We prayed together and placed kvitlach (messages of peace) in the crevices of the wall. This is how we began our Israel itinerary.

At Yad Vashem, Susan Wish (who had been a student in my first class in Holocaust studies at Heights High, and who participated in the first Journey of Conscience) chanted a heartfelt "Ani Maamin" in the Hall of Remembrance. Each student spoke, revealing what was most memorable about the journey to the Holocaust sites. We were then privileged to participate in seminars with Dr. Yitzchak Arad, director of Yad Vashem, a survivor of the Vilna ghetto and Holocaust historian; Shalmi Barmor, the educational director; and Efraim Zuroff, an educator and researcher (now Dr. Zuroff, director of the Simon Wiesenthal Center in Jerusalem). Antek Zuckerman (whose wife, Zivia Lubetkin, was known as the Mother of the Warsaw children) embraced us at Kibbutz Lohamei Hagettaot (survivors of the ghetto), which he and his wife founded in 1949. Antek Zuckerman touched our hearts. This was the man who, because of his Aryan appearance (light hair, light skin, tall, athletic looking) was the liaison between the survivors in hiding on the other side of the Warsaw Ghetto wall and the Jewish people imprisoned in the ghetto. He obtained small arms and munitions to prepare for the uprising, and secured food and supplies for those in the main bunker under the apartment at Mila 18 Street. He told us that in Israel they had turned their tragedies into joyous life experiences. He described the laughter of their grandchildren, the blooming kibbutz with large expanses of greenery, small houses

with trellises and plants, sophisticated farming, and small indus-
try projects. Jon Friedlander remarked that Antek was so quiet and
humble in his manner that it would be difficult to imagine him
fighting in the ghetto.

Two weeks of unbelievable life-impacting experiences. As we
boarded the plane for our return flight, Ken Myers, the first one
at the top of the stairs, turned to us and called out, "Hey guys,
the journey is over, but the conscience continues." This has become our motto for all successive journeys, eight thus far. Our
promise to convey what we have seen continues to be fulfilled.
Students, survivors, and teachers have spoken in 11 cities in the
United States and Canada before thousands of people of all faiths.
Small rural communities who had never heard of the word "Holocaust" now know about tyranny and dehumanization and how individual and world apathy can contribute to world catastrophe and
genocide. Our students, from succeeding journeys, have become
emissaries on college campuses—organizing Holocaust seminars
and planning programs for Days of Remembrance. Wittenberg
College, Trinity College, Tufts University, Northwestern University,
Youngstown University, Boston University, Ohio State University,
Cleveland State University and Miami University have all felt the
impact of our students.

The reactions of survivors to our Journey of Conscience was most
gratifying. Soon after the community had learned about our Holocaust Outreach program, Karola Edelstein, an Auschwitz survivor
working in our local bakery, came from behind the counter and
held my arm. She was tearful as she said, "We were seven girls on
our shelf in Birkenau. At night we would whisper, 'Who will ever
know what is happening to us?' I told them, 'And if they know, who
will believe?' " She hugged me and said, "Thank you for telling our
story."

Soon after our 1975 journey, Mrs. Edelstein wrote to *The Cleveland Jewish News*. We still have her letter:

Both my husband and myself are survivors of concentration camps. Most
of our families were killed there. What we remember very vividly is being brought there with the transports and being crowded into barracks.
No one knew what would happen to anyone the next day. But among
all the people, one thing was decided and repeated over and over—"Who-
ever survives this, tell the world what was done to us and why we were
killed." Mrs. Rabinsky is fulfilling the request of all those who were killed
in concentration camps. Through her efforts, a new generation will not
forget what happened and hopefully this will prevent it from happening again.

Our mission of Holocaust education became ever more compelling. Students responded with poetry, essays, research, and interviews with local survivors. Our classes began to publish journals of students' writings. One of the first publications, *Times of the Holocaust, No Excuse for Apathy*, evolved from research into newspapers and magazines of the years 1933–1945. Summaries of articles, noting sources and dates, resulted in a mature, revealing magazine. Yes, the world really knew what was happening in Nazi Germany. Pictures, original poetry, and essays enhanced the publication in 1976. Coeditor Judy Goldman (1976) wrote:

We must not forget the past for it is as much a part of us as the future is, as important as today. In our studies we surprisingly found an abundant amount of information screaming to the world what actually was occurring. Now we want to educate our generation to the extent of the Holocaust. Let us never again give apathy as our excuse. We have to make people aware that man is capable of losing his morality and humanity, not only the barbarians who took an active part in the atrocities, but also the ones who did nothing to help their brothers who fell victim to this disgrace. (p. 4)

Each class also embarked on a program of outreach education, which we deemed Our Journey of Remembrance.

Becoming Part of a Holocaust Education Network

Many opportunities for Holocaust education were gaining momentum. Mercy College in Detroit organized one of the first national conferences on the Holocaust in 1976. There, a gathering of pioneers in the field exchanged materials and ideas for curricula. Margot Strom and Bill Parsons (now with the United States Holocaust Memorial Museum) introduced their program, tested in junior high, which evolved into the successful Facing History and Ourselves. We, too, presented our program.

Two years later, in 1978, I participated in the Holocaust Education Conference in Philadelphia, organized by Dr. Franklin Littell. His message about the importance of integrity in education impacted on my teaching career in an important way. Dr. Littell had emphasized that the Holocaust reflected the corruption in education. Engineers, doctors, professors, skilled and trained in their professions, were the perpetrators of the Holocaust. Recently, in honor of Franklin H. Littell's eightieth birthday, I contributed to his *Festschrift*, a book of birthday letters entitled *A Modern Prophet*.

Dr. Franklin H. Littell has been a constant inspiration to me in my Holocaust education and Journey of Conscience ventures. His dynamism as a speaker and his message of Holocaust education outreach to people of all faiths are riveting. I carried his lessons to my students at Cleveland Heights High School and to the teacher workshops that I organized in our area. In 1987, we invited Dr. Littell to be the keynote speaker at the Holocaust Educators' Seminar at Cleveland Heights High School. More than 100 educators from secondary schools and colleges were inspired by Dr. Littell's challenge and charge to transmit the lessons of the Holocaust to our new generations.

The Journey of Conscience Continues

In 1979, 20 students, survivor Bertha Lautman, and I embarked on our second Journey of Conscience. This time we traveled in the summer and added Vienna and Budapest to our itinerary. We had studied about the Righteous Among the Nations and many of the rescue efforts. In Budapest we paid tribute at the life-size monument to Raoul Wallenberg, a Swedish dignitary who saved more than 100,000 Jews in safe houses during 1944–1945. Our group gathered in the courtyard of the majestic Dohaney Temple in Budapest to honor the courage of heroine Hannah Senesh in front of a plaque to her memory. A week later we met in Haifa, Israel, with Hannah's mother, Catherine; her brother, George; and sister-in-law, Ginosara. They spoke of Hannah's early life in Budapest, her determination to be a pioneer in the homeland of the Jews, and her bravery in parachuting into Yugoslavia as a member of the Jewish Brigade in a daring rescue mission. Twenty years later we still reminisce about this moving meeting.

Anticipating heightened community interest in our Journey of Conscience, a colleague suggested that a film crew follow us throughout our travels on the second journey in 1979. As a result, Dr. Alan Stephenson, of the local PBS station, and Dan MacDonald, cinematographer, filmed our ventures. The result was an award-winning production, *Tomorrow Came Much Later, A Journey of Conscience*. Television and movie star Ed Asner narrated the film. The title was picked up by Stephenson when he heard Bertha Lautman relate her story in the barracks in Birkenau. I remember her saying, "We all said, 'Tomorrow we'll be free. Tomorrow we'll go home.' But tomorrow came much later." Our students worked together with Stephenson to create the script. The film has been distributed and used in schools throughout the country. In a presentation to me, Judy Glickson, my colleague who initiated the production of the film, wrote this caption on a framed scene from the film: "To Dr. Leatrice Rabinsky whose

Journeys of Conscience have opened the doors to tomorrow for all who were her students."

Another memorable gathering took place in Vienna at the residence of Ambassador Milton Wolf (a Clevelander) and his wife, Roslyn. Friends of ours since college and through our mutual involvement in community activities, the ambassador and his wife were so gracious. They invited our journey group for a kosher Shabbat dinner at their home where a special guest was Simon Wiesenthal, Holocaust survivor and famed Nazi hunter. Christian and Jewish students joined together to welcome the Sabbath. Young Gary Robuck (now Rabbi Robuck of Congregation Shaarey Tikvah) chanted the *Kiddush* (sanctification prayer) and Simon Wiesenthal recited the blessing over the *challah* (Sabbath bread). Ambassador Wolf encouraged us to share our experiences about our journey through Poland. He also told us that the previous week he and his wife; President Carter, his wife, Roslyn, his daughter, Amy; and Russian Premier Leonid Brezhnev had met in this same room. They had all come to Vienna as part of the SALT II Conference. The next day, Simon Wiesenthal welcomed us to his office in Vienna. He shared many stories of the ongoing efforts of his Documentation Center to track down Nazi perpetrators of all levels wherever they may be throughout the world. Another monumental Journey of Conscience.

A SPECIAL EVENT IN JERUSALEM

More than 35 years after liberation, 6,000 survivors of the Holocaust gathered in Jerusalem from countries throughout the world. Ernst (Erni) Michel, the World Gathering chairperson, addressed the open meeting, telling of his vision as a 16-year-old concentration camp prisoner. He and his fellow *katzetniks* (concentration camp inmates) were determined to survive. "*Mir villen zei uberleben*" (We will outlive them). At that time, Erni pledged that someday all of the survivors would assemble in Jerusalem, in the homeland of the Jews. In 1981, the dream was realized. Hundreds of survivors came with their adult children who convened in an assembly of Second Generation members.

Every day was filled with events fraught with emotion. My husband and I participated as journalists representing *The Cleveland Jewish News*. Our Cleveland contingent, composed of the Kol Israel Foundation, survivors, and friends, brought an ambulance to give to the Magen David Adom (the Red Star of David) medical organization. One of the highlights of our visit was survivor Jack Beigelman's bar mitzvah at age 52 at the Western Wall. He had been a prisoner in the Lodz ghetto at age 13 and had never celebrated his special event. We were singing, dancing, laughing with joy, and crying as Jack chanted his prayers. A Jerusalem rabbi invited our entire group to his apartment in the Old City to continue the celebration.

Nor will we ever forget the other heartfelt events: Rose Kaplovitz having a reunion in Kibbutz Netzer Sereni with the "girls" from her children's home for orphans, established after liberation; the tragic news of the death of Antek Zuckerman at Kibbutz Lochamei Hagettaot where he had been overcome with emotion at the ingathering of survivors; the speech by Menachem Begin (then–prime minister of Israel) who spoke about the triumph of survival and the establishment of the Jewish State of Israel; the lighting of 6,000 *Yahrzeit* (memorial) candles at the Western Wall on the final night of the gathering; the intoning of the legacy of the survivors, which read in part:

We take this oath! We take it in the shadow of flames whose tongues scar the soul of our people. We vow in the name of dead parents and children. We vow, with our sadness hidden, our faith renewed. We vow we shall never let the sacred memory of our perished six million be scorned or erased.

and, the Pledge of Acceptance of the Second Generation, which read in part:

We accept the obligation of this legacy. We pledge to remember! We shall teach our children to preserve forever that uprooted Jewish spirit which could not be destroyed.

We shall tell the world of the depths to which humanity can sink and the heights which were attained, even in Hell itself. We are your children. We are here.

CONTINUING AND EXPANDING OUR HOLOCAUST EDUCATION EFFORTS IN CLEVELAND

Inspired and energized by this unforgettable ingathering we returned to Cleveland determined to intensify and expand our Holocaust education activities. Students at Heights High organized Holocaust Commemoration Week, which is still an annual program. Survivors, liberators, Second Generation speakers, panel discussions, and films are scheduled six periods a day throughout the week at Cleveland Heights High School.

Special tribute assemblies and luncheons honor distinguished guests, such as African American U.S. Army liberator Leon Bass and film star and Auschwitz survivor Robert Clary. Students begin months in advance preparing for this spring program. Hundreds of students participate in each day's program. Classes from area schools are invited to various assemblies. In addition, students create Holocaust education exhibits with posters, books, poetry, and essays. I was particularly proud of my class's project that was given a two-month exhibit period at the main library of the Cleveland Public Library.

At this point in time, we began to write, edit, and publish an annual magazine called *Journal of Testimony*. Poems, artistic interpretations of speakers' stories, photographs of sites of the Holocaust, and oral histories of survivors are included in each journal. Students of all nationalities and religions joined in every aspect of our efforts, and the magazine was a fulfillment of my earnest expectations.

Julie Roth's reflections, "My Father's Hands," were so searing and memorable that she was asked to read her poem to an all-school assembly during Holocaust Commemoration Week. The introduction and explanation were also riveting:

My father's hands are swelled from doing hard labor in Nazi concentration camps. He would like to be able to learn to play the violin, but the size of his hands makes it physically impossible. Because my father was deprived of an education he had to teach himself a trade when he came to America. He is a mechanic and his hands are never completely clean. In elementary school I was ashamed of these hands, but now I love them because my father's hands provide me with all I need.

Anxious to go beyond the classroom program, my students volunteered to help with the citywide *Yom HaShoah V'Hagvurah* (Holocaust and Heroes' Remembrance Day) annual meetings. In 1982 I accepted the position of program chair, an effort that continued for more than a decade. Throughout the years my students served in various capacities, distributing publicity flyers, ushering the night of the event, entering the creative arts and poetry competition, and walking with memorial candles in the March of the Generations.

A Journey of Conscience with My Former Students of the Second Generation

By 1983 many of my former students were adults, active in the Kol Israel Second Generation Foundation. They asked if I would lead them on a Journey of Conscience to the places of their birth in the former DP camps and to the sites of their parents' traumatic years during the Holocaust. Once again, survivor Bertha Lautman accompanied our group, but this time with her adult daughter, Alice Dickman. At an outlying cemetery near Munich, we conducted a moving memorial service with Lee Rosenberg chanting the Kaddish for the grandfather she had never known. This was the site of the burial in a mass grave of Dachau inmates who had perished in the last days before liberation. Lee's grandfather was among those who had died of illness and starvation at that time. Her father, Jack Wieder, was 16 years old when he had returned to the camp after labor and had found his father's body. It was just a few days before the American army liberated Dachau.

In Israel, we were honored to meet with Prime Minister Menachem Begin in his Knesset office. During our hour with him he congratulated the young people for their willingness to confront the places of their parents' Holocaust experiences. He shared his traumatic years in Warsaw. He also inspired us with his hopes that Israel would become a haven for all times for Jews who are oppressed anywhere in the world. Just a few weeks later, after the death of his beloved wife, Aliza, Begin left public life and went into seclusion.

A Holocaust Survivor Interview Project

In 1984, our local National Conference of Jewish Women (NCJW) undertook an ambitious project to interview local Holocaust survivors. This was part of a national effort of Yale University's Fortunoff Video Archives with Dr. Geoffrey Hartman as project director. I was asked to serve as cochairperson of the NCJW Interview Committee and to conduct seminars for prospective interviewers. Ultimately, we completed 137 oral histories. Each interview, most of which were three hours in length, was conducted at the television studio of our local Channel 5 station. Copies of the survivor testimonies were submitted to the Fortunoff Archives at Yale University and to Channel 5. Each survivor also received a taped interview.

I had the privilege of conducting seven oral histories. Soon after completing the project, I learned that Frieda Traub, a survivor whom I had interviewed, had passed away. Her daughter, Rivkah Traub Levitansky, has told me many times how precious that tape is. Every year on the Jewish fast day of *Tisha B'Av* (the ninth day of the month of *Av*, a solemn day of remembrance), the Traub family gathers to see and hear their mother's story of her family in Europe and the tragedy that consumed them in the Holocaust.

As a result of our NCJW effort, I was invited to participate in a Holocaust Educators' Conference at Yale University in 1984 and again in 1985. Part of my presentation was a lecture with slides about our Journeys of Conscience.

CONTINUING MY HOLOCAUST EFFORTS ON DIFFERENT FRONTS

In 1986, a significant honor was bestowed on my colleague, Holocaust author Bea Stadtler, and on me when we were appointed to the Chairperson's Advisory Council on Education of the United States Holocaust Memorial Council during the tenure of Elie Wiesel. In two successive years we met in Washington, D.C., with educators from all parts of the United States and with representatives from Yad Vashem in Jerusalem with whom we engaged in discussion about texts, survivors' testimony, and classroom strategies.

The 1980s also saw the two major conferences, one in Philadelphia and one in Washington, D.C., of the American Gathering of Holocaust Survivors. Students from my classes, together with members of the Kol Israel Foundation, attended each convocation. We will always remember Leon Faigenbaum, who wore his "Auschwitz cap" soiled beyond repair, and never took it off during the entire conference. Survivors embraced by the students stood before huge message boards filled with emotionally charged messages and pictures, such as: "I was in the orphanage in Malines, Belgium. Do you remember me?" and "I was separated from my sister in Shtuthof. Did you know her?" Some survivors wore front and back placards with their concentration camps' places of imprisonment, the years, and pleading questions such as "Were you there?" and "Did you know me?" We will never forget the husband and wife, who appeared at each conference with a large picture of a precious little girl, walking to every gathered group, asking, "Do you recognize our daughter? Did you ever see her? She was separated from us at the deportation." Such experiences conveyed a reality for my students that transcended classroom lectures and reports. Our Heights High students proudly presented an original artistic poster of commendation and congratulations on the occasion of the American Gathering of Holocaust Survivors in Philadelphia. Benjamin Meed, national president and dynamic leader of the survivors, accepted the gift and announced that the poster would be placed in the New York office of the American Gathering.

At this time, I became engrossed in works by Yehuda Bauer and Raul Hilberg. Bauer addressed the American Gathering in Washington and Philadelphia, and later I heard Hilberg at a Kent State Holocaust Educators' Conference. Each historian conveyed with accuracy and a riveting eye the unfolding tragedy of the Holocaust. Bauer's volume, *A History of the Holocaust,* was a valuable adjunct to my studies. There was a sustained intellectual quality to his work, conveying information with clarity. For years I have also appreciated Bauer's work, *The Holocaust in Historical Perspective.* I found Hilberg's tome, *The Destruction of European Jews*, especially helpful in preparing lectures for my students. Senior class members also appreciated Hilberg's clear voice as a distinguished historian.

DEVELOPING A HOLOCAUST CURRICULUM FOR THE OHIO COUNCIL ON HOLOCAUST EDUCATION

By 1986, a rewarding Ohio state effort in Holocaust education developed under the leadership of Governor Richard F. Celeste. More than 40 community leaders and educators of all faiths and ethnic backgrounds throughout the state convened at the state capitol to participate in the organization of the Ohio Council on Holocaust Education. It was an impressive meeting with a significant challenge proposed by the governor. He suggested that ultimately we would create a statewide Holocaust curriculum, which could be implemented in appropriate classes in secondary schools throughout Ohio. Max Friedman, past president of the Jewish Community Federation and revered communal leader, was elected president of the Ohio Council on Holocaust Education. We established a calendar of meeting dates and suggested activities to launch this project. I was asked to assume leadership of a challenging dimension of this effort, the Materials and Curriculum Committee. Many of the committee members were colleagues, friends, or acquaintances with whom I had previously shared classroom materials or who had joined with me as presenters at Holocaust conferences. I was also delighted to meet new colleagues and to learn of their teaching experiences. A bright young teacher, Carol Danks, from T.R. Roosevelt High School in Kent, Ohio, and I gravitated toward each other. I was delighted to learn that she had participated in Vladka Meed's Holocaust and Jewish Resistance Seminar in Israel. Our sessions were enhanced in many ways by Carol's insightful suggestions. She also shared valuable classroom experiences concerning her Holocaust unit at T.R. Roosevelt. In addition, Carol was jovial, perceptive, friendly, and most cooperative.

We became friends at once. It has been a privilege these many years to work in the field of Holocaust education with her.

Ultimately, I asked Carol to serve with me as coeditor of the final goal of our work, the Ohio State Holocaust Secondary School Curriculum. Carol agreed, and we proceeded to accomplish and publish our task with notable contributions from a vibrant committee. Volunteering their time and efforts to this important task, the 15 Ohio teachers and community leaders on our committee came from many cities between 1986 and 1988 to develop this curriculum— *The Holocaust: Prejudice Unleashed.*

Following our successful publication of the curriculum, first in 1989 and with a revision and reprinting in 1994, Carol and I teamed up to present several teacher workshops and seminars. Among the many places we presented at were Kent State University, the University of Toledo, the Detroit Holocaust Memorial Museum, the Holocaust Educators' Seminar in Flint, Michigan, and the Yad Vashem International Conference on the Holocaust in Jerusalem.

The Opening of the United States Holocaust Memorial Museum

In the spring of 1993 I had the opportunity to organize a Journey of Renewal to the opening of the United States Holocaust Memorial Museum in Washington, D.C. Survivors from the Kol Israel Foundation, members of the Second Generation, Heights High students, and area educators filled the bus for this pilgrimage. Despite the torrential rains, we sat for hours covered with rain gear in the vast plaza behind the museum building. We had come early, encouraged and guided by Bob Somers, Washington attorney, historian, and my former student and first Journey of Conscience participant. Heads of state, including Chaim Herzog, president of Israel, and government leaders were presented to the cheering crowd of thousands. Most impressive, however, was the message of Elie Wiesel, who is recognized by many to be the spokesman for the survivor community. He spoke of the victims of the Holocaust, abandoned by a silent world. He charged us to arrive at a moral reckoning and to dedicate ourselves to seeking justice for all oppressed people. He spoke of the genocide of the Jewish people, and as we had all learned earlier, while not all of the victims were Jews, all Jews were victims simply by virtue of their birth.

We were then permitted to visit the museum in shifts. Each component of the exhibit was compelling, an aggregate of artifacts, posters, and media segments of unusual scope. Unable to spend the time necessary to absorb all that we had seen or even to view many aspects of the exhibit, we were determined to return. Every year since, I have led a similar group, with many returnees, to the United States Holocaust Memorial Museum.

My Fifth and Sixth Journeys of Conscience

Our fifth Journey of Conscience took place in the summer of 1993. En route to Sosnowiec, the childhood city of three of our survivors, we stopped at the picturesque rural town of Chelmek, the home of Lola Mandelbaum's late husband, Sam. An aging farmer stopped as we exited the bus. Lola asked him if he remembered the Mandelbaum general store, saying that she was the wife of Sam. Staring at her strangely, he answered, "Yes, I remember, but you are not Sam's wife. You don't look like her." He had not known that Sam's first wife and child had been gassed at Auschwitz. Together with her son, Leo, who had come from Israel to join his mother, Lola found the courtyard and dwelling of her grandfather, where the family had always gathered for Shabbat. Together, they were permitted to enter and see the apartment.

Ann Perla, also from Sosnowiec, was not as fortunate in finding her childhood home. One of ten children, she and two sisters were the only survivors from a large family. Very disappointed and sad, Ann was comforted as we later chanted the memorial prayers for her family in the Jewish cemetery in Kraków. In Sosnowiec, Rose Kaplovitz led our group to the Jewish cemetery. Though most of the monuments were vandalized and broken, there was a postwar *matzevah* near the entrance on the site of a mass grave. Rose was sure that this was the mass grave where her 16-year-old brother and grandfather had been murdered and buried. We joined with Rose in a tearful intoning of the Kaddish.

Traveling to fulfill the mission of Esther Frank and her sister, Frances Neuman, we arrived at a small town, Klobusk. They were elated at finding the apartment of their grandparents where the extended family had always come for holiday celebrations. Their joy was dimmed, however, as they visited their childhood home and the neighbors whom they remembered came out to meet them and asked in an incredulous tone, "What? You are alive?" Esther and Frances felt that the neighbors sounded as if they were seeing ghosts, believing that all the Jews had perished.

Hoping to visit the grave of their grandfather who had died before the war, Esther and Frances asked directions to what had been

the Jewish cemetery in Klobusk. At the site, we found farmers
working the fields planted with cabbage, potatoes, and edged with
beautiful flowers. One farmer guided us to a lone *matzevah*, broken in two and lying on the ground, the only reminder that this
was once a Jewish cemetery. Survivor Alex Chrabry chanted the
Kaddish near this stone in memory of the grandfather and all those
whose graves had been ploughed under.

Philip Wexberg led us to Wadowice, his birthplace and also the
childhood home of the present pope, John Paul II. Together with
his son, Dr. Steve Wexberg, we stood at the site of Philip's synagogue that had been burnt by the Nazis. A children's day care center has been erected in its place. There is a plaque, however, on
the face of the building, commemorating the place of worship and
the Jews of Wadowice who had perished. In the reclaimed Wadowice
Jewish cemetery we honored the memory of Philip Wexberg's family.

Renewal for all of us took place in Israel. Our first visit was to
Yad Vashem in Jerusalem, where Abbi Akst chanted the Kaddish
in the Hall of Remembrance. Steve, Bryna, and Jaimie placed a
memorial wreath near the eternal flame, surrounded by the imbed-
ded stones naming the concentration camps we had visited. Soon
we were on the hills of Jerusalem, planting saplings in the forests
of the Jewish National Fund.

Unique to the 1993 journey was our visit to Denmark, to meet
with and honor the noble Danes who had saved more than 95 percent of their Jewish citizens from the Nazi onslaught. I had corre-
sponded with Preben Munch Nielsen, the president of *Sundets
Venner* (Friends of the Strait). This is the organization of people who
had been members of the Danish resistance and who had brought
the Danish Jews to safety in Sweden. Marcia Wexberg wrote in her
journal:

This past October (1993) marked 50 years since the Jews of Denmark
were warned in this synagogue (Jewish house of worship in Copenhagen)
of a planned Nazi roundup. Hidden in homes in the countryside, and
taken in fishing boats four or five at a time, across the waters, the Jews
found safety in Sweden. In the nearby Round Church (Trinitatus), Torah
scrolls were hidden from the Nazis throughout the war.

We then gathered in front of the Thomsen Inn next to the waters of the strait. We honored the memory of H.C. Thomsen, the
first of the Danes to take Jews across the strait to Sweden. Tragically, Thomsen was caught and met his death in Neungamme concentration camp.

Marcie Wahba had this entry in her journal:

After meeting with members of the Sundets Venner, all I can say is that I am in awe. They were brave beyond belief. They had more courage than most of Europe, and yet they swear up and down that what they did was what they had to do for their fellow humans.

Preben Munch Nielsen shared many of the resistance members' harrowing rescue ventures with us. He also spoke of the care which the Danes gave to the homes and property of the Jews (including mowing their lawns) who were taken to safety in Sweden. When the Jews returned to Denmark, they were able to move right into their dwellings without any difficulty. Our students asked, "Why did you do this?" "It was a matter of decency," answered Preben. I remember how, at our ceremony, Marcia Wexberg hugged Preben and tearfully said, "If there had been more like you, I would have had grandparents."

I have always been gratified that my classes in Holocaust education have been meaningful to Jewish and Christian young people as well as to students of diverse ethnic and racial backgrounds. Frequently, I receive letters and notes from class members who comment on how the Holocaust studies had motivated them to humanitarian activities. Particularly rewarding was a long letter in 1994 from Susan McGowan. Below are some of her comments:

Because of your class I wrote three Holocaust poems for my Writers as Readers class at college (Wooster). You gave me confidence in my writing, in my voice. The poems gave you the idea of taking me on your 1993 Journey of Conscience. Out of that trip came more poems which you allowed me to read at important sites like Auschwitz and Majdanek. My voice was growing stronger and you were speaking along with me. In the main section of my senior independent study project I am writing a Holocaust Requiem, poems about the Holocaust for each movement of the Catholic Requiem Mass. It is in this section that you have helped me the most. You made me feel that I had a right to discuss the Holocaust, a subject which so often is considered outside the realm of Christian understanding. You have treated me as an equal to those for whom the Holocaust runs in their blood. I have a soul, and I have a voice. And for that I will always be grateful to you.

Our sixth Journey of Conscience in 1995 had the added dimension of visiting the sites of *Schindler's List* in Kraków and Israel. We stared down into the area of the former Kraków ghetto just as Oskar Schindler had done as he watched the roundup of the Jews from the hill above the area. We toured Schindler's factory where he had created employment for more than 1,000 Jews whom he had saved from the concentration camps.

In Jerusalem's Catholic cemetery, we, too, honored the memory of Oskar Schindler as did the survivors in the final scenes of the film. One by one, we each placed a stone on Schindler's grave to say that we honor the memory of this rescuer.

THE LATTER HALF OF THE 1990s:
MY WORK CONTINUES

Each year there seems to be more opportunities for exploring and plumbing the depths of the Holocaust. Colleague Mary Chaitoff and I attended the first Hidden Child Conference in 1995 in New York City. Mary has also participated with me on five Journeys of Conscience. Rarely speaking of their traumas of separation from family, of bonding with new caregivers, hidden children were told, "You did not suffer in the camps. Keep silent." This was their first opportunity in an ingathering of hidden children to voice their anxieties and traumas. Only 200 participants were expected in the organizing months. More than 1,000 hidden children came from all parts of the world.

That same year I was asked to speak to the caregivers at our local Menorah Park Center for the Aging about the experiences and special considerations for aging Holocaust survivors. This preceded a visit by members of Menorah Park staff to the United States Holocaust Memorial Museum. A pacesetter in the care of residents who are survivors, Menorah Park's administration prepared a booklet, *Painful Memories*, that lists triggers related to concerned behavior of survivors of the Holocaust. In 1995, I presented this booklet to a seminar of physicians and nurses in Hadera, Israel, at Shaar Menashe Hospital, the largest mental health facility in the Middle East.

The following year, a remarkable opportunity was offered to Holocaust educators throughout the country: the Mandel Fellowship program at the United States Holocaust Memorial Museum. This was the first of six yearly study conferences and yearlong project development programs to be initiated and supported by the Mandel brothers of Cleveland. I was privileged to be a participant in the first year's cadre of 25 educators. Meeting for a week of intensive study, research, and lectures by world-famous Holocaust scholars, we prepared to develop our own innovative classroom project that would be presented at a concluding conference the following May. Rather than concluding, however, we, as Mandel Fellows, have been part of a nationwide network of serious Holocaust educators sharing, meeting, and presenting together at workshops and conferences—gaining momentum in our efforts every year. Kudos are extended to the Mandel Fellowship director, Steve Feinberg, a Holocaust educator of note and a skillful administrator.

At the conclusion of the 1996 academic year, I retired after 31 years of stimulating and happy years in the Cleveland Heights-University Heights school system. My Holocaust course continues to be taught, though, by my colleague Sol Factor.

It really wasn't retirement, but a change of venue. I continue to teach junior and senior students American and British literature and an intensive course, Confronting the Holocaust, at Fuchs Mizrachi, a private Jewish school that is prekindergarten through grade 12. Our program of Holocaust outreach to communal and school groups; the writing and publication of journals with oral histories of survivors, poetry, and essays, and the journeys to Detroit and Washington, D.C., are an integral part of the Holocaust studies program.

In the fall of 1996, I participated in the first International Conference on the Holocaust at Yad Vashem in Jerusalem. Carol Danks and I presented a workshop on implementing the Ohio curriculum, *The Holocaust: Prejudice Unleashed.* We shared specific lessons and successful classroom strategies, illustrating our guidelines with many of the projects created by our students.

Of particular interest was the eclectic assembly of world-renowned Holocaust scholars and educators. A special treat was the tour of the alleyways and byways of the Old City in East Jerusalem by our friend and colleague, Holocaust educator, writer, and editor, Dr. Samuel Totten of the University of Arkansas.

Another Journey of Conscience took place during the summer of 1997. Special highlights of this seventh journey of 23 participants were: making our first pilgrimage to Sobibor, now a forgotten, almost desolate concentration camp site, and being outraged at a costumed vampire figure being videotaped on a mound of human ashes; being welcomed to the History Museum of Zdunska-Wola by the mayor and curator who opened a wing to the Holocaust in honor of Gita Frankel; and embracing the last Jew of Mezherich, Menachem Kagan. For generations, Mezherich was a bastion of Polish Hasidic life. Now it is bereft of Jews. In Israel we heard from Rabbi Jonathan Friedlander, who participated as a 17-year-old in the first Journey of Conscience. He described how that journey had changed the direction of his life.

As with each journey, students wrote about their feelings and their projections for the future. Max Nathison wrote the following poem:

> Even flow.
> Consciousness.

       A stream that gathers from
       separated drops.

Looking to the future, Adina Bensoussan wrote, "People are for-getting, losing respect for what has happened in the Holocaust. It is our job, those who are fortunate enough to participate in such a journey, to make sure that people never forget."

In between organizing the Journeys of Conscience, I now had time to develop additional courses about the Holocaust, primar-ily for teachers. In 1998, 1999, 2000, and continuing through today, I have taught month-long evening courses for teachers and lay leaders at the Jewish Community Center of Cleveland. Among the topics have been: confronting the Holocaust (a chronology of events), history of antisemitism, documents of the Holocaust, he-roes and heroines of the Holocaust, and perpetrators of the Ho-locaust.

Our eighth Journey of Conscience took place in June and July 1999. In Amsterdam we were privileged to meet with Jacqueline Maarsens, childhood best friend of Anne Frank, mentioned numer-ous times as "Jope" in Anne's diary. She never knew that the Franks had gone into hiding, thinking they had left for Switzer-land. In Vienna we stood solemnly at the sculpture of the aged Jewish man scrubbing the sidewalk commemorating the humilia-tion of the Jews of Austria.

The uniqueness of this journey was also the bonding of Cleve-land generations—survivors and their Third Generation grand-children and educators and their grandchildren. Rose Kaplovitz and her husband, Jack Beigelman, and Roman Frayman were the sur-vivors accompanying, sharing, and inspiring us. An hour away from Vienna is the Mauthausen concentration camp with its quarries and the infamous 137 Steps of Death where inmates, emaciated and exhausted, carried heavy stones up and down the sharp stone stairs. Rose's grandchildren, Josh Kaplovitz and Jenna Gelin, held each other and sobbed as they stood in front of the Jewish monu-ment, an imposing gigantic concrete menorah. They spoke about their late grandfather, Henry Kaplovitz (Rose's first husband), who had been a prisoner in those quarries when he was the same age as they were now.

These are the words of Josh and Jenna:

We thought about what it would be like without a family, one that is as close as we are. Without a grandma or grandpa, aunt, uncles, parents, brothers and sisters and cousins. For all of those who have lost so much of their families in the Holocaust, there is no consolation, only the love of others. This is why we as a Jewish people are so much more than a people. We are a hand to hold, a shoulder to cry on, a family to depend on and a pride to carry on.

Completing the missions in Poland, Roman Frayman, who has been teaching about the Holocaust for 15 years, went to the city hall in Sosnowiec, the city where he was born. "Within the first hour, I touched a document I had waited to see for 54 years." It was the birth certificate of his baby brother, Haim Shaje Frayman, who died at the hands of the Nazis.

Rose Kaplovitz, also from Sosnowiec, found the marriage certificate of her parents in the same city hall. Rose had learned after the war that following her deportation to the Oberalstadt concentration-labor camp, the Sosnowiec ghetto of Shredula had been liquidated. Her parents had been deported to Auschwitz with other ghetto victims where they perished.

Now, the time has come to pass the mantle of Journey of Conscience leadership to a new generation. Of course, I shall still be in the vanguard of teaching, lecturing, studying, conducting workshops and seminars, and leading groups to the United States Holocaust Memorial Museum. It is imperative, however, to ensure that the Holocaust is remembered and studied long after the generation of survivors has passed on. I have been blessed with students who have assured me that they will protect and teach the lessons of the Holocaust. Marc Coles, for example, wrote recently:

Dear Dr. Rabinsky,

I am writing to you from Nijmegen, Holland, some 10 minutes west of the German border and 20 minutes south of the city of Arnhem, site of one of the most valiant attempts waged against the Nazis on Dutch soil (*A Bridge Too Far*) during the Second World War.

In reflecting on the significance of the Journey of Conscience in my life, I can state quite simply that the Journey altered the course of my life and was a critical factor leading to my decision to make Israel my home. As much as I learned to cry at Auschwitz, I learned the meaning of pride as we left behind the frozen steel wrought iron gates promising *Arbeit Macht Frei* and travelled directly to the Eternal City of Jerusalem, the place which has forever remained in the heart of our People.

Five years after the Journey, I returned to Jerusalem to teach about the Holocaust, guiding hundreds of American high school students through the Yad Vashem Holocaust memorial. On the evenings before the visit to Yad Vashem, I retold to these students the story of the Journey of Conscience through the slides I photographed during those frigid days of late December 1975. My personal encounter with the Holocaust became a solid personal bond with the State of Israel which I made my permanent home in 1982.

During the 1999 Journey of Conscience, Rabbi Gary Robuck was associate leader with me. When I asked him what the journey meant in his life, Rabbi Gary wrote:

In 1979 at the age of 18, a recent graduate of the Cleveland Heights High School, I was fortunate enough to be invited to participate in the Second Journey of Conscience under the direction of Dr. Leatrice Rabinsky. The Journey succeeded then even as it had on the first Journey and on six subsequent occasions, to inspire and to educate students regarding the horrors of the Holocaust in a way no other such experience could.

Due in no small part to the Journey's impact and Dr. Rabinsky's on-going encouragement and support, I soon after found my way first into the rabbinate and now am her successor, appointed to lead the next Journey of Conscience scheduled to depart in June of 2001. The Journey of Conscience has had a significant and long-term impact upon my life and work.

My consideration for issues related to Holocaust memory, my passion for Jewish education, and most recently, the successful creation of Face to Face, an original initiative in Holocaust education, each can be attributed to a great extent to the wisdom and vision of Dr. Rabinsky, a good friend and kind supporter.

It is worth noting that Face to Face is a remarkable program created by Rabbi Gary Robuck that I helped initiate, and is now run by Dr. Sharon Faigin. Both Sharon and Gary were on my 1999 Journey of Conscience. They bring students (by word of mouth) from public, private, and parochial schools to the Shaarey Tikvah Congregation. Rabbi Gary Robuck introduces them to traditions and rituals of Judaism, and they view *Daniel's Story*, a film about the chronology of the Holocaust as seen through the composite experiences of a young boy. The students meet with a survivor who presents his/her Holocaust experiences, engage in dialogue with the survivor, tour Face to Face's minimuseum of Holocaust memorabilia on the synagogue's premises, and have lunch at the synagogue with volunteer synagogue members and sometimes with students from the area's Jewish day schools. This is an enriching program of rapprochement with young people sharing ideas and experiences. Each year thousands of students are involved in the program. For me, this is a very rewarding fulfillment of a legacy of Holocaust education, which I pass on to my former students.

I write with a sense of *nachat* (limitless pride), knowing that our young people will embrace the legacy of the Holocaust, transmitting the responsibility with heartfelt care.

REFERENCES

Evans, Becky, and Goldman, Judy (Eds.) (1976). *Times of the Holocaust — No Excuse for Apathy*. Cleveland, OH: Shofar Publishing.

Tomorrow Came Much Later, A Journey of Conscience. 1980. 60 min., col. Originally distributed by Coronet Films. For current information on obtaining the film, contact the producer and director of the film, Dr. Alan Stephenson. Write to him in care of John Carroll University, 20700 North Park Boulevard, University Heights, Ohio 44118.

Chapter 7

~

The Call of the Story

Karen Shawn

The Holocaust has shadowed and shaped the last half of the last century; the impact of its stories remains immutable. So it is not surprising that those who know the power of this watershed, either through surviving it, inheriting its legacy, or simply hearing about it in school, should wonder about those who choose to spend their lives in the field of Holocaust education.

"How did you get involved in teaching about the Holocaust?" This is the perennial question people ask me, the supersessional query that has replaced and outlasted earlier ones. No one asks me any more, for example, if I know what I want to be when I grow up. Nor does anyone ask me these days if I am going to keep my own name when I marry, or whether I'm going to let my teenager drive at night, or how it feels to be the mother of the bride, or how my husband and I are managing our empty nest. People have even stopped asking me what it's like to be a new grandmother. Stage specific, such questions ceased as I outgrew them. But for the past 15 years, people have consistently sought to discover the circumstances of my encounters with the subject of the Holocaust, to understand what underlies the choice I made to dedicate myself to teach and design curriculum about the Shoah, the death of the European Jewish community.

"Are your parents survivors?"

"Were you born in a displaced persons (DP) camp?"

"Did you lose family in the Holocaust?"

"Is your degree in history?"

"Were you influenced by a particular book?"
And of course, from students: "Are you Jewish?"

The questions are straightforward, but to shed light on why and how I came to do what I do, they require complex answers. As Carl Friedman (1996) makes clear in her novel *The Shovel and the Loom*, "a person is who he is" because of "who he has been [and] with whom and where he [has] been. He was the words he had heard and the voices with which they had been spoken; he was the images he had seen, the smells he had smelled, and all the hands that had touched him." (pp. 24, 26)

My parents' touch was, of course, the most profound. My parents were not survivors, nor were my grandparents, all four of whom came to America with two of their parents and a large assortment of other relatives during the first decade of the twentieth century to escape the pogroms of their native Russia.

I was not born in a DP camp, but rather in the capital city of Albany, New York, to a very loving, middle-class, highly educated, assimilated but culturally committed Jewish family. In my childhood, at my mother's insistence, we were members of a Conservative *shul*, but my father saw no need to send us to Hebrew school, or to attend services for more than the obligatory High Holy Day devotions. He himself taught Jewish history at our local Reform congregation and we eventually joined that *shul*, which he continued not to attend, despite my mother's urging.

Both of my parents came from large and extremely close-knit families who had known one another since childhood, and my sister, my brother, and I grew up surrounded by adoring grandparents, aunts, uncles, and cousins of all ages. Whatever extended family we had lost in the Holocaust have always been lost to us; as far as I can remember, neither European relatives nor the Holocaust was discussed in any detail in my house.

As a 13-year-old, I did receive *Anne Frank: The Diary of a Young Girl* (1952) as a birthday present from an aunt, and read it in one sitting. But reading and rereading the diary alone in my room, I regarded it as more than the introduction to the Holocaust my aunt may have meant it to be. Self-involved, rebellious, and yearning to be free of my mother's constraints, I fancied that Anne was a teenager much like me, that her struggles mirrored my own. We both adored our fathers, despaired over our mothers, and had sweet and obedient older sisters. We were both Jewish, chatty, good in school, and sometimes defiantly rude. We both kept a diary and wrote short stories. I, like Anne, had a crush on a boy named Peter.

Of course, Anne was in hiding from the Nazis in the middle of World War II, her world destroyed and her life endangered. I recognized that, and understood, conceptually at least, the anti-semitism that fueled Anne's enemies. But in my insulated, drama-soaked state of early adolescence, I somehow was able to hold in abeyance the very real context of her suffering, and focus instead on those aspects of Anne's story that rendered it personally and immediately relevant.

Louise Rosenblatt (1976), in her seminal text, *Literature as Exploration*, reminds us that a young adolescent's reactions to literature "will inevitably be in terms of his own temperament and background," that a young reader's "primary experience" of literature will have meaning "in these personal terms and no others . . . no matter how imperfect or mistaken." (p. 51) She concludes, somewhat understatedly, "Undoubtedly, these may often lead him to do injustice to the text." (p. 51)

For me, Anne had more connection to Holden Caulfield, the protagonist in J.D. Salinger's *Catcher in the Rye*, than to the stacked, naked bodies or the striped-suited, skeletal remnants of the Holocaust I had seen in the newsreels of the 1950s. I never discussed the diary in the context of Holocaust history, so Anne remained what I needed her to be at that time.

My degrees are not in history, but my father, of blessed memory, majored in history and economics, and had taught those subjects at Alfred University in New York, in the 1930s. Of all my childhood teachers, he was the only one who ever made history come alive to me, the only one who understood what James F. Moore (1988), in his essay "Crossing the Experience Barrier: Teaching the Holocaust to Christian Students" affirms, that "there is no entirely pure history," that all "history bears a story. . . . Mere confrontation with facts as they can be reconstructed will tell a story for each student who hears those facts. . . . Each assemblage of facts is already a shaping of the history into a particular story." (p. 156)

My father was a consummate storyteller; a raconteur, people called him, and from infancy on I was regaled and mesmerized by his tales. In my childhood they frequently centered on the history of Albany and the people who populated its poorest neighborhoods, and often included dramatic accounts of his own history juxtaposed with his dreams and aspirations for us, his three beloved children.

His only rival storyteller was my mother, a gifted and inexhaustible reader, writer, and primary source of morality tales. She read to me to get me to sit still, eat, behave, go to sleep, and sometimes just to amuse and enthrall me. Fairy stories, folktales, fables, nursery rhymes, poetry, children's classics, stories of Sholom Aleichem — every day my life was enriched by her reading.

She made up stories as well. Our favorite main characters, and her most enduring, were twins, Henry and Penelope, who didn't listen to their parents, got into trouble, had near-death experiences, and learned new and vital lessons as a result. Henny and Penny stood too close to the stove, ran across the street without looking, accepted rides from strangers, and hid in leaves piled high in their driveway just as their father was due home from work. But they were always rescued from almost inevitable disaster just in time ("Thank God!" my mother would have their mother say) and learned never, ever, to do such a thing again.

With such parents, it is not surprising that I would grow up to teach the Holocaust, the most consuming and powerful story of our time. But how was it possible that I never learned about it in any meaningful way from them?

My parents' philosophy of child rearing was reflective of the European Jewish tradition that learning should be associated with sweetness. On their first day of school, Jewish children were dressed in new clothes, carried to their classrooms by a rabbi or learned man, and given a rolled paper cone filled to the brim with sweets, apples, and nuts. When children were ready to learn the *aleph-bet*, the Hebrew alphabet, mothers baked cookies in the shape of each letter, topped them with honey, and sent them to the teachers to give to the children as they learned. That is what my parents wished for their children: that our learning would always be as sweet as honey cookies, that our childhood knowledge would include only the goodness in the world.

Life can be hard, my parents knew from firsthand experience, so childhood must not be. They had had to bear adult burdens at a tender age; their children must never be made to do the same. There was time enough for worry, they knew, and childhood was fleeting under the best of circumstances. Let children be children as long as they can, they felt; and they devoted themselves to protecting us, physically and emotionally, to ensuring us a happy, carefree, secure, and loving childhood.

My parents spoke only in Yiddish about family travails, illnesses, financial worries. Any arguments they had were behind closed doors. They never left us in the care of someone who was not a family member, even for an evening, and, until we were teenagers, they never took a vacation without us. As children we did not attend funerals, even when our own grandparents died.

Of course, the world was full of dangers that might threaten a child, and some of them we had to know about to remain safe. But

Henny and Penny taught us that if we listened to our parents, did the right thing, and were always very careful, nothing bad would happen to us. We rejoiced in the stories' happy endings, but took them for granted.

The Holocaust was over. It had not directly affected my parents or their families, and did not then threaten us. Its sinister, dark reality had no place in our world.

At no time did I make a conscious decision to be a teacher. My father was a teacher, so I had wanted to be one for as long as I can remember. I knew from my parents' tales and talents that history could fascinate me, that I could learn a great deal from the experiences of ordinary people who came alive through the details of their daily lives. Hearing about their relationships, struggles, dilemmas, and decisions, sometimes reconstructed from what we could surmise about them, sometimes from their own words, allowed me to enter their world and make sense of the context in which they lived.

But in class after class in junior high and high school I felt alienated and bored as teachers spoke of decades and centuries, battles lost and empires won, compacts signed and treaties broken, revolutions and conquests, rulers and heroes, expeditions and territories, and dates, always dates: 1066, 1215, 1492. In the survey courses I encountered each year, I was exposed to great leaders and history's vast sweep, to eras and cycles and movements. But I wanted to understand history one moment, one day, one person at a time. In college I minored in psychology and majored in English, where I slaked my thirst for stories and the people and meanings behind them.

I became an English teacher in Lawrence Junior High School on Long Island, New York, imbued with my parents' sense of literature, history, and the inviolate nature of childhood. But curriculum demands shaped my performance, and my ideals were quickly replaced by the realities of the mandated grammar, spelling, vocabulary, composition lessons, and weekly tests. My seventh and eighth graders busied themselves with workbook skill-building drills; they read the anthologized stories for the sole purpose of being able to give the "right" answers to the required questions on each last page. My supervisor was delighted with me, and told me I was well on my way to becoming a master teacher.

In 1971, not long after I began teaching, a passage, author unknown, circulated among the staff:

I have taught in high school for ten years. During that time I have given assignments, among others, to a murderer, . . . a thief and an imbecile.

The murderer was a quiet little boy who sat in the front seat and regarded me with pale blue eyes; . . . the thief was a gay-hearted Lothario
with a song on his lips; and the imbecile, a soft-eyed little animal seeking the shadows.

The murderer awaits death in the state penitentiary; . . . the thief
. . . can see my room from the county jail; and the gentle-eyed little
moron beats his head against a padded wall in the state asylum. . . .
I must have been a great help to those pupils—I taught them the rhym-
ing scheme of the Elizabethan Sonnet and how to diagram a complex
sentence.

While others shrugged off the words with rueful head shaking,
the essay's painful acknowledgment of futility touched me; the
author could have been I. I began to reexamine what I actually did
as a teacher and what I might and should be doing, a study that
would ultimately change my life.

I enrolled in a master's degree program, taking education courses
first at Brooklyn College and later at Teachers' College at Columbia
University. But only when I discovered the faculty and philosophy
at New York University (NYU) were my intuition and upbringing
validated. Under the expert and caring tutelage of Professors Harold
Vine and Marilyn Sobelman, I discovered the "personal growth
through English" paradigm, which became the hallmark of my
teaching. I invested my energies in the design and implementation
of an "emergent" curriculum that encouraged multiresponses expressed through a variety of modes. With authors John Dewey,
Louise Rosenblatt, James Britton, James Squire, James Moffett,
John Dixon, Alan Purves, Stephen Tchudi, Ken Macrorie, Jerome
Bruner, Norman Holland, and others, in concert with my professors, providing the theoretical underpinnings, my teaching of language and literature became focused on, and reflective of, the needs
of my students. With a new English department supervisor in place
and my growing ability to explain the theory behind my practices,
I was able to align much more closely what I knew to be right with
what I did in the classroom.

But when, in the early 1980s, I began to teach the Francis
Goodrich and Albert Hackett (1956) play, *The Diary of Anne Frank*,
required reading from our literature anthology, I was stymied by
the problems that arose. I took pains to introduce the feisty Anne
and her family within the proper context of the Holocaust, the history of which I had finally learned, albeit cursorily, through my own
reading. But my eighth graders asked questions to which I had no
answers. I was now a doctoral student at NYU, focusing on curriculum development in English education, not on studying the Holocaust. How could I respond to students' questions about Anne's

life and death when I myself did not understand the tragedy that engulfed her? How could I go beyond the strength, courage, and rebelliousness of Anne the adolescent to introduce and explore the more authentic and meaningful picture of Anne, the Jewish victim of Nazi persecution? How could I teach about the one and a half million other young victims and still allow my children to be children? The grim recognition of my vast ignorance of this subject became yet another catalyst for what would be my initially tentative forays into Holocaust history.

In the summer of 1985, my husband and I embarked on a three-week adventure to Israel sponsored by the Jewish National Fund, an experience that allowed us to get to know Israel through touring and "working the land." Based for two weeks at the Rosenblatt, a small hotel in Nahariya, a favorite vacation destination in the north of Israel, we spent each morning clearing brush from what was to become a local picnic area and planting seedlings at a nearby kibbutz's tree nursery. Each afternoon we toured the Galilee, the Golan Heights, and the surrounding towns and cities.

One of those afternoons led us to Beit Lohamei Haghettaot, the Ghetto Fighters' House, a Holocaust memorial museum built in 1949 by survivors of the Warsaw Ghetto Uprising. I wandered throughout the hot, silent building for hours, trying to understand what I was seeing in this, my first visit to a museum that told the story of the Holocaust and, within it, the meaning and scope of Jewish resistance. Jewish resistance? The concept was new to me. I had never thought of such a possibility. What I knew of the Holocaust was what the Nazis had done, and how some Jews, such as Anne and her family, had hidden, trying to keep sane in a world gone mad. But to understand the events from a Jewish point of view? Remarkable.

On Friday nights, our group of 25 or so hurried back to the hotel to shower and dress. Once in the lobby, hair and eyes shining, we welcomed Shabbat, the girls and women lighting the squat white candles that sat on a large silver tray in the now-bustling lobby. Some women, their hair covered with a hat or a circle of white lace, waved their hands around the flames of the candles, covered their eyes, and swayed, whispering the blessings and their own private prayers. I watched them, envious of their competence and comfort in a language and tradition of which I knew nothing.

The lobby soon filled with greetings of "Shabbat Shalom!" as men returned from evening prayers, ready to eat. They sang the blessings over the sweet reddish brown kiddush wine, and passed a full silver goblet around the table for us to sip. Many guests washed their hands and fell silent before they salted and ate the golden challah, two loaves hidden until then under a painted silk cloth. These ancient rituals, new to me, kindled a spark long dormant in my soul.

Much of our last week was spent in Jerusalem.

"One does not travel to Jerusalem, / One returns. / One ascends / the road taken by generations, / the path of longing / on the way to redemption. / One brings rucksacks / stuffed with memories / to each mountain / and each hill." So wrote the Yiddish poet Yitzhak Yasinowitz in his poem "To Jerusalem" (translated by Miriam Grossman), and so I felt. Jerusalem was my heritage unearthed; finally, I had come home.

I returned as well to the story of the Holocaust. My guide at Yad Vashem, Jerusalem's state-sponsored memorial museum and documentation center, was a survivor. The graphic black-and-white photos and text panels came alive through his gentle commentary.

"I remember this happening in our house," he said softly, pointing to one in the list of laws drafted at Nuremberg. "Our maid had to leave us—she had taken care of me since I was born—but she had to leave because the Nazis said she could no longer work for a Jewish family."

"Here," he said, stopping before a grainy photograph of a pit filled with bodies, "here is where my family is buried."

The experience left me aching and yet consumed with the need to know more about this catastrophe. I spent hours at Yad Vashem and in every part of the city, new and old, walking, listening, learning, sitting at cafes, juxtaposing Jewish history with Jewish present and future, attempting to place the 12-year Shoah (1933–1945) within the context of thousands of years of Jewish life and the vital, vibrant community that was the modern Jerusalem. At the same time I questioned my place and my future in the Jewish rhythms and rituals I was discovering.

The summer was ending. As surely as I knew I had to leave, I knew I would return.

My parents had driven from Florida to Brooklyn for my homecoming, and we spent our first full day together regaling each other with anecdotes about our Israel experiences. My husband's and mine were recounted with immediacy and intensity, while my parents' memories of their several trips were tempered with thoughtful reflection and a poignant drive to return yet again.

As I talked passionately about the moments our photographs captured, and tried to express my longings, both to return to Israel and to learn more about the Holocaust and the role of Judaism in my life, I was overcome with emotion. My tears surprised us all into silence, until my father got up from the kitchen table to hold me in his arms.

"I knew you would feel this way," he said. "I've been waiting for you to understand." He wanted to continue our talk, he assured me, but he wasn't feeling well, and thought he'd lie down.

That night, on our physician's insistence, we took him to the hospital. He was feeling better, so I sat at his bedside and talked, as I had many times before, about the gifts he and my mother had given me. After his varied and successful career in education at the high school, college, and graduate school level, my father retired from the New York State Department of Education as an associate in the Department of Mental Retardation (called today, I imagine, Special Needs). His life revolved around helping those less fortunate than he was, making a contribution to society, and he made it clear that this was a mandate for Jews. He had made me a proud Jew, bringing me up to understand the importance of the contributions the Jewish people had made to the world, well out of proportion to our numbers, and to affirm the centrality of Israel in our lives.

My parents had instilled in all three of their children and their granddaughter the necessity of a good education, the one thing that no one could take from us. They imbued us with an all-embracing love for our extended family and for the Jewish people, and an understanding of our obligation to live a life of service, to help those in need, and to treat everyone, regardless of race, class, or position, with respect and kindness.

Despite my father's rejection of formal observance of a traditional Jewish lifestyle, he was the consummate Jewish educator, living, not just teaching, his idiosyncratic understanding of Jewish values. He gave fully and joyfully of himself to his family, students, colleagues, community, and, of course, to Jewish causes, a variety of local Jewish institutions, and Israel, always Israel.

When my parents moved to Florida, my mother, always the more traditional of the two, began to attend synagogue services regularly. My father was drawn to Jewish learning, studying Hebrew and the Bible and even reading a prayer book on those mornings my mother went to services. His knowledge of Jewish history was vast, and in addition to his scholarly essays, he wrote a column in his local paper on little-known facts about the Jews. He learned to bake challah. In his painting class he captured bearded rabbis and the arches of ancient synagogues. He toyed with the idea of returning to his birth name, Olshansky, deciding he regretted giving in to the economic and political pressures of Albany in the early 1930s to

change it to the less-Jewish sounding "Shawn." He compromised
by adopting "Schaum" as his penname.

He had spoken to me of all this, of the profound importance that
Judaism had for him, of the defining nature of Jewishness in his
life. But my recognition of myself as a Jewish woman, rather than
as a woman who happened to be a Jew, came late, only during this
summer in Israel.

"I knew you would understand," my father said. And, finally, I
did.

As we sat and reminisced, I parceled out still more photographs,
each with its attendant story. We would go there to Haifa and there
to Netanya and there to Tel Aviv together, we assured each other,
sketching out the details of a future family trip.

But it was not to be. Four days later, still in the hospital await-
ing a diagnosis, my father suffered a fatal heart attack.

What would his monument be? What could I do to ensure that I
would uphold the ideals he had bequeathed to me? I had desire,
but no knowledge; the melody, but no words. I was firmly rooted
in my Jewishness, but only through a kind of osmosis: through
the foods I ate, the company I kept, the intonations and inflections
of my speech, the causes I supported, my understanding of who
we were in and how we were seen by the world, my collective memories, and now, my commitment to Israel. Only this last root seemed
tangible, a likely place to begin to commemorate my beloved father,
my teacher.

But how would I return to Israel? I was still in mourning. I could
not and did not want to go back as a tourist; I wanted to work or
to learn. When, almost a year later, a notice appeared in a teachers'
newsletter offering summer fellowships to study the Holocaust and
Jewish resistance at Yad Vashem and at the Ghetto Fighters'
House, I applied and was accepted.

This summer study fellowship was led by Vladka and Benjamin
Meed, survivors of the Warsaw ghetto, who understood early on the
importance of helping American teachers learn the history of the
Holocaust, and who had the foresight, commitment, courage, and
resources to realize their dream.

Vladka Meed, vice president of the Education Chapter of the
Jewish Labor Committee, and Ben Meed, president of the American Gathering of Jewish Holocaust Survivors, worked in conjunc-
tion with the American Friends of the Ghetto Fighters' House, the
United Federation of Teachers, and the American Federation of
Teachers to offer summer fellowships to public schoolteachers to
study the Holocaust in Israel for three weeks. When I was fortunate enough to be chosen in 1986, there were 42 of us represent-

ing 13 states. Today there are close to 700 graduates from 48 states, Washington, D.C., and the Virgin Islands.

Vladka and Ben were our guides, mentors, teachers, mother and father. Vladka and Ben were parents in the image of my own; they took on the responsibility of worrying for and about all of us. We were not to be burdened by any problems that might arise during the trip. Since our subject was so painful, they wanted us to have only the best accommodations, so we stayed at the five-star Carlton Hotel in Nahariya, three blocks and three stars away from my first home in that city, the Hotel Rosenblatt. Vladka never left us during the day, ensuring that each lecturer would be scrupulous both in presentation and timeliness. She did not want us to stray from our hotel at night, feeling that we were safest when we were all together under her watchful eye. She wanted us to learn of Jewish life before and during the Holocaust, not just of death, so she invited survivors to tell us of their childhoods in pre-World War II Poland and to entertain us with Yiddish music and songs from their cities and villages as well as their ghettos and camps. And she talked, quietly, modestly, about herself and her life before, during, and after the Holocaust, helping us to understand that the Holocaust was a chapter in, rather than the entire story of, the life of a survivor.

A teenager during the Holocaust, Vladka had been a courier who traveled between the Aryan and the Jewish sides of the Warsaw ghetto. Living with false papers under an assumed name, Vladka worked to find a haven for Jewish children secreted out of the ghetto even as she smuggled information and dynamite into the ghetto as part of the underground resistance movement. I had seen her photograph the previous year in the museum's section on resistance; now she was my teacher and mentor.

In addition to her stories of her own active resistance, Vladka introduced me to the concept of spiritual resistance. She talked of rabbis and teachers who risked their lives to teach when schools were forbidden, of children who smuggled potatoes by burrowing through openings in the ghetto wall when smuggling was punishable by death, of men and women who danced in the ghetto courtyards on Jewish holidays despite the threat of fatal beatings. With each reminiscence, Vladka helped me to understand that resistance could be defined as anything one did to stay alive. She, along with our host, the director of the education department of the Ghetto Fighters' House, Simcha Stein, underscored the importance of teaching the concept of spiritual resistance to a generation of students who had never heard of it.

In addition to classes with Vladka and Simcha, I studied with historian Dr. Yehiel Yanai and other luminaries, such as Dr. Nili Keren. Keren, a historian and teacher of teachers, presented a unit on children's dilemmas, making the point that children might most comfortably learn about this subject through the stories of children who lived during the Holocaust. This was a simple and obvious premise and yet none of us had raised it until Nili made her graceful and fluid presentation.

At Yad Vashem I met the world's preeminent Holocaust scholars and recorded their every word. Professor Yehuda Bauer sat calmly behind a small table and, lecturing without a note, introduced me to the varying conditions in each ghetto that helped to shape the Jewish Councils and their leaders. With balance and brilliance he helped me to understand the dilemmas in which councils were placed and the issues to consider when trying to understand their actions.

Professor Emil Fackenheim introduced me to what he termed "the 614th Commandment": "Jews are forbidden to hand Hitler posthumous victories." This distinguished, gray-bearded, gentle man helped me to understand my parents' insistence that we embrace our heritage as he explained that

after Auschwitz, we are commanded to survive as Jews, lest the Jewish people perish. We are commanded to remember the victims of Auschwitz, lest their memory perish. We are forbidden to despair of humanity and escape into cynicism or otherworldliness, lest we cooperate in delivering the world over to the forces of Auschwitz. We are forbidden to despair of the God of Israel, lest Judaism perish. (personal class notes, July 1986)

Shalmi Barmor, then the director of the Department of Education, expanded my nascent understanding of the concept of spiritual resistance as he spoke about the variety of Jewish responses to the situation in which Jews found themselves. "Not *kiddush hashem*, martyrdom in the name of God," he insisted, "but *kiddush hachaim*! We will hang on to life!" He paced back and forth across the classroom, his passion ensuring that we would remember his every word. The teachings of these men and a dozen others laid the foundation of the career I would subsequently build.

In both museums I also met Holocaust survivors. Each day I listened raptly to their remarkably detailed accounts of their experiences; each night I read whatever memoirs of young people I could find in the museum bookshops and libraries. From these talks and books I learned to speak of the one and not just of the six million, to portray the Jews as vital and vibrant and not just as victims.

The testimonies of Anushka Freedman, Ruth Elias, Ruth Brand, Gabriel Dagan, and Vladka Meed, and the writings of Sarah Neshamit (*The Children of Mapu Street*), Isabella Leitner (*Fragments of Isabella*), Clara Isaacman (*Clara's Story*), Livia Bitton Jackson (*Elli: Coming of Age in the Holocaust*), and Edith Baer (*A Frost in the Night*) are just a handful of countless stories whose impact allowed me a much-needed catharsis and served as well as a catalyst for my immersion in the field.

I mourned both my father and the six million that summer. In their memory, and for the survivors I met and befriended, I committed myself to teaching what I had learned. As much as I might wish to help my students taste only the sweetness and see only the good in the world, that was no longer an option. I no longer had the choice of whether or not to tell them about the Holocaust; the survivors' voices, as well as my father's, chorused the imperative. I could choose now only how to tell them about it, and help them to explore its significance.

Once back in my eighth-grade English classroom, I began our Holocaust unit by introducing some of the literature I had read that summer, planning to offer a developmentally appropriate story of one or two young people. But my newly acquired knowledge haunted me. I felt compelled to tell my students the historical facts I had learned and to exhort them to remember. I presented a traditional historical overview and told of the horrors still so vivid to me. My goal was no longer to protect my students' adolescent sensibilities. Instead, perhaps exorcising my own demons, I thought I could measure my success by the numbers of students who cried.

And they did cry, and they did remember—gas chambers, piles of shoes, wedding rings, hair—but they didn't begin to understand. They didn't know why it happened, or how it was humanly possible, or why people didn't help, or why it was different from any number of other genocides. Smothered by graphic details, frustrated by their unmanageable and contradictory feelings of outrage and impotence, confused and overwhelmed by the immensity of the events, many students rejected further learning. It was too much for them, they would say, and too terrible; they simply could not learn any more about the subject.

In my zeal to share with them the nightmare in history I had been told, I had put aside what I had learned from my parents, Vladka Meed, and Nili Keren. In my attempt to do justice to the memories of the victims and the survivors, I had forgotten that adults do not share their nightmares with children.

Why was I trying to teach them everything I had learned? They had the rest of their lives to study this subject, I reasoned, and, if

I did my job correctly, they should want to. I came to see that I would have to find an older audience if I needed to teach this subject in depth. My need to teach it was most assuredly not their need to learn it.

There is a story of a little girl who one day asked her mother where she came from. The mother knew that this question was inevitable, and she was ready, although she never expected to hear it from so young a child. She took out the books, sat down with the child, and told her everything she thought a modern mother should say about where babies come from. When she finished, she asked her daughter if she had any questions. The child shrugged. "I asked Grandma where she came from and she said, 'New York.' "

Primed as I was to answer my students, I was misunderstanding their questions, which demanded far simpler responses than I had been wont to give.

Still at NYU, I changed the focus of my doctoral thesis in curriculum development from an examination of teachers as curriculum developers to an exploration of the use of literature as an age-appropriate means of introducing the Holocaust to middle school adolescents.

I returned to Israel for the next two summers to study both the Hebrew language and the Holocaust. At the Ghetto Fighters' House, once again in the company of Simcha Stein, Ben and Vladka Meed, and their latest group of teachers, I listened to more history lectures and survivors' testimonies. I spent weeks at Yad Vashem, examining the English-language Holocaust curricula stacked on the shelves of its Pedagogic Center, sent there by American teachers who were proud of them. As I mastered the history, I rejected the majority of the curricula I read, for they did no more than recreate my own unsatisfactory high school experience by offering ways to help students memorize key names, dates, and places. Some even resorted to crossword puzzles and 50-question, fill-in-the-blank or multiple-choice worksheets. Many recreated as well my unsatisfactory teaching experience by presenting to middle school students in depth and gruesome detail, the mechanics of the Final Solution.

Each fall I returned to my classroom and, through trial and error, analyzed various methods and materials and compared my findings with colleagues from the summer seminars. One of my primary goals was to find ways to make both the history and the literature of the Holocaust accessible, to help students make sense of what they saw, heard, and read. I wanted students to analyze and reflect on events of the Holocaust, and on the relationship between these events and personal and societal decisions and values. I wanted to increase their knowledge of Holocaust history

in an incremental, age-appropriate way, but I also wanted them
to ponder its significance, its implications for them as young people
who live in its shadow. I began to develop a sequential, literature-
based approach to teaching.

Realizing that the personal growth model of education, with its
focus on the importance of meaning-making, was uniquely appropriate for teaching the Shoah, I strove to make my classroom a
caring community in which students were empowered to explore
what they read, viewed, and heard with the goal of making information personally meaningful and significant. They were encouraged to respond to texts, videos, survivors, and the Second
Generation—the children of survivors who also had stories to tell—
in personal journals, through conversation, and through a variety
of creative arts projects. They were encouraged to contextualize
Holocaust literature and testimony by reading the appropriate and
relevant historical background.

In 1988 I met Dr. Dennis Klein, then the director of the Anti-
Defamation League's (ADL) Braun Center for Holocaust Studies.
After hearing me speak at a symposium on Holocaust education,
he invited me to put my theories into practice and write a textbook
that would illustrate my ideas of using age-appropriate stories to
complement history. Only I could fully appreciate the irony in his
charge that the book was to be about Anne Frank, to commemorate what would have been her sixtieth birthday.

I worked closely with the warm and supportive Dr. Klein, a meticulous historian and editor, and in 1989, the ADL published my
textbook, *The End of Innocence: Anne Frank and the Holocaust.*
Using excerpts from Anne's diary as points of departure throughout each of five lessons, the text explored only those issues and
events of the Holocaust that related directly to Anne's life. This
exploration in turn provided the counterpoint to Anne's voice, enabling students to connect certain global events with their direct
and specific effects on one young girl, her family, and the citizens
of Germany and Holland, the two countries in which she lived. My
goal was to help students understand both Anne and the world that
shaped her. An appendix of 23 related-literature excerpts, including testimony, memoirs, and poetry, helped to put a human face
on the historical abstractions.

That year as well I was awarded a Mt. Scopus Fellowship from
the Melton Center at Hebrew University, which allowed me to take
a year off from my teaching to live and study in Jerusalem for six
months. At the university, I was blessed with the opportunity to
be mentored by the scholarly, eloquent Dr. Ze'ev Mankowitz, professor of history at Hebrew University. In his packed lecture hall

and under his tutorial expertise, I immersed myself in the history of the Holocaust. At Yad Vashem I studied again with Shalmi Barmor, Dr. Bauer, Dr. Fackenheim, Dr. Keren, and others, including Dr. Mordecai Paldiel, the gentle, soft-spoken director of Yad Vashem's Department of the Righteous among the Nations. Dr. Paldiel taught me the importance of offering an alternative to despair by providing stories of heroism and courage and righteous acts. At Yad Vashem I was privileged to hear guest lecturers such as Dr. Christopher Browning, then-professor of history at Pacific Lutheran University in Tacoma, Washington, and author of *Ordinary Men: Reserve Police Battalion 101 and the Final Solution in Poland*; and Dr. Ephraim Zuroff, historian, director of the Simon Wiesenthal Center in Jerusalem, and noted Nazi hunter. *Finally*, I was learning history as my father would have taught it.

I spent countless hours in pedagogic discussions with Shulamit Imber and Safira Rapoport, leaders and innovators in Yad Vashem's education department. I participated in a semester-long pedagogic workshop designed and run by the charismatic Shulamit. Through our dialogues and debates, I cemented my convictions to avoid the subject altogether in the primary grades, and to limit the scope and the depth of a middle school curriculum. I became convinced of the importance of teaching young adolescents about the rich and vibrant European Jewish life before the Holocaust, and of helping them understand the Jewish response to the catastrophe by providing stories of the daily life of Jewish children during the early and middle years of the Holocaust. Stories of Jewish life, not death, would be my focus.

With the patient guidance and exacting instruction of Ze'ev Mankowitz, I designed and taught a postgraduate course in the literature of the Holocaust at the World Union of Jewish Students in Arad, a development town south of Jerusalem. With the support and encouragement of education director and teacher Shalmi Barmor, I developed a literature unit to complement a Yad Vashem poster series.

During the final month of my fellowship, I audited an intensive three-week seminar on Holocaust history at Yad Vashem. Led by the brilliant, iconoclastic young scholar Ya'acov Lozowick (now Dr. Lozowick, the director of the Yad Vashem Archives) and attended by some 25 professors and scholars from England, America, Australia, and South Africa, the course was rich in history. But it was bereft of pedagogy, the component crucial for American middle and high school educators slated to come for the summer version. I submitted my critique to Shalmi, in charge of the winter and summer seminars.

"You think the course needs the perspective of an American educator?" he asked.

"That's the only thing it lacks," I answered. "Teachers will learn what to teach, but they need someone to help them articulate their goals, and explore methods and materials appropriate for their classrooms."

"Would you come back this summer and do it for us?" he asked, and my heart stood still. I left Israel in February and returned in July as part of the staff of the Yad Vashem Summer Institute for Teachers from Abroad, a position I would hold for ten years. Ya'acov Lozowick, my teacher, became my mentor, supporter, and friend.

The first summer workshops were held in my rented apartment in Talbieh, a centrally located neighborhood in Jerusalem. Two times a week, after an entire day of history lectures, the ten or so teachers in the group made their way to our two-hour sessions. We snacked on grapes, pretzels, nuts, and cookies, drank gallons of grapefruit and orange soda, and shared questions and concerns about methods and materials. The debates were friendly but fierce. Do we teach about the death camps in grade five? Can we ask survivors to limit and focus their classroom testimony? If we have only a class period or two to talk about the Holocaust in an eighth-grade world history survey, what do we include?

And we didn't talk about history, but rather devoured short stories and poetry that might help our students enter the darkness without falling into the pit that lay in wait for them. Every session ended with the same refrain, "I don't know what I would do without this chance to talk about teaching!"

That fall I completed my dissertation and returned to my eighth graders. But as opportunities to work in the field of Holocaust education presented themselves more frequently through requests for articles, teachers' guides, parent and teacher workshops, and consulting positions for both the ADL's Braun Center and the American Friends of the Ghetto Fighters' House, the more I wanted to devote myself to that teaching. When, in 1993, the offer came from the Moriah School of Englewood, a modern Orthodox Jewish day school, to design and implement a new Holocaust studies program to be housed in a newly built, state-of-the-art Holocaust Study Center complete with performance and exhibition space, I accepted the position eagerly.

Of equal importance was the opportunity such a position afforded me to work in an observant community, to experience firsthand what such a commitment would entail and the effect it would have on my life. As my knowledge of the Holocaust had grown, so had my interest in embracing a more traditional Jewish lifestyle. Each

Friday night my husband and I lit Shabbat candles; each new Jewish song led to another. Each Hebrew word and blessing I learned was motivated by, and was a memorial to, my father and the Jews of the Holocaust.

Thus, learning about the Holocaust, in part, served to deepen my connection to Judaism. Equally true is that the closer I came to living an observant Jewish life, the more I felt the imperative to remember and to teach this chapter of Jewish history.

Each summer in Israel I designed and implemented pedagogic workshops for both the Yad Vashem Institute and Vladka Meed's seminars. As much as the teachers loved the intimacy of the minicourse in my apartment, the new director of the Summer Institute, Ephraim Kaye, felt the sessions should be held at Yad Vashem. He wanted to counter, and rightly so, the attitude of some of the Summer Institute's attending professors who regarded methodology as "fluffy stuff." He encouraged me to hold the sessions at Yad Vashem during the day, lengthen some of them to four hours, align them more closely with the course curriculum, and open them to college teachers as well as those in middle and high school. By doing so he felt we would make the statement that an educational-methods course was an integral and legitimate component of Yad Vashem's history seminars. The sessions were now attracting up to 25 participants each summer, and I somewhat reluctantly exchanged the intimacy of our earlier gatherings for the professionalism and status of a Yad Vashem conference room.

The most consistently troubling issue each year for the majority of teachers was that of when and what to teach elementary school children. Readings by child psychologist Dr. David Elkind, essayist and social commentator Charles Krauthammer, and NYU Professor of Education Dr. Neil Postman became, at the teachers' request, part of my core curriculum.

In *The Hurried Child: Growing Up Too Fast, Too Soon*, Elkind (1988) posits that the trend toward teaching young children "the wrong things at the wrong time for no purpose" (p. xi) is an outgrowth of the "superkid" phenomenon. Parents insist that their children are precociously competent and can therefore be "hurried" into learning and doing. Teachers valued this book for its broad application as well as its specific implications for Holocaust education in schools where state mandates have encouraged some teachers to accept the concept of "superkid," and to introduce their youngest children to subjects previously considered taboo. The "superkid" paradigm allows such teachers (and politicians) to rationalize what is really their "need to teach" as students' "need to know."

Essayist Charles Krauthammer (1995) laments, "Teaching the most wrenching social history to the very young assaults their innocence by deliberately disturbing their cozy, rosy view of the world. . . . They live only once, and for a very short time, in a tooth-fairy world. Why shorten that time further?" (p. 80)

In discussing the price of the openness and candor of today's society, Neil Postman (1982) reminds us in *The Disappearance of Childhood* that "certain facets of life—its mysteries, its contradictions, its violence, its tragedies . . . are not considered suitable for children to know; [and] are, indeed, shameful to reveal to them indiscriminately." (p. 15) He adds, "It is clear that if we turn over to children a vast store of powerful adult material, childhood cannot survive. By definition adulthood means mysteries solved and secrets uncovered." (p. 88) "How have we forgotten this?" the teachers wondered each year.

At home I was now the regional director of educational outreach for the American Society for Yad Vashem, and consultant to the American Friends of the Ghetto Fighters' House. In these roles I conducted educational workshops in New Jersey, wrote curriculum, offered support and guidance to graduates of the summer programs, and served as a resource for potential participants.

At the Moriah School I initiated a sequential curriculum in which the history of the Holocaust is not introduced until fifth grade and then only from 1933 to 1939. Even through the eighth grade, our students are taken "up to the camps but not inside"—my parents' philosophy adapted to the subject of the Holocaust, and reconfirmed by the historians and educators at the Ghetto Fighters' House. In our curriculum, literature introduces and accompanies the historical content, for

history, by its nature, attempts to express and interpret factual and inter-related general totality; well-rendered literature, paradoxically, may offer a more accessible sense of an event because the knowledge it may have the potential to impart is personal knowledge, immediate individual apprehension of the meaning of a complex idea, event, experience, or emotion. (Farrant, 1989, p. 25)

For primary school students, I introduced the concept of Holocaust Education Readiness Activities. Bolstered by the ideas of Drs. Elkind and Postman, and of course the wisdom of my parents, I encouraged teachers in grades one through four to avoid teaching the Holocaust and to examine instead its underlying themes as a way of laying the groundwork for future learning. For example, students explore, through story, discussion, and the arts, the concept of memory and the crucial role it plays in our individual and communal lives. Another unit examines the centrality of intergenerational dialogue in their lives, focusing on the relationship between grandparent and grandchild and the rich heritage of family stories they share with joy and pride.

In keeping with these themes that form the foundation of our Holocaust education program, and still convinced of the power of the story, I conducted a writing workshop for survivors, the Second Generation, and seventh graders. The result was an anthology entitled *In the Aftermath of the Holocaust: Three Generations Speak* (1995).

The encouragement of my principal at that time, Rabbi Harvey Silberstein, and of several graduates of the summer seminars, led me to begin in 1995 the Holocaust Education Consortium, an invitational gathering of Israel-educated teachers, administrators, and resource center personnel who would come together yearly for a weekend of study and collaboration. The consortium was designed to provide a professional forum for structured peer support and problem solving, and for exploring and developing the best materials and practices. It has become a small but committed national network of affiliated, Israel-educated pedagogues who implement and improve Holocaust education in their schools and communities, and who have become devoted mentors to me and each other.

In 1995, the Ghetto Fighters' House opened Yad Layeled, the only Holocaust museum in the world designed specifically for children in grades four through nine. Because its educational philosophy had become mine, I encouraged a partnership between it and the Moriah School. Thanks to the foresight, openness, and collaborative spirit of Director Emeritus Monia Avrahami; the current director, Simcha Stein; and the executive director of the American Friends of the Ghetto Fighters' House, Debbie Nahshon; the partnership has become a cornerstone of our curriculum.

As part of the opening ceremonies of Yad Layeled, the Moriah School presented the art work of our fifth graders, who had drawn their responses to a survivor's testimony under the guidance of their teacher, Margo Zomback. The 24 drawings were hung in the museum's classroom gallery throughout its first year, allowing our students the unique opportunity of seeing their work displayed in a world-class museum.

Over the course of several years we worked cooperatively to develop the International Book-Sharing Project, an outgrowth of work begun at the Moriah School. This project pairs American and Israeli students in a discussion of Holocaust literature conducted via the Internet. Through the vision and dedication of the director of the Yad Layeled Pedagogical Center, Dr. Moshe Shner, and museum educators Miri Kedem, Tali Shner, Beth Seldin Dotan, Varda Shiff, and Puriya Lichi, and with generous support from Moriah parents Mark and Anita Sarna, the project has grown from a three-classroom literary response unit to a 60-school international adventure.

In my third year at the Moriah School, I was asked if I would accept the position of assistant principal for secular studies for the junior high school. I would remain as director of Holocaust studies, albeit with far fewer responsibilities, and would take on the administrative duties necessary as the school expanded yearly, now close to 1,000 students. I hesitated only long enough to consider whether I would be able to do justice to both positions and then accepted, a decision for which I am grateful each day.

My husband and I now live in a New Jersey community where we have found the support and opportunities for learning that have enabled us to live a fully observant Jewish life. I have built for my father and for the six million the only monument I could: I am teaching and transmitting my Jewish heritage through my lifestyle and my work.

I do what I do today because of where and with whom I have been. I am the words I have heard, and the voices with which those words have been spoken. I am the images I have seen, and all the hands that have touched me.

REFERENCES

Baer, Edith (1980). *A Frost in the Night: A Girlhood on the Eve of the Third Reich.* New York: Pantheon Books.

Elkind, David (1988). *The Hurried Child: Growing Up Too Fast, Too Soon.* Reading, PA: Addison-Wesley Publishing Company, Inc.

Farrant, Patricia A. (1989). "On the Necessity of Reading Holocaust Literature," pp. 23–29. In *Peace/Shalom After Atrocity.* Greensburg, PA: The National Catholic Center for Holocaust Education, Seton Hill College.

Frank, Anne (1969). *Anne Frank: The Diary of a Young Girl.* 8th ed., trans. B.M. Mooyart-Doubleday. New York: Washington Square Press.

Friedman, Carl (1996). *The Shovel and the Loom.* New York: Persea Books.

Goodrich, Frances, and Hackett, Albert (1956). *The Diary of Anne Frank.* New York: Random House, Inc.

Isaacman, Clara (1984). *Clara's Story.* Philadelphia, PA: Jewish Publication Society of America.

Jackson, Livia Bitton (1980). *Elli: Coming of Age in the Holocaust.* New York: Times Books.

Krauthammer, Charles (1995). "Hiroshima, Mon Petit." *Time,* March 27, p. 80.

Leitner, Isabella (1978). *Fragments of Isabella.* New York: Dell Publishing Co.

Meed, Vladka (1979). *On Both Sides of the Wall: Memoirs from the Warsaw Ghetto.* New York: Holocaust Library.

Moore, James F. (1988). "Crossing the Experience Barrier: Teaching the Holocaust to Christian Students," pp. 155–167. In Zev Garber (Ed.) *Methodology in the Academic Teaching of the Holocaust.* Lanham, MD: University Press of America.

Neshamit, Sarah (1970). *The Children of Mapu Street.* Philadelphia, PA: Jewish Publication Society.

Postman, Neil (1982). *The Disappearance of Childhood.* New York: Delacorte Press.

Rosenblatt, Louise M. (1976). *Literature as Exploration.* New York: The Modern Language Association.

Yasinowitz, Yitzhak (1995). "To Jerusalem." In *Jerusalem Day.* New York: Israel Information Center, p. 19.

Chapter 8

~

Why?

Samuel Totten

FORMATIVE YEARS

What prompts one to become immersed in a field that inevitably forces him/her to probe the darkest recesses of the human condition? There are no easy answers, and it is a question I've pondered over long and hard. It is also a question I have personally and frequently been confronted with over the past two decades by other academics, friends, and relatives. More specifically, I have been asked: "What drives you to think, write, and teach about such issues?"—such issues being the deprivation of human rights and genocide, in general, and the Holocaust, in particular.

Many are simply curious as to why one would dwell on and obsess about such horrific matters. Others, though, seem to find it odd, even aberrant, as if there were possibly something innately wrong with an individual who dedicates, day in and day out, so much of his time and energy to such work.

While I can pinpoint the exact location and evening of the awakening of my vital concern over the deprivation of human rights, which gradually evolved into my becoming immersed in the field of genocide and Holocaust studies, the underlying reason for my obsession with those who are ill-treated is painfully personal and thus much more difficult to reveal.

I grew up in a household in which violence, racism, and to a certain extent, antisemitism, were pervasive. My father, a grossly overweight man with a horrible temper, was a police officer in East Los Angeles, California. A rough-and-tumble area, it was primarily composed of stockyards, meat-packing houses, industrial plants, and impoverished residents, most of whom were blacks and Hispanics. In Los Angeles in the 1950s, at least from what I gleaned from my father's conversations with my mother and other officers who visited our house, meting out "street justice" by cops was fairly common then, if not the norm. That included threatening, slapping, and, if "need be," beating suspects with fists and blackjacks— in some cases, *literally*, to a pulp—and then arresting them. While my mother, brother, and I were technically his "loved ones," my father meted out the same sort of brutal treatment in the house as he did on the street. I suspect that the endless beatings, the profanity-laced ranting and raving, the smashing of anything in his way, and the pervasive terror induced by him were more frequent at home than they were on the street. Due to sheer fear, no one in the house dared attempt to quell his actions. And no one came to our assistance. Not our relatives, not the neighbors, not our teachers, and certainly not the local police.

As long as I can remember, verbal assault and physical violence ruled our house and our existence. A day did not go by that either my mother, brother, or I was not screamed at, slapped, punched, pounded, bitten, or hit with whatever was in reach (a dinner fork or knife, an ashtray, a splintered piece of furniture, a screwdriver's or a hammer's handle). And my father didn't stop there. As he broke our bodies, he—to a profound extent—broke our spirits.

When I was in first grade and about six years old, my father, in a rage, punched me and broke off my front tooth. When my brother was about eight, my father, who was eating dinner by himself in the living room, called my brother in to do something, but out of earshot my brother wasn't sure what was wanted and when he asked for clarification, my father, enraged, stabbed him just above the eye with a fork. To this day, the scar from that attack is visible on my brother's face. When my brother and I were teens, my father broke my mother's arm, and when she returned home from the hospital that evening, he smashed the cast, breaking her arm yet again.

Anything and everything seemed to set off this violence: if someone spilled a glass of milk at the dinner table, if he perceived a slight, if he didn't like the look on one's face, if he didn't like an answer to a question, if someone didn't do something exactly the way he wanted it done. Indeed, he often became enraged over anything, everything, and nothing.

Few, if any, days went by without my father maligning someone who crossed or simply irritated him, and this generally resulted in his referring to the spurned individual as a nigger, spick, kike, or dirty Jap. And generally *mf* or *gd* (the words, not the initials) preceded each of those terms. At the same time, my father ceaselessly, proudly, and hypocritically proclaimed his "great" friendships with Mexicans and Jews. However, his ugly epithets contradicted such claims and, in fact, mirrored his misanthropy toward most who were "different." He particularly loathed blacks and only referred to them as "niggers." When my brother and I were in high school, a never-ending threat of his was, "You can marry anyone you want but if you marry a nigger don't show your face on this doorstep, ever!"

The violence was always brutal, but as my brother and I moved into our teens and got bigger and stronger, the beatings became more severe. It was almost as if he were saying to us, "Don't even think about challenging me!" During these years, it was not uncommon for him, especially when he was in a paroxysm of rage, to choke us nearly into unconsciousness.

And then, what seemed almost inevitable happened: furious at my brother and I for disagreeing with him over a minor matter, he rushed into his bedroom, grabbed one of his many pistols, and then, terrorizing us, along with our mother, for several hours, he threatened to kill all three of us. Screaming at us as he wildly waved his pistol about, he threatened to blow off our *mf(ing)* heads. As for reporting the incident to the police, it never entered our heads; for we *knew* that, if we did, he would hunt us down, and the next time there would be no miracle.

I often ponder how my brother and I survived such an ordeal more or less intact. Actually, more often than not, I feel as if my very being has been torn and shredded to such a point that it will forever remain in tatters. Indeed, my father almost totally and single-handedly seems to have extinguished any *joie de vivre* that I might have experienced in my life.

The saving grace of our childhood, though, was our mother—a kind, gentle, and loving woman. Caught in a nightmare from which she could not extricate herself or her children, she still genuinely cared for everyone and tried to protect her sons to the best of her ability.

The point of this painful and embarrassing confession is that I entered the field of genocide studies with a marrow-deep disdain for those who brutalize others. I also have a deep and abiding concern for the victims of brutes. That is the foundation on which my subsequent and lifelong concern about human rights and genocide is built. It is a foundation that is rock solid, and one that always keeps the *individual victims* at the forefront of my mind and heart.

Let no one mistakenly assume that I am equating, in any way whatsoever, that what my mother, brother, and I experienced over a period of roughly 18 years is analogous to what victims of genocide suffer. That would be—and this is the understatement of understatements—a ludicrous and totally fallacious analogy, and one that would minimize the catastrophic horror of genocide. What I do understand, though, is how people can be terrorized and cowed. I also understand, to a certain extent, and at the gut level, the bystander syndrome. Likewise, I received an early education in a perverse version of the primacy of "sovereignty" and "internal affairs."

The Null Curriculum

During homeroom period in junior high we were allowed to do homework, read, or daydream—anything really, as long as we were quiet. I frequently found myself thumbing through my literature anthology to find something to read; during the course of my seventh and eighth grade years I probably read, on my own, excerpts of *The Diary of Anne Frank* three or four times or more.

That was my sole introduction to anything about the Holocaust throughout my entire junior high, high school, and university years. While I took numerous social studies and history courses at Laguna Beach High School—everything from world history to American history to American government, and even an elective entitled Chinese History—I do not recall a single mention of the Holocaust. And not even in college, during which I started out as a history major but switched to English, do I recall a single instance of a mention of the Holocaust.

For all intents and purposes, my junior high, high school, and college curricula constituted, at least when it came to the subject of the Holocaust, the "null curriculum." Stanford University professor of education, Elliot Eisner (1979), comments about the null curriculum as follows:

What schools do not teach may be as important as what they do teach. I argue this position because ignorance is not simply a void, it has important effects on the kinds of option[s] one is able to consider; the alternatives one can examine, and the perspectives with which one can view a situation or problem. (p. 83)

WORKING ON THE BEHALF OF PRISONERS OF CONSCIENCE

I graduated from college in 1972 with a B.A. in English, and after a year and a half in graduate school, I moved to San Francisco.

Taking up residence in a seedy hotel on the periphery of Chinatown, the St. Paul on Kearny Street, I immersed myself in a daily routine: up by 6:00 A.M., on the trolley car out to the San Francisco State University library by 7:30 A.M., five hours of writing, a cheap dinner at the Ding Ho cafe in the heart of Chinatown, and evenings spent reading at Lawrence Ferlinghetti's City Lights Bookshop, located in North Beach and only minutes by foot from my hotel. Each evening I sat at one of the many tables situated in the basement of the store and proceeded to read from about 7:30 P.M. to 11:00 P.M. Roughly five months into this routine, the cover of a magazine, *The New Republic,* that had been left on the table caught my eye. In bold letters splashed across its cover was: "'Torture in Chile' by Rose Styron." That article virtually changed the course of my life.

Not three paragraphs into the article, I was devastated. First, I was dismayed to discover the brutal treatment to which some individuals were being subjected by their own governments. Describing the treatment of a 20-year-old student who was falsely arrested for revolutionary activity, Styron (1976) reported that "For 45 days Pedro was subjected to a range of tortures standard in places like Chile, Uruguay and Brazil, from intensive electroshock to the wet and dry 'submarines.' In the wet submarine the bound victim is held upside down, totally immersed in a nameless liquid or excrement, to the brink of drowning." (p. 16) Continuing, Styron (1976) asserted that "Others fear death if their releases are delayed, dying from too much electroshock and too many beatings, as did . . . Roseta Marinetti, who died on a Mexican operating table, her insides destroyed, the wires still in her vagina . . ." (p. 17) That such brutality and deprivation of one's basic human rights existed in the late twentieth century astounded me. Little did I know how naive I had been up to that point.

As far as I am concerned, no one should be subjected to torture. Period. That said, it was still astonishing to learn that the aforementioned victims had not threatened to commit nor had they committed a capital crime or threatened violence against the existing government. Rather, these people were brutalized either because of their suspected or actual associations with certain individuals and/or organizations, their attempt to gain civil or human rights protection for marginalized groups, or for a comment they had made about some facet of the government.

I was also devastated by my own ignorance. I prided myself on being well read, and interested in and aware of key social problems. Obviously, I was not as well read or informed as I had thought. And, as previously mentioned, I was also abysmally naive about the ways of various governments in the world. Why, I also wondered, hadn't I learned about any of this in high school or college?

Styron's piece concluded with a note about the work and efforts of an organization called Amnesty International (A.I.), which worked on the behalf of what it deemed "prisoners of conscience." It was an organization about which I was intent on learning more.

Early the next morning, I walked to the San Francisco branch office of A.I. and informed the person at the front desk that I wished to do volunteer work for A.I. The tasks offered to me—collating and stapling reports and other tedious and mindless tasks—did not, however, appeal to my burning desire to do something of consequence, and thus I declined the offer. On the way out, I gathered information about A.I.'s organizational structure and purpose as well as numerous reports it had generated on the plight of prisoners of conscience across the globe. In my heart and mind, I knew that someday I would work for A.I. in a capacity other than collating and stapling papers.

It was during this same period that I read Viktor E. Frankl's *Man's Search for Meaning: An Introduction to Logotherapy* (1969). It, too, prodded me to question why I had not been introduced to anything about the Holocaust in high school or at college. In retrospect, I am fairly sure that Frankl's harrowing story of life and death in Auschwitz planted the seed for my later work in the field of Holocaust education and the study of first-person accounts of genocidal acts in the twentieth century.

A year and a half later, in May 1976, I moved to Eaglehawk, Victoria, Australia, to teach English (literature, composition, and grammar) at an Australian junior high/high school. Shortly after my arrival, an article appeared in *The Melbourne Age* regarding the work of the Australian A.I. secretariat office in Melbourne. That day I contacted the office and offered my services. I was enthusiastically encouraged by the dynamic A.I. Secretary Leonore Ryan for Australia, to establish an Amnesty "adoption group," which worked on the behalf of political prisoners by "adopting" a prisoner's case and writing to the government on his/her behalf, calling for fair treatment of the individual and/or his/her release. Within the next month I formed a core of individuals, most of whom were Australian teachers living in and around the Eaglehawk/Bendigo area of Victoria, who were willing to dedicate time to A.I.'s work. For the next year and a half that I resided in Australia, I dedicated my energy and effort to establishing an active adoption group. In doing so, I put in many hours chairing our adoption group meetings, studying a wide range of global human rights issues, prodding our members to write scores of letters on the behalf of "our" prisoners of conscience (for example, a teenage Indonesian political prisoner incarcerated on Buru Island and a political prisoner held by the Soviet Union), writing newspaper articles on A.I.'s work, and planning and conducting fund-raising ventures and public education forums.

While A.I.'s headquarters in London generally encouraged each member of an adoption group to send at least one letter a month to the authorities holding "his/her" prisoner(s) of conscience, I periodically organized writing sessions during which each member of our group would write ten letters apiece to different authorities within the same regime. As a result, we sometimes sent over 200 letters at a time to a single government, calling on the powers that be to release "our" prisoner.

During this period, A.I. released a report on the use of torture by governments, which was of epidemic proportions. That report still gnaws at me and, though a cliché, it constantly forces me to reflect about where we, humanity, are on the continuum of being civilized.

The power of A.I., I came to believe, was its ability to harness the care, determination, and energy of tens of thousands of people across the globe to work on the behalf of others who had had their rights trampled as well as the individual face it placed on those being violated of their rights. The former galvanized a massive force to work for the universal protection of international human rights, while the latter never allowed us to forget why we worked as hard as we did: the unfortunate—and often horrific—plight of individual human beings who, just like us, had aspirations, hopes and dreams, desired a life bereft of fear and threat, and, when beaten, tortured, and maimed, felt all of the pain and horror that we, too, would, not to mention the terror and humiliation.

While residing in Australia I became interested in and alarmed by the status and ill treatment of the Aboriginals. I read as much as I could about their plight, and spoke to state legislators about the fact that their (Aboriginals') land, which they considered sacred, was being mined for uranium. More rarely, during my travels to Queensland and the Northern Territory, I spoke with Aboriginals regarding their situation.

The images of the "humpies" (rickety abodes made of corrugated tin, boards, cardboard, and other rough materials) in the dusty streets of Alice Springs and the people, most of whom were unemployed, sitting and talking in small groups in the sweltering heat, with the occasional pair of men arguing or sole individuals stumbling down the street inebriated, have never left me. Forced into a sedentary way of life that was foreign to them and then left, with little to no support—other than the dole, which just seemed to fuel their problems—the result was an abysmal existence.

One evening a member of the Australian Parliament, who touted himself as a "Friend of A.I.," attended one of our local adoption group meetings. When I broached the issue of the deprivation of human rights of the Aboriginals—that their ancestral land was being gobbled up by the government for uranium mining, and that their quality of life was well below that of the average Australian— he simply excused the government's position. He asserted that "the Aboriginals are different from you and me; they have different needs, wants, and goals." I contested his position but to no avail. Disturbingly, most of the other members of the adoption group were so enamored by this suave and "important" man that they were either blind to or gladly overlooked his hypocrisy and sickening double standards.

It was during my work with A.I. in Australia that I became interested in and vitally concerned about the concept of "internal affairs": many, if not most, nations that are accused of human rights violations cavalierly dismiss "outsiders'" concerns by asserting that the issue (whether it be prolonged incarceration of an individual without a trial, or torture or murder of their citizens) is an "internal matter." This same concept, as I was to discover later, has also been used and abused during periods of genocidal actions by many governments. It is an issue I address in a book I am working on that deals with the intervention and prevention of genocide.

It was also during this period that I began teaching about the deprivation of human rights to my students at Eaglehawk Junior/ Senior High School. In part, my students read and discussed A.I. reports on the ubiquitous deprivation of human rights (including the epidemic use of torture by various governments across the globe), and a wide array of articles and atrocities (including mass killings of various victim groups). We also read and discussed such literary works as Aleksandr Solzhenitsyn's *One Day in the Life of Ivan Denisovich*.

I do not recall teaching anything about the Holocaust during this period of time. Part of that may have been due to my immersion in and obsession with the issue of the deprivation of international human rights. It may also have been because the school was bereft of any materials about the Holocaust, and that since I had a strong collection of information on human rights I simply focused on that issue. While I did not have a formal name or concept for it then, what I was basically attempting to do by addressing human rights issues with my students was to overcome the previously mentioned null curriculum.

At the end of my stint in Australia, I traveled across sections of Asia, the Middle East, and Africa. As I did so, I continued, in a voluntary capacity, my work with A.I. In Nepal, I met with a local A.I. adoption group, which was composed of lawyers, businessmen, and an airline pilot, concerned about the plight of political prisoners in their own country. They complained bitterly that the American ambassador to Nepal, a Mr. Heck, had been quoted in a local paper as stating that ". . . the Panchayat system of Nepal is the effective means for mobilization of people for national development." The local A.I. members felt that he was seriously undermining concerned citizens' attempts to move toward a democratic state. Subsequently, I met with Ambassador Heck, and that meeting constituted my second personal encounter with the machinations of bureaucratic double-talk vis-à-vis the issue of human rights. During the course of the meeting, the ambassador and his aide repeatedly asserted that all was more or less well in the kingdom of Nepal, despite the fact that citizens met punitive measures for criticizing the monarchy, individuals were not allowed to organize clubs or volunteer organizations without government permission, and those who pressed for democracy faced imprisonment. Toward the conclusion of our discussion, the ambassador said, "You know, Nepal really isn't so bad. It only has 12–15 political prisoners." When I informed him that just the week before, A.I. had issued a report asserting there were 150–200 political prisoners in Nepal, the ambassador's aide, a young woman, piped up: "Those 100 or so people aren't prisoners. They're merely in detention waiting for trial." The ambassador agreed. When I pressed them about the fact that many had been incarcerated for months, and some for years, and that they were housed in a prison, it did not phase or alter the ambassador's or his aide's grotesque argument. Ironically, just the week before, President Jimmy Carter had delivered a speech before the Indian Parliament, in which he declared the following:

There are those who say that democracy is a kind of rich man's plaything—and that the poor are too preoccupied with survival to care about the luxury of freedom and the right to choose their government. This argument is repeated all over the world—mostly, I have noticed, by persons whose own bellies are full and who speak from positions of privilege and power in their own societies. Their argument reminds me of a statement by Lincoln—"Whenever I hear anyone arguing for slavery, I feel a strong impulse to see it tried on him." . . . To quote Gandhi, "No principle exists in the abstract, without its concrete application, it has no meaning."

Following my meeting with the ambassador, all of my subsequent meetings with the Nepalese human rights members were held in different locations, for the latter feared that the secret police may be following me. On my way to meetings with the members, which I always got to on foot, I was directed by them to periodically stop on a corner or just around the turn of a corner to check to see whether I was being followed. As ridiculous as I felt doing it, I honored their request, for it had been made in such a serious manner. Once, in fact, I had the distinct impression that I was being followed, and, as a result, I did not continue on to the meeting place.

During my last meeting with the A.I group, one of the members said, "Who would've imagined that somebody like you would show up in our country and call on an ambassador to defend his statements in the press. It's probably the first time it has happened here."

THE HOLOCAUST, ETHNOCIDE, APARTHEID, OTHER GENOCIDES

Continuing my travels, I landed on Kibbutz Barkai in the north central region of Israel, between Hadera and Afula. With a fellow who had recently fled political turmoil in Uruguay and whose best friend was in prison there, and likely being tortured by government officials, I began the rudimentary work of establishing a kibbutz-based A.I. adoption group. During our meetings in the evening, Jony filled me in on what a state under siege really meant. His stories were raw reminders of what I had read in Styron's article, two years previous.

On the kibbutz, an older man, in his late fifties or early sixties, ran the laundry. A survivor of the Holocaust, he rarely, if ever, spoke to anyone. All sorts of rumors about him were afloat among the volunteers, including one that what he had experienced during the Holocaust had so traumatized him that he basically existed but did not enjoy any aspect of life. It was possible, of course, that he was simply a taciturn individual, and had always been one and would have been whether he had experienced the Holocaust or not. The fact is, I never discovered the real truth behind his silence, but while on the kibbutz, and all of these years later, his silence haunted and still haunts me. The very fact that what he experienced may have molded his silence is what haunts me most.

On a break from working and living on the kibbutz, I visited Yad Vashem, the Holocaust Martyrs' and Heroes' Remembrance Authority in Jerusalem. I will never forget that foggy morning, walking past a pile of Uzis that a group of soldiers had placed in front of the museum door. The photographs of the Nazis mocking and humiliating old men on the streets of Germany and Austria during the early and middle years of the Holocaust, the other types of abject brutality to which the Jews were subjected, the bureaucratic and systematic approach to the extermination of a people, the silent weeping of other museum patrons, and the guttural voices of those who tried to comfort their grieving companions left me in a conflicted state. On the one hand, I felt like screaming endlessly, while on the other, I desired to be totally alone with my thoughts. Returning to my room at the Petra Hotel, just inside the Jaffa Gate of the Old City, I sat staring into space mulling over what I had just experienced.

Possibly because of my passion for literature, a statement I read in the exhibit at Yad Vashem has stayed with me all of these years. Made by Heinrich Heine, a German poet of Jewish origin, it read: "Where one burns books, one will, in the end, burn people." Pondering that assertion, along with the actions of the Nazis, planted the seed, I believe, for my interest in and current study about potential early warning signals vis-á-vis genocide.

The day after I returned to the kibbutz, Palestinian terrorists landed on a beach in northern Israel, killed a young woman, and hijacked a bus. In the ensuing melee, 24 people were killed. At 1:30 A.M. the next morning, I awoke in order to go to work in the "chicken house," where a group of volunteers and members of the kibbutz first corralled and cajoled hundreds of chickens into a small area, and then grabbed the chickens and loaded them into plastic boxes. The boxes were piled high on a flatbed truck and taken to Jericho where they were sold to local Arab merchants. As I made my way, in the pitch-black morning, down the hill from the volunteers' small, crude wooden cabins, which had served as the original housing for the founding members of the kibbutz, my fellow volunteers and I, who were usually only half awake and totally silent on our trek to work, made a point of jabbering loudly in English while making sure we also mentioned the names of well-known volunteers. We knew that as a result of the recent terrorist incident, many kibbutizniks had been placed on guard duty with Uzis and we were fearful that one or more of them might be a bit nervous and trigger-happy.

A few days after returning from Yad Vashem, I visited the kibbutz's small library where I came across Elie Wiesel's *Night* (1969), an account of his horrific experiences during the Holocaust. One image, in particular, was seared into my mind: "Not far from us, flames were leaping up from a ditch, gigantic flames. They were burning something. A lorry drew up at the pit and delivered its load—little children. Babies! Yes, I saw it—saw it with my own eyes . . . those children in the flames" (Wiesel, 1969, p. 42). "*Where was humanity?*" pounded in my brain. Not incidentally, upon my return to the States a year later, I enrolled in an M.A. program in English and undertook a study of the motifs of silence and testimony in Wiesel's fictional works.

Leaving Israel, I traveled to southern Africa where I crisscrossed portions of the Kalahari Desert with a close friend, Robert Hitchcock, an anthropologist, who was conducting research into the living patterns of the Basarwa (Bushmen), both the sedentary and the nomadic. During these trips Hitchcock filled me in on how large landowners, many of whom were high government officials, restricted the Basarwa's natural movement patterns, including their hunting rights, thus dramatically and disturbingly altering their traditional way of life. As we visited borehole after borehole, where sedentary Basarwa tended cattle for cattle barons and from which the men traveled to South Africa to work in mines, the stories of how the Basarwa were forced to adopt and adapt to a sedentary way of life clearly revealed what it meant for a traditional way of life to gradually be eroded into oblivion.

On one trip I saw firsthand the way of life that was being wiped out. For days, we searched for a group of nomadic hunters and gatherers, and what I witnessed when we finally located them was something out of another world. In a diary I kept, I wrote:

Mogabe [our interpreter who spoke Basarwa] emerged from the bush with five male hunter/gatherers, all in traditional garb—their huge stomachs looking as if they were pregnant, dressed in a skin fashioned like a jockstrap around their genital area, the rest of their body (torso, legs, feet) all bare, and their buttocks hanging loose . . . They led us to their camp, where even the tiniest of children and babies have huge stomachs, all dressed in skins, the women with straps crossing their bellies but their breasts totally exposed. Mothers carry their babies in pouches either slung over the back or on their sides. The older people's skin is extremely wrinkled; especially their stomachs, which are comprised of a series of hard ridges running from just below their belly buttons to their lower chest cavity. Their camp overlooks a pan, allowing them perfect access for spotting game.

They've only been in this camp two days, which is comprised of two natural windbreaks (trees), two camp fires, skins drying in trees, and their tools—hand-crafted axes and sticks with long flat ends that serve as scrapers and diggers with which they dig for roots and scrape out the melons they forage—and weapons, several sets of tiny bows and arrow.

The life of the people I met and spoke with, and the scenes I witnessed—the dismemberment of an eland that they had killed illegally; the boiling of the meat on an open fire; the making of *biltong* by hanging strings of meat on bushes serving as makeshift racks; the hunting of a lion with the barefoot Basarwa; the stories about *Quai* or the location where their relatives and ancestors go when they die—were, literally, slowly but inexorably being extinguished by "progress" and the greed of the leaders of the government of Botswana who established cattle ranches for their own benefit.

On several of these journeys, while sitting on the back of our truck as we crashed through the bush and drove across long stretches of desert, I engaged in conversations with a young paleontologist, Henry Bunn, about the plight of the Yanomami in South America, and, later, with Hitchcock about the plight of the Aché in Paraguay. Along with the aforementioned experiences, these discussions broadened my awareness regarding egregious human rights violations, and especially ethnocide and genocide. Years later, Hitchcock and I would collaborate on a number of projects related to the issue of genocide. (See, for example, "Confronting Genocide and Ethnocide of Indigenous Peoples: An Interdisciplinary Approach to Definition, Intervention, Prevention, and Advocacy" in Alexander Hinton (Ed.) *Annihilating Difference: The Anthropology of Genocide.* Los Angeles and Berkeley: University of California Press, 2002.)

While in Botswana I made a trip into South Africa where, hitchhiking across small swaths of it—from the border of Botswana, outside Gaborne, to Johannesburg and from Johannesburg to Pretoria and from Pretoria to the border of Kruger National Park, then down toward Swaziland and back through Johannesburg before heading back to Botswana—I witnessed firsthand what life under apartheid meant for millions of people of color. One of the most bizarre incidents I experienced was early in my trip when I entered a liquor store to purchase drinks for myself and the fellow who had given me a ride from the South African/Botswana border to Johannesburg. The "bottle shop" was very long and very narrow with a counter that divided the customer's side from that of the proprietor. Fronting the wall behind the counter where the proprietor stood was a floor-to-ceiling and wall-to-wall mirror, and directly in front of the mirror were shelves on which all of the bottles and cans of various shapes and sizes containing colorful hues of liquids were neatly stacked. Approaching the cash register, I asked the man behind the counter for two beers. Brusquely and in a strongly accented voice that was difficult to understand, he said something like, "You know not here," and he whipped his arm behind his body. Having no idea what he meant, I asked for two beers again, but this time altering and slowing my words. Angrily, he repeated the exact same words and jerked his arm around in the same motion as before. Baffled, I started to ask again, but this time he yelled "Get out!" As I exited the door and turned back to look at what I thought was a crazed proprietor, my eye caught the entrance of another liquor store directly next door. Entering, I was momentarily shocked, thinking I had somehow entered the original liquor store. I hadn't. Rather, this second one was a mirrored reflection of the other, with the exact same counter, mirror, and, as far as I could ascertain, the same bottles and cans in exactly the same spots on the shelves. The only difference was that behind the counter was a different man, a white—not a black—man. This was my simple but profound introduction to apartheid's separation of the races.

But there was more. Much more. As I continued my short journey in South Africa, I came across everything from articles in the newspaper about black people who had horribly burned their faces while attempting to bleach their skin white in order to "pass," to repetitive "conversations" with Afrikaners about the "dire need" to maintain a separation between blacks and whites and how they (the speaker and his brethren) were armed and ready for any attempted black-based revolution. Most of the latter individuals were extremely kind to me—putting me up for the night, driving me out of their way, introducing me to other folks who put me up and/or showed me around their part of the country—but that kindness clashed with the ugliness of their words, thoughts, and epithets about their fellow black South Africans.

I returned to the States during the summer of 1978. That summer I wrote to A.I.-USA in New York City with the suggestion that they hire me to set up university, college, and high school adoption groups across the country. I said fair remuneration would be the same (low) pay I would receive as an English teacher in California, plus the cost of travel. I also noted that I was interested in and willing to develop a human rights curriculum for use in high school settings. I received a polite note informing me that while both ideas were interesting, neither was a high priority of A.I.-USA.

THE BEGINNING OF MY HOLOCAUST EDUCATION EFFORTS

That same summer, I read about the establishment of the U.S. President's Commission on the Holocaust and was interested to discover that, as part of its work, it had formed an Education Committee. Somehow, I obtained the membership list of the Education Committee of the U.S. President's Commission on the Holocaust and wrote a series of letters informing the various members that I was interested in assisting the committee in any way I could with its mission. Out of the 13 or so individuals I wrote to, I received a single reply—a very kind and encouraging letter from Holocaust scholar Harry James Cargas. He stated that the committee was at the most incipient stage of its work, but that he would gladly keep me informed of its efforts. Many years later, I had the great pleasure of communicating with him again in regard to some specific educational issues related to the Holocaust, and every single time I wrote him he wrote a helpful and encouraging letter back to me. Early in my career, I consciously promised myself that should I ever reach a point where I was asked by others for assistance with their work in the field of human rights or Holocaust education I would make a point of emulating the kindness, thoughtfulness, and helpfulness of Harry James Cargas. To the best of my ability, I have tried to keep that promise.

Ultimately, I took a teaching job in a northern California high school. During the course of the 1978–1979 academic year, I continued to incorporate human rights issues into my students' English curriculum, but also added the issue of the Holocaust. My volunteer work with A.I. continued unabated.

In retrospect, how I went about teaching *Night* to my students that first time left a lot to be desired. As far as I can remember, I believe I neglected to provide a historical context for the piece of literature. I'm not even sure that I provided, at a minimum, some sort of time line that would have assisted the students to have at least placed the events in some sort of rough chronological context. The saving grace, I guess, is that I did involve the students in ample discussion, as opposed to lecture, and attempted to the best of my ability to welcome and answer their questions. Still, all in all, today I would look askance at such a meager approach.

At the conclusion of the study, I invited a Holocaust survivor who resided in San Francisco to speak to my class. From the outset of the academic year I had subscribed to the *Martyrdom and Resistance* newsletter published by the International Society for Yad Vashem, and had come across a story about the San Francisco-based survivor (whose name, unfortunately, I cannot recall). When several of the social studies and English teachers in the school heard about the survivor's pending visit, they asked me if their students could attend the talk. In light of the general rudeness and lack of interest in academics displayed by a vast number of the students at Esparto High School, I was extremely leery of agreeing to such a request. However, after being convinced by the principal that I should agree, we ended up allowing two additional classes of students to join us for the talk. Much to my astonishment, all of the students — even those who were generally the most rowdy — remained rapt throughout the survivor's talk, and during the question-and-answer period many asked intelligent and probing questions. At the conclusion of the session, the students gave our guest a warm round of applause and then surrounded her both to thank her for speaking to them and to ask her additional questions. The session was a revelation to me on a couple of levels. First, it proved to me that if students are truly engaged in something important to them, even the most "disinterested" student will be attentive. Second, even the rudest students can act in a civil fashion when they deem it important to do so. As for the value of having a survivor speak to a class, I became utterly convinced that such sessions were invaluable. Indeed, I believe to this day that the session we held that afternoon was quite possibly the highlight of many of the students' educational careers in that school. In fact, the thank-you letters that my students wrote and sent to the guest stated as much.

During the course of this academic year I completed my M.A. in English, and my culminating project for a class on biography and literature was a study of the writings of Elie Wiesel. That academic year I read all of his fiction and nonfiction, interviews with him by such figures as Harry James Cargas, and literary criticism of his works. To say that it was an enlightening, moving, and draining experience would be a gross understatement.

During the spring of 1979 I applied for a summer position as a volunteer in the Washington, D.C.-based office of the newly formed President's Commission on the Holocaust. Deputy Director Michael Berenbaum, who eventually played an instrumental role in the development of the U.S. Holocaust Memorial Museum (USHMM) and served as its first director of research, said that I was welcome to assist a paid intern in conducting a survey about what universities and colleges across the United States were doing in the way of Holocaust education. While all the tasks were basically the same as those offered me by the A.I. office in San Francisco years earlier — that is, collating and stapling papers, filling and addressing envelopes — I accepted the offer and was glad I did, for each and every day I gained knowledge about widely different aspects of the Holocaust.

Unfortunately, I didn't get to know Michael Berenbaum very well as he was always extremely busy and under a lot of pressure. In addition to working on a host of issues related to the Council's work, he was also at the beck and call of Elie Wiesel, the chairman of the President's Commission on the Holocaust, who was leading the Council's members on a fact-finding trip to various Holocaust sites across Europe. At the end of my tenure in the office, just before I was to return to Israel in order to teach at the American School, Michael kindly gave me a copy of his new book on Elie Wiesel, *The Vision of the Void: Theological Reflections on the Works of Elie Wiesel* (1979), and wished me well in my future endeavors. Little did we know then that our paths would cross again, almost a decade later, when he was the director of research at the USHMM and I was one of its early educational consultants.

At the end of the summer, I wrote my first article on an issue of the Holocaust, which was about the seemingly cavalier and mindless way that many politicians, educators, and writers bandied about such phrases and admonitions as, "Those who do not remember the past are condemned to repeat it," "Never forget," and "Remember!" when speaking or writing about the Holocaust. Many, if not most, I argued, who used such phrases seemed unaware and/or unconcerned that genocide was a fact of life in the post-Holocaust world. Through their overuse — and here I explicitly exclude the use of such phrases by Holocaust survivors, for if anyone has a right to use them, they do — such powerful thoughts had become little more than clichés. To use such expressions in a mindless and clichéd manner, I asserted, was an insult to every victim of every genocide. It constituted a callous disregard for what needed and must be done to staunch contemporaneous situations possibly slouching toward genocidal atrocities.

A FORTUITOUS MEETING

In 1979 I began teaching at the Walworth Barbour American International School (WBAIS) in Kfar Shmaryahu, Israel. It was a year during which I continued to work on the issue of international human rights and continued to educate myself about the Holocaust, and it included numerous trips to Yad Vashem.

Daily, I picked up the school's mail from the small postal office in the tiny village just up the hill from the school. The postmistress, a small, weary-looking woman in her late forties or early fifties, but who always had a smile and a friendly "Shalom!" for me, was a Holocaust survivor who had crudely drawn blue numbers tattooed on her arm. Every time she handed me the bundle of mail, the sight of the tattoo caught my eye. Just the thought that a certain group of people had the gall and power to tattoo another for the purpose of identification and dehumanization sickened me. And the fact

194

Remembering the Past

that this kind woman had to go through life with that tattoo, a daily
reminder to herself and everyone else that she had been subjected
to such ignorance and ugliness, made me ache. Oddly, the tattoo
reminded me of the blue markings stamped on slabs of meat that
my father would bring home from the stockyards in the city where
he was a police officer. That just heightened my sense of what the
Nazis were about—the degradation, the depersonalization, and the
treatment of people as if they were not human.

During the course of the year I taught Wiesel's *Night* to my sopho-
more students, this time using a booklet from Yad Vashem to
provide a historical context of the period, and upon the conclusion
of our study, I took the students to Yad Vashem to tour the museum. Disappointingly, I discovered that many of the students who
had attended WBAIS for an extended period of time (over a period
of five years or more) were extremely blasé about studying the Holocaust and/or touring Yad Vashem. In fact, some stated overtly
that they were "tired of hearing and reading about the Holocaust,"
noting that they had "studied" it in the fifth, sixth, and eighth
grades. When I queried them about historical aspects of the Holocaust, they had little knowledge and thus I had to wonder what
they had studied and "learned" in the past, not to mention the
value of it. At the same time, it made me ponder the value of
teaching something so complex to students who were so young
(especially those at the fifth-grade level). It also made me question
the sagacity of teaching the same subject over and over again to
the point where the students were not moved by the events but
rather put off by the entire subject.

During that same year, I also developed and conducted a simple
questionnaire about what the junior high students at the school
knew about the Holocaust and discovered that their knowledge
base was extremely scant. I used the data collected from the survey in a talk I gave on Holocaust education to Professor Israel W.
Charny's university students who were from the United States and
were spending their junior year abroad at Tel Aviv University.

During this period I also decided to undertake a study about the
Holocaust's impact on survivors' religious beliefs. In order to do
so, I developed a lengthy questionnaire that I planned to use to
conduct interviews of the survivors and placed a notice in the
English version of the *Jerusalem Post* asking for survivors to contact me if they were interested in being interviewed. Within a week
of the publication of the notice, I began to receive many hand-
written notes from survivors informing me a little about their background as well as the notification of their willingness to be
interviewed for the study. However, about a month into the project,

just as I was beginning to set up interviews, I received the following note in the mail: "Pilgrim, your journey has ended." Below the comment was the title and author of a book that had just been published, *The Faith and Doubt of Holocaust Survivors* by Reeve Robert Brenner. Thus ended that project.

Midway through the year, a chance meeting with a student's father was to result in another change in my life. That man was the previously mentioned Dr. Israel W. Charny. As a colleague at the school introduced us, he informed Charny that I was his son's English teacher and told us that we (Charny and I) shared an interest in the issue of international human rights. Following a quick exchange, during which Charny, a clinical psychologist, mentioned he was in the process of completing a book on genocide (ultimately published as *How Can We Commit the Unthinkable? Genocide, The Human Cancer*, 1982), we agreed that we needed to get together. As I was to discover later, he was also engaged in planning a pioneering conference on genocide that was ultimately held in Israel in 1982. Throughout the rest of the academic year, Charny and I discussed various human rights issues, shared information about mutual projects, and became close friends. From the outset, what most impressed me about Israel, and drew me ever closer to him, was his rare combination of sharp intellect, deep passion for life, forthright honesty, and abiding care for humanity. Over the years he has become one of my dearest friends as well as my mentor in the field of genocide studies. It was a fortuitous meeting and the beginning of a lifelong friendship that I shall always cherish.

It is not too much to say that had I not met Israel W. Charny, I may never have entered the field of genocide studies; indeed, I probably would have focused solely on human rights issues and Holocaust education, which would have been fine, of course. Instead, over the years, I have basically focused my attention on two different areas: the narrower field of Holocaust education and the broader field of genocide studies. (It is worth noting that over and above my meeting Israel Charny and the influence of his work in the field of genocide studies on my thinking, there are three major reasons why I gradually moved into the field of genocide studies: (1) It seemed that few people were cognizant of and/or cared about the fact that genocide was an ongoing blight in the post-Holocaust world; (2) many, if not most, human rights activists were not addressing the issue of genocide, and thus one genocide after another was being perpetrated and no one was doing much of anything to attempt to stanch and/or prevent such acts from taking place; and (3) while a fairly sizable group of educators were developing curricula and teaching about the Holocaust in their classes, few, if any, were addressing the issue of genocide.)

Focusing on the Motivations, Actions, and Lives of Social Activists

My year in Israel proved to be extraordinary for numerous reasons, including the fact that I met and became friends with so many fascinating individuals who either were or were on the verge of becoming scholar-activists in an eclectic range of fields. In addition to befriending Israel Charny, who was at the incipient stage of his career in becoming one of *the* pioneers of genocide studies, I had the great pleasure and honor to meet and become friendly with the following individuals: Bill Frelick, who had been on the board of A.I.-USA before moving to Israel for several years and who would eventually become a research associate at the U.S. Refugee Committee; Bruce Hoffman, a U.S. citizen and a Ph.D. candidate at Oxford University who was conducting research on the Irgun, who would later become an internationally respected expert on terrorism and a researcher/administrator with the terrorism division at the Rand Corporation; Laurie Wiseberg, the cofounder of Human Rights Internet, whom I met at an A.I. meeting in Tel Aviv; and a woman named Rebecca (whose last name I cannot recall), who was a graduate of Cornell University and was working with the Red Cross in the refugee camps in the Gaza Strip.

During the course of the year in Israel I began to ponder what it was that drove certain individuals to commit their lives to working on a single social issue and/or on the behalf of others. I was also curious as to what drove them, in the first place, to choose their specific fields of endeavor. As I thought about such issues, I often reflected on my own story and began to ask various folks to share theirs with me. Shortly after my return to the United States I decided to conduct a series of oral histories with social activists in various fields (for example, human rights, civil rights, peace, environment, alternative sources of energy, antinuclear power, antinuclear weapons, antinuclear power *and* weapons, poverty, tax reform) in order to ascertain what motivated such individuals to become activists. My ultimate goal was to publish a book of their stories. During the first year of the project I found myself, again, teaching English at Esparto High School, and thus I began conducting the oral histories in northern and then southern California. By the end of the academic year my then-wife (Martha Wescoat Totten) and I had met and interviewed an eclectic range of people.

Among the more interesting individuals of whom I, personally, conducted oral histories were: Kristin Selvig, the daughter of a former
FBI man, who, following a Christian calling, was protesting against
nuclear weapons proliferation by committing acts of civil disobe-
dience and was spending an ever-increasing amount of time in jail;
Madeline Duckles, a middle-aged woman who had become active
in the anti–Vietnam War movement and ended up traveling to Vietnam in order to bring Vietnamese children, who had been disfig-
ured as a result of the war, to the United States for medical
treatment. Her story of bringing the children into her home to live
during their stay in the United States was extremely moving, especially that of the story of Twee, a little girl who, when told she
was about to return home to Vietnam, asked Madeline, "But Missy
Duckles, who going to find car keys for you?" And I'll never forget
meeting and speaking with Earle and Barbara Reynolds, peace
activists who had sailed into atomic bomb testing zones in the
Pacific on their sailboat, *The Golden Rule*, in order to protest the
development, testing, and deployment of atomic and hydrogen
bombs. And over the next three years—one of which was spent
traveling across the United States interviewing activists in New
Mexico, Texas, Louisiana, Alabama, North Carolina, Washington,
D.C., Maryland, New Jersey, New York, Connecticut, Massachusetts, and elsewhere (and meeting folks from other states in
such hubs as Washington, D.C., and New York City)—I interviewed
over 200 individuals, among them: William Sloane Coffin (the fiery
former chaplain at Yale University and then current minister at
Riverside Church in Manhattan); Amory Lovins (the environmen-
talist); James Lawson (a minister and noted civil rights pioneer and
activist); Kanji Kuramoto (a survivor of the atomic bombing of
Hiroshima); Jack Anderson (the indefatigable investigative re-
porter); Barry Commoner (the tireless and influential environmen-
talist); Helen Caldicott (a pediatrician and one of the most well
known and outspoken opponents of the nuclear arms race); Philip
Morrison (who was a member of the Manhattan Project and supervisor of the assembly of the atomic bomb that was dropped on
Nagasaki, and, then, as a professor of physics at M.I.T., an active
opponent of the nuclear arms race); Jim Wallis (a minister and
founder of the religious/activist group known as Sojourners); Eddie
Albert (a well-known actor who used his fame to fight successfully
for the cleanup of the Pacific Ocean off the coast of southern California); and Buckminister Fuller (inventor of the geodesic dome,
noted author, explorer—a modern renaissance figure, who was
involved in all sorts of environmental activist activity).

Among the many and varied places I conducted the interviews were: the end of a dock at the Presidio in San Francisco (with a civil disobedient who was with Greenpeace); a mosquito-ridden, rickety porch somewhere in the backwoods of Alabama (Judy Cumbee, an antiwar activist); John Kenneth Galbraith's office at Harvard University, during which he pulled the plug of my recorder out of the socket as he was peeved with my "irritating" follow-up questions; the waiting room at the Port Authority in New York City (with Randy Kehler, an antinuclear activist on his way to a conference); the edge of an airport luggage conveyor belt in La Guardia Airport (with Rosalie Bertell, a nun and antinuclear activist on her way back from a hearing); a shabby, two-story house in Washington, D.C. (with homeless advocate, Mitch Snider, during which homeless people in various states noisily passed through the hallway); and a bench in Central Park, near the old dairy (with scientist and antinuclear activist Ernest Sternglass).

The three years spent on the book was an education that I could not have obtained anywhere else. My two- to three- to four-hour meetings with these individuals, each of which was taped and immediately transcribed, was often, at one and the same time, inspiring, saddening, hopeful, joyous, and optimistic.

Interestingly, when I called Ralph Nader, the consumer advocate and founder of Public Citizen, and asked him if he would be willing to have his story included in the book, he chastised me for even working on such a project and asked scathingly "whether I wanted to provide the opposition with inside information they'd love to have." That is as close as I got to Nader, until years later when I worked as an editor for his Critical Mass Energy Project in Washington, D.C.

Unfortunately, we never found a publisher for the complete book of oral histories. Many publishers suggested that we cull the book down into separate books, which we finally did. That said, we ended up publishing only one book—*Facing the Danger: Interviews with 20 Antinuclear Activists* (Trumansburg, New York: The Crossing Press, 1984). It included just 20 of the over 200 oral histories we conducted during the project.

My belief in the value and power of personal stories ultimately led me, years later, to develop a major annotated bibliography on the first-person accounts of genocide in the twentieth century. It also led to my working on this book, *Remembering the Past, Educating for the Present and the Future: The Personal and Pedagogical Stories of Holocaust Educators*, and another, *Pioneers of Genocide Studies* (2002).

INFLUENCES OVER THE YEARS

When Ernest Hemingway was asked once who had influenced him as a writer, he began naming off one author after another and went on and on and on. I feel much the same way in regard to my efforts as a Holocaust educator. There have been so many who have influenced my thinking and efforts that to even attempt to list names runs the risk of leaving out a large number of individuals. That said, among those who stand out in my mind at this point in time as critical influences are the following: Raul Hilberg, Sybil Milton, Christopher Browning, Henry Friedlander, Michael R. Marrus, Donald Niewyk, Lucy S. Dawidowicz (all of whom are/were historians or political scientists); Elie Wiesel, Primo Levi, and Victor Klemperer (survivors-authors); Harry James Cargas, Michael Berenbaum, John Roth, Franklin H. Littell, Lawrence Langer, Deborah Lipstadt (scholars in fields other than history and political science); and William S. Parsons, Stephen Feinberg, William Fernekes, and Karen Shawn (educators). Some of these individuals, such as Henry Friedlander, really belong in two or more of the categories, for in his case, not only is he a renowned historian, but also a survivor of the Holocaust and the author of an early and seminal essay on Holocaust education.

As one might imagine, some researchers, survivors, and educators have impacted me more than others, and I shall, as succinctly as I can, mention how the latter have influenced me in various and significant ways. Hilberg's magisterial *The Destruction of the European Jews* (1985) has had an immense impact on my understanding of the Holocaust as well as on the way in which I teach and write about it. Herein, I shall only mention a couple of the most important points and perspectives that I gleaned. The first chapter ("Precedents") in volume one of *The Destruction of the European Jews*, was critical to my understanding of the longtime antagonism against the Jews by others and why that was so. This is, I believe, absolutely essential information that students need to understand, otherwise the Nazis' thinking and actions appear to have occurred in a vacuum of sorts. Indeed, Hilberg's comparison and contrast of "Canonical and Nazi Anti-Jewish Measures" (1985, pp. 11–12) and the "Pre-Nazi and Nazi Anti-Jewish Measures" (p. 14) is nothing short of enlightening. Particularly revealing and illuminating, for me, are the following statements by Hilberg at the beginning of his three-volume work. First, "[s]ince the fourth century after Christ there have been three anti-Jewish policies: conversion, expulsion, and annihilation. The second appeared as an alternative to the first, and the third emerged as an alternative to the second" (1985, p. 8). And second,

The Nazi destruction process did not come out of a void; it was the culmination of a cyclical trend . . . The missionaries of Christianity [begin-
ning in the fourth century after Christ in Rome and continuing through
the next twelve centuries] had said in effect: You have no right to live
among us Jews. The secular rulers who followed had proclaimed: You
have no right to live among us. The German Nazis at last decreed: You
have no right to live. (1985, pp. 8–9)

Also influential on my understanding of the Holocaust was what
Hilberg called "the structure of destruction," which he notes "un-
folded in a definite pattern: definition, expropriation, concentration, annihilation" (1985, pp. 53, 54). As Hilberg goes on to explain:
"[at] first sight the destruction of the Jews may have the appearance of an indivisible, monolithic, and impenetrable event. Upon
closer observation it is revealed to be a process of sequential steps
that were taken at the initiative of countless decision makers in a
far-flung bureaucratic machine." (1985, p. 53) Again, what I've
mentioned and delineated here is only the tip of the iceberg in regard to what I've gleaned from Hilberg. I firmly believe that it is a
must read for anyone who is serious about teaching the Holocaust
in an accurate and pedagogically sound manner.
Another key text for me was Hilberg's *Perpetrators, Victims, Bystanders: The Jewish Catastrophe, 1933–1945* (1992). It clearly
discusses who was included in each group, what they did and did
not do, and why. Speaking of the three groups, Hilberg says, "Each
saw what had happened from its own, special perspective, and each
harbored a separate set of attitudes and reactions." (1992, p. ix)
Going on to speak about the perpetrators, he notes, "The work was
diffused in a widespread bureaucracy, and each man could feel that
his contribution was a small part of an immense undertaking. For
these reasons, an administrator, clerk, or uniformed guard never
referred to himself as a perpetrator" (Hilberg, 1992, p. ix).
Speaking of the victims, he comments as follows:

To be defined as Jews, they only had to have had Jewish parents or grandparents. . . . The victims, as a whole, have remained an amorphous mass.
Millions of them suffered a common fate in front of pre-dug graves or in
the darkness of hermetically sealed gas chambers. . . . Yet the impact of
destruction was not simultaneously the same for everyone. There were,
first of all, people who left in time—the refugees. The vast majority, who
stayed or were trapped in place, included grown men and women, whose
respective encounters with adversity were not identical. Some of the married Jews were in a special category, because they had non-Jewish partners. Jewish children had lives and afflictions all their own. The quandary
for Christians of Jewish descent is a story in and of itself. The community as a whole was stratified from top to bottom in terms of wealth and

income, and in many situations these material distinctions mattered a great deal. Even more significant were differences of personality traits. Whereas most victims adjusted themselves step-by-step to the increasing stringency of deprivation and loss, there was a minority, however small, that did not share the adaptations of the multitude. The inability or refusal to become reconciled to the assault gave rise to a variety of reactions, from suicides to open rebellion. Finally, a remnant of persisters and resisters were found alive in the liberated camps and woods — survivors. (Hilberg, 1992, pp. x–xi)

Of the bystanders, he perspicaciously notes:

Most contemporaries of the Jewish catastrophe were neither perpetrators nor victims. Many people, however, saw or heard something of the event. Those of them who lived in Adolf Hitler's Europe would have described themselves, with few exceptions, as bystanders. They were not "involved," not willing to hurt the victims and not wishing to be hurt by the perpetrators. Yet the reality was not always so uncomplicated. Much depended on the relations of various continental European nations with the Germans and with the Jews. These bonds or fissures could facilitate or hinder action in one direction or another. . . . In some areas, bystanders became perpetrators themselves. In many regions they took advantage of Jewish misfortunes and seized a profit, but there were also those who helped the hunted. . . . (Hilberg, 1992, p. xi)

For educators, of course, the key here is the critical need to assist students to make distinctions in regard to why and how people behaved the way they did, and to assiduously avoid describing or perceiving any group as monolithic.

As for Lucy S. Dawidowicz (1986), her concept that the Germans were fighting two wars — the world war and a war against the Jews — also impacted my thinking in a significant manner. To view the Nazis' actions against the Jews in this manner emphasized, for me, what I've come to think as the "total war" against the Jews in an age of "total war."

Illuminating Dawidowicz's concept of a war against the Jews is the following observation by Berenbaum (1993), from his outstanding book entitled *The World Must Know: The History of the Holocaust as Told in the United States Holocaust Memorial Museum*: "Nazi Germany became a genocidal state. The goal of annihilation called for participation by every arm of the government. The policy of extermination involved every level of German society and marshaled the entire apparatus of the German bureaucracy." (p. 106) And illuminating the last point about the German bureaucracy is the following point, which is absolutely crucial for students to understand, "four hundred separate pieces of legislation enacted between 1933 and 1939 [by the Germans] . . . defined, isolated, excluded, segregated and impoverished German Jews" (Berenbaum, 1993, p. 22). (Note: I personally think that one of the best—that is, most readable, informative, detailed, and engaging— books that teachers can possibly use in the classroom [that is, to actually have the students read from cover to cover] is Berenbaum's *The World Must Know*. This recommendation is based on my own experience of having used it twice with different groups of high school students, once during a two-week summer program and once during a semester-long course on the Holocaust.)

Over the past 30 years I have come across one statement after another by Elie Wiesel that has, if you will, impregnated my thinking about the Holocaust. One is as follows: "While not all victims [of the Nazis] were Jews, all Jews were victims, destined for annihilation solely because they were born Jewish. They were doomed not because of something they had done or proclaimed or acquired but because of who they were: sons and daughters of the Jewish people" (Wiesel, 1979, p. iii). This states as clearly as anything I have ever read as to who constituted the main target of the Nazis as well as that which constituted the Nazis' primary goal.

Another statement, which for me graphically illustrates the systematic, sustained, and unprecedented nature of the Holocaust is as follows:

The Nazis' aim was to make the Jewish world shrink—from town to neighborhood, from neighborhood to street, from street to house, from house to room, from room to garret, from garret to cattle car, from cattle car to gas chamber. . . .

And they did the same to the individual—separated from his or her community, then from his or her family, then from his or her identity, eventually becoming a work permit, then a number, until the number itself was turned into ashes. (Wiesel, 1984, p. 1)

Victor Klemperer's magnificent two-volume diary—*I Will Bear Witness: A Diary of the Nazi Years, 1933–1941* (1998) and *I Will Bear Witness: A Diary of the Nazi Years, 1942–1945* (2000)—provided me with unique and powerful insights into what daily life under the Nazi dictatorship was like for Jews. Indeed, the diaries are packed with revelatory insights, and it is my sense that no teacher should attempt to teach about the Holocaust until he/she has read this two-volume set. Then and only then will he/she begin to have a sense as to how important it is to teach their students about the early years of Nazi rule; it is the only way that the students will even begin to understand the insidious and incremental horror of what it meant to live under a totalitarian and racist regime whose every move was aimed at suffocating the very life out of a group of people (the Jews).

A brief excerpt from the first volume of Klemperer's diary provides a glimpse into the illuminating nature of Klemperer's insights. He writes: "Yesterday, as Eva [Klemperer's wife] was sewing on the Jew's star, I had a raving fit of despair. . . . Yesterday shut in all day in glorious weather, in the evening sneaked out for a couple of minutes. . . . Every step, the thought of every step, is desperation" (1998, p. 434). Like little else I have read, Klemperer's diary delineates in heartrending detail the meaning of being singled out in a society primed to look down upon, ostracize, and despise the "other."

In regard to my thoughts about and work in the field of Holocaust education, Henry Friedlander's "Toward a Methodology of Teaching about the Holocaust" (1979) provided me with a keen sense as to the complexity of teaching the Holocaust and the various ways in which one could approach such a complex topic. It also provided me with ample food for thought in regard to the critical need to teach this history with great care. A passage that I frequently revisit is the following:

The problem with too much being taught by too many without focus is that this poses the danger of destroying the subject matter [the Holocaust] through dilettantism. It is not enough for well meaning teachers to feel a commitment to teach about genocide; they also must know the subject. . . .

The problems of popularization and proliferation should make us careful about how we introduce the Holocaust into the curriculum; it does not mean we should stop teaching it. But we must try to define the subject of the Holocaust. Even if we do not agree about the content of the subject, we must agree on its goals and on its limitations. (Friedlander, 1979, pp. 520, 522)

As for William S. Parsons, one of the cofounders of the influential Facing History and Ourselves program, the first director of education at the USHMM, and now its chief of staff (and I should add, a close friend of mine), he made me appreciate the critical need to make what he refers to as careful "distinctions" about events, actions, decisions, issues, and perspectives when considering any piece of history, not just the Holocaust. This very concern became one of the key tenets in the *Guidelines for Teaching about the Holocaust* (1993) that we coauthored for the USHMM.

Another crucial way in which I was influenced by Parsons is his "mantra" about the need, in the best sense of the word, to "complicate students' thinking." As we argue in *Guidelines for Teaching about the Holocaust*, teachers and students need to: "avoid simple answers to complex history" (Parsons and Totten, 1993, p. 3), appreciate that "just because [an event] happened, does not mean it was inevitable" (Parsons and Totten, 1993, p. 3), "make careful distinctions about sources of information" (Parsons and Totten, 1993, p. 4), "avoid stereotypical descriptions" (Parsons and Totten, 1993, p. 4), and "contextualize the history" one is teaching and/or learning about (Parsons and Totten, 1993, p. 5).

A FOCUS ON TWO FIELDS: HOLOCAUST EDUCATION AND GENOCIDE STUDIES

Following my year back in California, I decided to earn an advanced degree in curriculum and instruction at Teachers College, Columbia University. It was four years well spent. Indeed, during my matriculation at Columbia, I was blessed to have many fine professors, among them Maxine Greene (philosophy of education), Lawrence Cremin (history of education), and Dwayne Huebner, Ann Lieberman, and Karen Zumwalt (curriculum and instruction). The only drawback, and I consider it a major one, is that my dissertation committee did not agree to allow me to conduct a study of the focus, methods, and efficacy of Facing History, the noted Holocaust education program based in Brookline, Massachusetts. I'm not sure it ever understood the real focus and broad outreach of Facing History, and, in retrospect, I think I should have been more persuasive and insistent. Instead, I conducted a study of educational efforts surrounding the issue of the nuclear arms race.

During this same period, I completed my book *Facing the Danger*. While writing my dissertation I worked, as previously mentioned, for Ralph Nader and then, for a year, as the English teacher at the U.S. House of Representatives Page School. At the Page School I had the students in my World Literature course read *Night* as well as a number of key essays on the history of the period. It was a small class of five students, but the discussions were intense.

While teaching English at the Page School, I served as the guest editor of various publications (including *Social Education*, the official journal of the National Council for the Social Studies, and the *Social Science Record*, the journal of the New York State Council for the Social Studies), addressing issues germane to human rights, Holocaust, and genocide education. For the various special issues, I solicited essays from such notable scholars, educators, and activists as Israel W. Charny, Bill Frelick, Maxine Greene, Richard Hovannisian, Isabel Letelier, Herbert Kohl, Aryeh Neier, William S. Parsons, and Ginetta Sagan. Parsons still gets a good laugh when he recalls that I addressed my initial letter to him in the following manner: William S. Parsons, Facing the Danger and Ourselves. I inadvertently used the title from my book on nuclear issues in place of his organization's correct name, which was Facing History and Ourselves.

In 1985, Israel W. Charny solicited a contribution from me for the series' inaugural edition of his *Genocide: A Critical Bibliographic Review* (1988). More specifically, he requested a chapter on literary works and films that addressed the issues of the Holocaust, genocide, and the nuclear threat. The resulting chapter was so long (over 60 pages) that Charny decided to have me divide it into three distinct chapters: "The Literature, Art, and Film of the Holocaust," "The Literature, Art, and Film of Genocide," and "The Literature, Art, and Film of Nuclear and Other Futuristic Destruction."

In 1987 Bill Fernekes, an outstanding teacher and social studies supervisor at Hunterdon Central High School in New Jersey, organized a panel discussion on human rights at the annual National Council for the Social Studies Conference, which was being held in Dallas. In addition to himself, Fernekes invited both William S. Parsons, codirector of Facing History, and me to serve on the panel. Parsons, a charismatic and confident character and speaker, impressed me immensely with his knowledge, his speaking skills, his obvious love of teaching, and his *joie de vivre*. That evening, Fernekes, Parsons, and I, along with several other individuals, including Steve Feinberg, then a junior high teacher in Massachusetts, went out to dinner at a Mexican restaurant. As the evening went on and the discussion flowed easily from one topic to another—human rights, the Holocaust, the art of teaching, Facing History's work—I remember thinking that down the road, somehow, some way, I needed to hook up with these individuals again on mutual projects.

My work on behalf of prisoners of conscience and my obsession with all of the voices that were silenced as a result of genocide in this century prompted me to undertake a three-year project, beginning in the late 1980s, that resulted in the development of the first bibliography in any language to focus on first-person accounts of various genocidal acts committed in the twentieth century. Among the genocidal acts addressed in *First-Person Accounts of Genocidal Acts Committed in the Twentieth Century: An Annotated Bibliography* (1991) are: the German slaughter of the Hereros, the Ottoman Turks' genocide of the Armenians, the Soviet man-made famine in the Ukraine, the Soviet Union's Great Purge, the Soviet Deportation of Whole Nations, the Holocaust, the Indonesian genocide of Communists and suspected Communists, the genocide in Bangladesh, the genocide of the Hutus in Burundi, the Indonesian genocide in East Timor, the Khmer Rouge-perpetrated genocide in Cambodia/Kampuchea, and the genocide of various indigenous peoples across the globe.

Throughout this three-year project I continued reading theoretical works on genocide as well as on the history of individual genocidal acts (including the Holocaust), but, primarily, I focused on the reading of literally hundreds of first-person accounts, many of which were extremely graphic in their description of the brutality and horror faced by the individual victims. The book's section on the Holocaust, alone, numbered 182 pages. During the reading of these accounts, I periodically found myself staring into space, devastated that human beings—*just like me, just like all of us, of flesh, bone, heart, mind and soul*—were subjected to such hatred and brutality. During these periods, I pondered the fact that the greatest lesson from past horrors had not yet been learned—that *those individuals, groups, and nations that are able to do so must reach out to potential victims* before *they, the victims, are subjected to such horrifying treatment.*

Also in the late 1980s, I called Bill Parsons and asked him if he would be interested in coediting a special issue of *Social Education* on "Teaching About Genocide." He said he would be, and thus for the next two years we worked closely together, talking on the phone at least several times a week, in creating and editing the issue. It was the first in the National Council for the Social Studies' nearly 60-year history to dedicate a total issue to the focus of genocide theory and multiple genocidal events. Over and above soliciting and editing all of the articles, Bill and I also wrote a piece entitled "Teaching and Learning About Genocide: Questions of Content, Rationale, and Methodology." Among the many contributors to the special issue were Leo Kuper, Israel W. Charny, Rouben Adalian, René Lemarchand, Ben Kiernan, Sybil Milton, Henry Friedlander, Geoffrey Hartman, Deborah Lipstadt, William Fernekes, and Margaret Drew.

During this period, Parsons was working for the United States Holocaust Memorial Council, the organization that was responsible for the development and erection of the USHMM. In late 1989, Bill brought together a team of educational consultants for the council in order to begin to develop outreach programs on Holocaust education. By this time I was a tenure-track assistant professor in the Department of Curriculum and Instruction at the University of Arkansas. Interestingly, in addition to myself, the two other members of the five-person team were Steve Feinberg and Bill Fernekes. Just as I had once hoped would happen, those of us who had gone out to dinner back in 1987 in Dallas were united to work on a number of key projects. The other individual joining us was Grace Caporino, a high school English teacher and longtime Holocaust educator from New York.

For the next several years, the team was flown into Washington, D.C., for many meetings at the council's headquarters. During those meetings, we discussed, along with Sybil Milton, a Holocaust historian who would become the museum's senior historian, and various archivists, what was needed to encourage teachers both to teach their students about the Holocaust and to teach it in an accurate and pedagogically sound fashion.

Ultimately, the team worked on the development of: a poster series for classroom use, which was based around actual artifacts in the USHMM's permanent exhibit; a set of guidelines for teaching about the Holocaust; a teacher's guide to accompany a film entitled *Daniel's Story*, which conveyed the history of the Holocaust from a young person's perspective; and a series of nationwide workshops.

Beginning in 1994, the museum began its National Conference for Educators, which was held twice during the course of the summer. Approximately 100 teachers from around the country attended each three-day session. The presentations were given by the four educational consultants (Caporino, Fernekes, Feinberg, and Totten), William S. Parsons (by then, director of education at the USHMM), Sybil Milton, and several Holocaust educators who worked for the USHMM (for example, Shari Rosenstein Werb, David Klevan, Warren Marcus, and Marcia Sabol). Among the sessions initially offered at these conferences were such basics as "Questions of Rationale, Methodologies, and Content," "Developing Curriculum: High School," "Developing Curriculum: Middle School," "Holocaust History," "Using USHMM Educational Resources," "Interdisciplinary Approaches Using Literature," and "Survivor Testimony in the Classrooms." At the initial conference Sybil Milton gave a fascinating and learned talk entitled "Helping Students Learn about Holocaust History" at which hundreds were in attendance.

Eventually funded by the Belfer family, these summer conferences became known as the Belfer Conferences. I presented at the first three conferences (generally at least one session on the use of first-person accounts and another session on the use of literature). In subsequent years, the presenters were primarily composed of museum personnel and teachers who had successfully completed a program that Steve Feinberg eventually headed up, the Mandel program.

One of the many highlights of working on the initial team of consultants was getting to know and work with Sybil Milton. A noted
Holocaust historian, Sybil astounded us all with her encyclopedic
knowledge about the Holocaust. With no intention whatsoever of
trying to impress us with her erudition, she would, whenever there
was a question about a particular historical event, issue, or arti-
fact, provide us with a detailed and almost spellbinding historical
lesson. At heart, she was a natural and wonderful teacher. Not only
did she love knowledge, but she loved to share it and engage in
dialogue with others about it. What I found particularly admirable
about Sybil was that this highly respected scholar, who had her
hands full with all sorts of pressing and complex assignments,
spent inordinate amounts of time with us, the educational consultants, in order to assist us to develop the best pedagogical tools
possible. Unfortunately, not many other historians or political scientists have followed in her footsteps; that is, one who graciously
gave of her time and energy to see to it that educators were provided with the best advice and assistance possible in their endeavors to teach the young about this history.

As serious as our work was and as serious as we were in undertaking it, humor would surface periodically. For example, none
of us will ever forget the morning when Sara Bloomfield, who is
now the Executive Director of the USHMM, brought a museum archivist into a meeting of the educational consultants. After introducing us to the archivist, who was going to be working with us
on the development of the poster series, Sara began, counterclock-
wise, introducing all of the educational consultants to the archivist, first mentioning our names and then our affiliations. First,
she introduced Grace Caporino, next Bill Fernekes, then Steve
Feinberg, and then me. However, in introducing me, she said, "And
this is Sam Tottenberg, from the University of Arkansas." As a gale
of laughter burst out across the room, Feinberg, a real character
and a quick wit, bellowed, "That was the quickest conversion I've
ever seen." And with that, the room exploded into paroxysms of
laughter.

Ultimately, I was asked to take the lead on the development of
the guidelines for teaching about the Holocaust. It must be duly
noted, though, that while I took the lead, all of the aforementioned
consultants, along with William S. Parsons, Sybil Milton, and Sara
Bloomfield, participated in the development of the guidelines. It was
truly a team effort. Over the course of a long, hot summer in
Fayetteville, Arkansas, I put in ten hours a day for several months
working on various versions of the guidelines, and continued the
work well into the next academic year. The guidelines were edited

and vetted by various individuals at the museum, including Bill Parsons and Sara Bloomfield. The guidelines were subsequently published in booklet form under the title *Guidelines for Teaching about the Holocaust* (1993). Now in its fifth printing, it has been disseminated to several hundred thousand educators across the United States and other parts of the globe.

During my work on the guidelines I reviewed all of the individual lessons, units, and curricula I had collected over the years — including some that were first developed back in the 1970s by various agencies in Philadelphia, New York, and Los Angeles. As I studied the materials, it became increasingly evident that many of the individual lessons, and not a few of the curricula developed by various state departments of education, were, in one way or another extremely weak.

More specifically, I discovered that many were rife with historical inaccuracies, with tremendous gaps in the way the history was portrayed (for example, one state curriculum suggested that the Nazis' rise to power began in 1935 and, accordingly, that is exactly where the curriculum began, starting out with a discussion of the implementation of the Nuremberg Laws), and were often pedagogically unsound (for example, while some included gimmicky activities like simplistic crossword puzzles and picking the word out of a series of letters (for example, "find the word Nazis in the letters kdjhglknazisilkghh, and circle it"), others included simulations (for example, drawing a large rectangle in a classroom or playground and then pretending to cram all the students into it) that suggested once the students took part in them they "would have a real sense as to what the actual victims experienced during the Holocaust." A vast number of curricula primarily focused more on the "what, where, and how" of the Holocaust while totally overlooking the why, thus leaving students with little to no sense as to why the perpetrators believed or acted in the way they did or why the Jews and certain others were targeted as victims. Furthermore, many of the learning activities in the lessons, units, and curriculum were "set" at the lowest levels of the cognitive domain in Bloom's taxonomy; that is, at the knowledge and comprehension levels, thus requiring memorization but little to no analysis, synthesis, or evaluation during the course of study.

All of these findings influenced not only what we eventually addressed in the *Guidelines for Teaching about the Holocaust*, but also the work I was to undertake over the course of the next decade. More specifically, I made the conscious decision that, in addition to my work on various genocide-related projects, my main work in the field of Holocaust education was going to focus on (1) creating and publishing materials that would assist teachers to develop and implement pedagogically sound and historically accurate lessons and units on the Holocaust, and (2) on writing and publishing critiques of contemporary lessons, units, and curricula on the Holocaust—noting the strengths and weaknesses of the latter and commenting on the critical need to develop historically accurate and pedagogically sound materials for use in the classroom.

Two other events along the way corroborated, for me, the need for such a focus. First, during the course of one of our face-to-face semiannual meetings about a book we were working on (which was eventually entitled *Teaching and Studying the Holocaust*), both Bill Fernekes and Steve Feinberg suggested that we seek permission from the Association for Holocaust Organizations (AHO) to include its recently published booklet, "Evaluating Holocaust Curricula: Guidelines and Suggestions" in our book. I stated that before making the request, I wanted the opportunity to examine the instrument. Much to my dismay, the guidelines were so general that they would have been virtually useless in assessing the value of any Holocaust lesson or curriculum. To convince Fernekes and Feinberg of my concern, I wrote a rather lengthy critique and sent it to both of them with a note that I did not want to see the instrument included in the book as it would taint the value of it. Upon reading my critique, both graciously agreed to forego their initial request. Subsequently, I wrote a much longer and more detailed critique of the instrument and presented my findings at a Holocaust conference in Jerusalem.

My sense then, and remains to this day, was that if such knowledgeable and savvy educators as Fernekes and Feinberg would settle for such a weak instrument, indeed, even to the point of including it in a book they were editing, then there was little doubt in my mind that many other educators, without the same strong knowledge base, would attempt to use the instrument. In doing so, I feared, not only would they not gain a sense as to the strengths and weaknesses of any curriculum but that they might settle for something that was inferior, based on the false notion that the instrument they were using to assess the curriculum "suggested" that it (the curriculum) was adequate for use in a classroom setting.

Second, at the twenty-ninth Annual Scholars' Conference on the Holocaust and the Churches on Long Island in New York, a Holocaust educator from a Holocaust center in New Jersey approached me and asked if I would read a recent article she had published as she wanted feedback on her ideas. I agreed to do so, and read the paper on the flight back to Arkansas. Again, much to my dismay, the paper made recommendations that I found nonsensical and irresponsible. The paper basically called for teachers to teach about the Holocaust at the K–4 level. It also asserted that teachers at the K–4 level who were interested in teaching such subject matter needed to make a case for the importance of such work. Vehement in my disagreement with her premise, I wrote a strong rebuttal and notified her of the fact that I intended to submit it to the same journal that published her essay. Distraught, she argued that I had no right to write and publish a rebuttal since she had simply asked me to read the piece. I replied that had she not published the paper I would never have written and submitted a rebuttal for publication, but since the article was in the public domain I had every right to publish a rejoinder. My article was published as "Should There Be Holocaust Education for K–4 Students? The Answer Is No!" in the National Council for the Social Studies' journal, *Social Studies and the Young Learner*. To be fair, I informed the publisher that the author of the original piece was not pleased that I planned to write a rebuttal, and the publisher stated that in all fairness the original author should be allowed to write a rejoinder to my piece. Ultimately, the other author chose not to write a rejoinder.

Interestingly, the two aforementioned articles spawned a minidebate. First, I received a long letter from a German Holocaust educator, Heike Deckert-Peaceman, with the Fritz Bauer Institute, who offered counterpoints to my arguments. I responded to her letter with my own counterarguments. My article, the two aforementioned letters, plus a third that Deckert-Peaceman wrote to me, all ended up, somehow, on the Internet. Several months after the above correspondence, I was contacted by Warren Marcus at the USHMM and asked if I would be willing to speak at a two- to three-day seminar at the museum on the topic of "age-appropriate Holocaust education." He explained that, along with me, he was inviting Ms. Deckert-Peaceman from Germany, the original author of the piece to which I responded, and Karen Shawn, a noted educator from New Jersey. I agreed. As of July 2002 and because of a conflict in schedules, the seminar has not yet been held.

Anyhow, within a year of the publication of my annotated bibliography of first-person accounts of genocide in 1991, I developed a proposal for a book composed of scholarly essays and first-person accounts about genocidal incidents perpetrated in the twentieth century. A key motivation was to see the voices of the victims and survivors of various genocides in print and available to educators at the secondary and university levels, as well as to the larger public. Another goal was to provide educators and others with essays written by noted scholars that clearly delineated the various historical trends and other key factors that eventually culminated in the perpetration of a particular genocide. In order to assist students to gain an understanding of the "why" behind such events, educators need to be cognizant of and conversant with such trends and factors. Bereft of such an understanding, teaching and learning about genocide become not much more than hand-wringing over horrific wrongs. Ultimately, William S. Parsons, Israel W. Charny, and I coedited *Genocide in the Twentieth Century: Critical Essays and Eyewitness Accounts* (New York: Garland Publishing, Inc., 1995). In 1997 it was updated and reissued as a paperback entitled *Century of Genocide: Eyewitness Accounts and Critical Views* (New York: Garland Publishing, Inc.). The latter has been used as a text in various courses on genocide, including those taught by: Roger Smith, Professor of Political Science at William and Mary College; Mary Felstiner, Professor of History at San Francisco State University; Joyce Apsel, Adjunct Professor of History at New York University; Henry Huttenbach and Carol Rittner, respectively, in the Master of Arts Program in Holocaust and Genocide Studies at the Richard Stockton College of New Jersey in Pomona; Paul Bartrop, Adjunct Professor of History at Bialik College in Victoria, Australia; and Rhoda Hassmann, Professor of Sociology at McMaster University in Hamilton, Ontario, Canada.

In 1993, I approached Steve Feinberg about the possibility of coediting a special issue ("Teaching about the Holocaust") of *Social Education* for the National Council for the Social Studies. I wanted to work with Steve because he knows the history of the Holocaust like few other educators (indeed, it was not uncommon for Steve and Sybil Milton to get into passionate discussions and arguments over a piece of the history, with Steve often being correct in his assertions.) And like me, he's a stickler for detail and accuracy.

Steve readily agreed, and for the next year and a half we solicited, edited, and wrote articles for inclusion in the special issue. The issue, which was awarded an EdPress Award, included essays by such noted scholars and educators as Ina R. Friedman ("The Other Victims of the Nazis"), Alison Owings ("Women in Nazi Germany: Denial by Any Other Name"), Nechama Tec ("Altruism and the Holocaust"), Margaret A. Drew ("Incorporating Literature into a Study of the Holocaust: Some Advice, Some Cautions"), Carol Danks ("Using Holocaust Short Stories and Poetry in the Social Studies Classroom"), and Paul Wieser ("Antisemitism: A Warrant for Genocide," "The American Press and the Holocaust," and "Hitler's Death Camps"), among others.

Over breakfast one morning in 1994 in Washington, D.C., with Steve Feinberg and Bill Fernekes, I broached the suggestion that we should coedit a book on Holocaust education. Both liked the idea, and that morning, before we left for a meeting at the USHMM, we worked out a rough draft of what we thought such a book should include. Over the course of the next six months, we traded ideas back and forth, constantly honing the outline of the book. By the time we submitted the book proposal to the publishers, we were in agreement that (1) while the book should have a practical focus, it must be undergirded with a sound theoretical base; (2) that the contributors to the book must be highly respected educators with long and solid track records in teaching the Holocaust in a pedagogically sound and historically accurate manner; (3) in addition to separate chapters on such concerns as instructional issues and methods, we needed to include a strong chapter on rationales for teaching the Holocaust as well as a strong chapter on the historiography of the Holocaust; and (4) we would take as long as need be—and not rush the process in order to meet an arbitrary deadline—in order to develop the strongest book we possibly could.

Six years later, after many ups and downs (some authors dropped out of the project after being asked to revise an essay for a third or fourth time, thus forcing the editors to search for new authors for certain chapters; the editors decided to add several chapters late in the project—including a chapter on primary accounts and a second chapter on the use of films), the book was published under the title *Teaching and Studying the Holocaust* (Boston, MA: Allyn and Bacon Publishers, 2001). Unfortunately, midway through the project Bill Fernekes felt compelled to drop out as one of the coeditors, but did remain as the coauthor of the lead chapter in the book.

Steve Feinberg and I were extremely pleased with the final product and proud of the efforts of the fine group of contributors we brought together to make the book a reality, among them being: Steve Cohen, Judith Doneson, William Fernekes, Karen Shawn, Paul Wieser, and Shari Rosenstein Werb.

In 1997 I decided to edit yet another book on Holocaust education, but this time with the singular focus of teaching Holocaust literature. That book, *Teaching Holocaust Literature* (Boston, MA: Allyn and Bacon Publishers, 2001), includes essays about how different Holocaust educators have taught their students in grades 7 through 12 various novels, short stories, poems, and plays. Those who contributed essays were Rebecca G. Aupperle, Elaine

Culbertson, Carol Danks, Margaret Drew, Beth Dutton, Bill
Fernekes, Karen Shawn, and Samuel Totten.

A year later (1998), I decided to write my own book on Holocaust
education in order to bring together a series of essays I had published over the years as well as to address numerous issues I had
not addressed in the first two books. It is entitled *Holocaust Education: Issues and Approaches* (Boston, MA: Allyn and Bacon,
2002). A number of the essays address the critical need to teach
the Holocaust in a pedagogically sound and historically accurate
manner—a motif that was interwoven through much of my work
in Holocaust education throughout the 1990s. More specifically,
among the topics, issues, and approaches addressed in this book
are: the critical need to establish a strong foundation for the study
of the Holocaust; focusing on essential issues and topics for a study
of the Holocaust; the common misconceptions and inaccuracies
that plague Holocaust education; the need to "complicate" students'
thinking vis-à-vis the history of the Holocaust; the problematic use
of simulations in an attempt to convey historical experiences; and
the imperative to avoid clichés when teaching this history.

Beginning in 1999, I was asked to serve on the American Com-
mittee for the planning of the Annual Scholars' Conference on the
Holocaust and the Churches, one of the longest running and most
esteemed Holocaust conferences held in the United States. I was
proud to serve on such a committee, along with others such as
Judith Doneson, Zev Garber, Stephen Haynes, Henry Huttenbach,
Mary Johnson, David Patterson, Abraham Peck, Carol Rittner, and
Richard Rubenstein.

Backtracking a bit, I should note that beginning in the late 1980s
and continuing throughout the 1990s, and at the behest of Israel
W. Charny, I also undertook numerous projects on the broader
topic of genocide with the Jerusalem-based Institute on the Holocaust and Genocide. Initially, I served as contributing editor to the
institute's newsletter, *Internet on the Holocaust and Genocide*, then
as coassociate editor of *The Widening Circle of Genocide*, volume
three in the institute's Critical Bibliographic Review series, and finally, as coassociate editor of the *Encyclopedia of Genocide*.

In 1995, I was asked by the USHMM to develop a lecture series
on genocide in the twentieth century. A seven-part series entitled
"Genocide and Mass Murder in the Twentieth Century: A Histori-
cal Perspective," it included talks by Robert Conquest, Alison Des
Forges, Helen Fein, Merle Goldman, David Hawk, Barbara Harff,
Raul Hilberg, and Richard Hovannisian.

In 1999 I volunteered to serve as the book review editor of the new *Journal of Genocide Research*, which was founded by Professor Henry Huttenbach.

THE DEVELOPMENT OF AN ANNUAL HOLOCAUST EDUCATION CONFERENCE IN ARKANSAS

In March 1993, a local educator who was associated with one of Arkansas's educational cooperatives asked me if I would support her effort to obtain monies that would enable her to attend the National Endowment for the Humanities's Holocaust summer institute. I suggested that it might be more worthwhile in the long run to obtain funding to support the development of a local conference for teachers. I stated that in doing so, she could provide a valuable service to scores, if not hundreds, of teachers in our area. Agreeing with me, we decided to call a meeting of local educators who might be interested in creating such a program. The result was the establishment of the Arkansas Holocaust Education Committee (AHEC) in 1993. From the beginning the committee was composed of local high school, junior high, middle school, and elementary teachers, university faculty (from the College of Education and the German department), and local community members (including a survivor of the Holocaust and a liberator of the camps).

For the first two years, AHEC offered a conference in the fall and in the spring. Then, due to a tapering off of participation by teachers at the spring conference, it was decided to offer one session a year in November. Over the years AHEC has offered ten conferences that have involved hundreds of teachers. The first conference was held on October 7, 1994, and included an eclectic group of presenters: William S. Parsons, director of education at USHMM, who presented an informative keynote address entitled "Teaching and Learning about Genocide and the Holocaust"; Arnold Kramer, director of technical services at the USHMM; Dr. Mark Cory, professor of German and director of humanities at the University of Arkansas; Dr. Evan Bukey, professor of history at the University of Arkansas; Professor Diane Blair, professor of political science at the University of Arkansas, Fayetteville; Herb Graver and Nate Blumenthal, two residents of northwest Arkansas who were involved in the liberation of the Nazi concentration camps; and Samuel Totten.

Among the many scholars, educators, and survivors who have presented at various conferences over the years are: Dr. Michael

Berenbaum, director of research at the USHMM; Dr. Samuel Oliner, a survivor and researcher in altruistic behavior during the Holocaust years; Johanna Reiss, Holocaust survivor and author of *The Upstairs Room* and *The Journey Back*; Dr. Beverly Asbury, university chaplain and director of religious affairs at Vanderbilt University; Stephen Feinberg, social studies teacher at Wayland Middle School and an educational consultant to the USHMM; Dr. William R. Fernekes, social studies supervisor at Hunterdon Central Regional High School in Flemington, New Jersey, and an educational consultant to the USHMM; Mary Costanza, a specialist on art and the Holocaust; Shari Werb, a teacher educator at the USHMM and a specialist in art and music about the Holocaust; Carol Danks, an English teacher at Roosevelt High School in Kent, Ohio, and one of the codevelopers of the State of Ohio's Holocaust curriculum; Sidney Finkel, a Holocaust survivor; Irene Gut Opdyke, who, as a Polish Catholic teenager, risked her life to protect Jews marked for death by the Gestapo; Dr. Jacob Boas, author of *We Are Witnesses: Five Diaries of Teenagers Who Died in the Holocaust*; Paul Wieser, social studies director for Pendergast School District in Phoenix, Arizona; Max Notowitz, a Holocaust survivor of the Pustkow concentration camp and 21 months in the forest; and Warren Marcus, coordinator of school and adult programs in the education department at the USHMM.

Out of this effort, I ended up teaching a summer school course to high school students (grades 9–11) enrolled in a special program at the University of Arkansas for students who, should they choose to do so, would be the first in their families to attend college. The class met five days a week for three hours a day over a course of two weeks. As the course text, I used Michael Berenbaum's *The World Must Know*, which was a resounding success. Many of the strategies that I used in this course are highlighted in the text I coedited with Stephen Feinberg, *Teaching and Studying the Holocaust* and in the book I edited, *Teaching Holocaust Literature*.

Another course was also developed as a result of AHEC's work— a semester-long, elective course for juniors and seniors at Springdale High School in Arkansas. I codeveloped the course with a high school English teacher who had participated in Vladka Meed's highly acclaimed Holocaust education program, which tours Poland and Israel and involves talks by noted Holocaust educators. Approximately 15 students enrolled in the course. Using Berenbaum's *The World Must Know*, plus a number of key essays by such scholars as Raul Hilberg, Michael R. Marrus, Christopher Browning, Franklin H. Littell, and Israel Gutman, we examined the history of antisemitism, Jewish life and communities in the pre-war years, the rise of the Nazi party, the Nazi takeover of Germany, the incremental assault on Jews in Nazi-controlled territory, the Nuremberg Laws, *Anschluss*, the Evian Conference, *Kristallnacht*, the "euthanasia" of the mentally and physically handicapped, the formation of the ghettos, the breakout of World War II, the actions of the *Einsatzgruppen*, the Wannsee Conference, the development of the killing centers, and the mass murder of the Jews and others. Throughout, we examined the unique role of the perpetrators, collaborators, and bystanders, all the while emphasizing that none acted in a monolithic fashion. We did the same with the targeted groups—the victims and survivors. It was a course that involved ample discussion, some lectures, student research projects, guest speakers, key films, and a lot of wrestling with tough questions and horrific facts and issues.

While the students got a lot out of the course and it was a real pleasure working with them, coteaching the course was extremely difficult. The teacher did not know the history as well as I thought he should, and he was more prone to lecturing while I was in favor of a much more hands-on, minds-on approach.

THE FIRST TWO INTERNATIONAL HOLOCAUST EDUCATION CONFERENCES AT YAD VASHEM

In October 1996 Yad Vashem, The Holocaust Martyrs' and Heroes' Remembrance Authority, held its first international conference ("The Holocaust in Education"), and in October 1999 it held its second international conference ("The Memory of the Holocaust in the Twenty-First Century: The Challenge for Education"). I attended and presented at both conferences.

At the first conference (which had attendees from Israel, the United States, Australia, England, Canada, Japan, South Africa, Russia, and Germany), I presented a paper that analyzed and critiqued the Association of Holocaust Organization's instrument entitled "Evaluating Holocaust Curricula: Guidelines and Suggestions." The first evening, during which I met up with old friends Carol Danks and Richard Flaim, and met, for the first time, the wonderful Leatrice Rabinsky, there was a gathering in a massive amphitheater on the grounds of Yad Vashem and a talk by the then Prime Minister Binyamin Netanyahu. There was also a very moving and haunting reading of "Crazy," a short story by Ida Fink.

What the organizers of the conference neglected to inform the potential speakers is that their proposals to do a presentation would appear—*exactly as they had originally submitted them*—in a conference booklet that would be handed out to all participants.

Had I known that, I would have been more judicious in the tone of my proposal. That is, my tone would have been much less harsh in its condemnation of the extremely poor quality of the instrument as well as in its questioning of the judgment of those who wrote it, published it, and disseminated it for use by educators across the globe. Furthermore, and even more embarrassingly, the conveners of the conference neglected to inform me that the two individuals who had developed the instrument were going to be at the conference giving a talk *on the value of their instrument*. And to make matters even worse, the conveners had neglected to inform the two other individuals and me that our talks were to be given in the same room during the same time period (a three-hour time period during which five talks were presented). And finally, we were not told that our talks would be given back-to-back, with the two developers of the instrument going first, followed by me. As one can imagine, there was great tension—for all three of us were caught in a most uncomfortable situation. The two talks were presented; the give-and-take by the audience was probing and interesting, but the final outcome was less than satisfactory. There was not enough time to truly go through the instrument point by point, though most participants seemed to appreciate my various concerns. The two developers, as one might surmise, were extremely put out by the whole situation and felt that they had been set up. I felt much the same way. (For my analysis of the instrument, see "A Holocaust Curriculum Evaluation Instrument: Admirable Aim, Poor Result," in the *Journal of Curriculum and Supervision*: 148–166.)

At the second international conference (which had a greater representation from even more countries than the first), one of the most informative and best-presented talks was "Who Knew What, When, and Where about the Murder of European Jewry?" by Professor Michael R. Marrus.

In addition to giving my talk, "Reader-Response Theory and Holocaust Literature," I, along with Israel W. Charny and Marc Sherman (a librarian at Tel Aviv University and a member of Charny's editorial team) manned a booth that informed the participants about the soon-to-be-published *Encyclopedia of Genocide*. In between a trip to the Dead Sea with Israel W. Charny (during which we were halted in the middle of the Judean Desert by a police roadblock as a robot was moved into place in order to blow up a suspicious package) and a trip to the Gaza Strip on my own, I spent the warm Jerusalem days of October sitting in my hotel room at the famous and beautiful Jerusalem YMCA, proofing the final version of the over 1,000-page *Encyclopedia of Genocide*.

ADDITIONAL PLANS

At the Second International Conference on the Holocaust and Education at Yad Vashem, Dr. Marcia Littel, the director of the Master of Arts Program in Holocaust and Genocide Studies at the Richard Stockton College, invited me to spend a year at Richard Stockton as the Ida E. King Distinguished Visiting Scholar of Holocaust Studies. I told her I was honored to be asked (especially in light of past holders of the Distinguished Visiting Scholar position—Franklin Littell, Carol Rittner, Henry Huttenbach, and Michael Berenbaum), but that I could not even consider such an offer for at least two years as I was in the middle of completing several books on the Holocaust and genocide. She kindly agreed to consider me in the future. So, that is one possibility down the road. Should I actually accept the position, I hope to primarily teach courses on Holocaust pedagogy, and on the intervention and prevention of genocide.

Early in 1999 I decided that once I had completed the four books I was working on about Holocaust education (including the one in which this essay appears), I was going to shift all of my attention to writing about the intervention and prevention of genocide. In November 2000 I signed a book contract with Greenwood Press for a new book on the intervention and prevention of genocide and submitted proposals out for two other books on genocide.

CONCLUSION

As we enter the twenty-first century, my primary focus, then, will be on the intervention and prevention of genocide. On one front, I plan to focus on how the work of human rights organizations—particularly nongovernmental organizations—and the work of genocide organizations can merge certain aspects of their work in order to intervene and/or prevent genocide from taking place. On another front, I plan to continue to study, write about, and contribute to the work on the intervention and prevention of genocide. A project I hope to undertake in the near future is the editorship of volume five of *Genocide: A Critical Bibliographic Review*, whose focus will be the intervention and prevention of genocide.

I also plan to continue to focus on other issues that consume me—many of which, in fact, complement the latter: what genocide means to the individual victim; the bystander syndrome and the need for a universal political will not to allow genocide to simply take its course; the need to take seriously the admonition that in certain dire situations, such as genocide, it is imperative that free

nations serve as their brothers' and sisters' keepers; the need to
move from lip service to serious and concrete efforts to staunch
genocide before it happens; and the critical need to educate the
general populace about genocide and its many ramifications, thus
heeding Ben Whitaker's insightful point that "Without a strong
basis of international public support, even the most perfectly
redrafted [U.N.] Convention [on genocide] will be of little value. Con-
ventions and good governments can give a lead, but the mobilization of public awareness and vigilance is essential to guard against
any recurrence of genocide and other crimes against humanity and
human rights" (Whitaker, 1985, p. 42).

REFERENCES

Berenbaum, Michael (1979). *The Vision of the Void: Theological Reflections
    on the Works of Elie Wiesel.* Middletown, CT: Wesleyan University
    Press.
———. (1993). *The World Must Know: The History of the Holocaust as Told
    in the United States Holocaust Memorial Museum.* Boston, MA: Little,
    Brown and Company.
Charny, Israel W. (1988). *Genocide: A Critical Bibliographic Review,* vol.
    1. London and New York: Mansell Publishers and Facts on File.
Charny, Israel W. and Rapaport, Chanan (1982). *How Can We Commit
    the Unthinkable? Genocide, the Human Cancer.* Boulder, CO: West-
    view Press.
Dawidowicz, Lucy S. (1986). *The War against the Jews, 1933–1945.* New
    York: Bantam Books.
Eisner, Elliot (1979). *The Educational Imagination: On the Design and
    Evaluation of School Programs.* New York: Macmillan.
Frankl, Viktor E. (1969). *Man's Search for Meaning: An Introduction to
    Logotherapy.* New York: Washington Square Press.
Friedlander, Henry (1979). "Toward a Methodology of Teaching about the
    Holocaust." *Teachers College Record,* 89(3): 519–542.
Hilberg, Raul (1985). *The Destruction of the European Jews,* vol. 1. New
    York: Holmes and Meier Publishers, Inc.
———. (1992). *Perpetrators, Victims, Bystanders: The Jewish Catastrophe,
    1933–1945.* New York: HarperCollins Publishers.
Klemperer, Victor (1998). *I Will Bear Witness: A Diary of the Nazi Years,
    1933–1941,* vol. 1. New York: Random House.
———. (2000). *I Will Bear Witness: A Diary of the Nazi Years, 1942–1945,*
    vol. 2. New York: Random House.
Marrus, Michael R. (1987). *The Holocaust in History.* New York: Meridian.
Parsons, William S. and Totten, Samuel (1993). *Guidelines for Teaching
    about the Holocaust.* Washington, DC: United States Holocaust
    Memorial Museum.
Styron, Rose (March 20, 1976). "Torture in Chile." *The New Republic*
    174(12): 15–17.

Totten, Samuel (1991). *First-Person Accounts of Genocidal Acts Commit-
ted in the Twentieth Century: An Annotated Bibliography.* Westport,
CT: Greenwood Press.
———. (1999). "Should There Be Holocaust Education for K–4 Students?
The Answer is No!" *Social Studies and the Young Learner,* Septem-
ber/October, 12(1): 36–39.
Whitaker, Ben (1985). *Revised and Updated Report on the Question of the
Prevention and Punishment of the Crime of Genocide.* E/CN.4/
Sub.2/1985/62, July 1985. Submitted to the United Nations Sub-
commission on Prevention of Discrimination and Protection of Mi-
norities of the Commission on Human Rights of the United Nations
Economic and Social Council. Geneva, April 1985.
Wiesel, Elie (1984). "All Was Lost, Yet Something Was Preserved." Review
of *The Chronicle of the Lodz Ghetto, 1941–1944. New York Times
Book Review*: 1, 23.
———. (1969). *Night.* New York: Avon.
———. (1979). "Preface." *Report to the President.* Washington, DC:
President's Commission on the Holocaust.

(Note: For a more detailed discussion of my work in the field of genocide studies,
see my essay "A Matter of Conscience" in Samuel Totten and Steven Jacobs' (Eds.)
Pioneers of Genocide Studies. Westport, CT: Greenwood Press, 2002.)

Chapter 9

~

That We Do No Less

Paul Wieser

It may have been the swastika on the cover that caught my attention. It was so long ago, I do not recall. As I thumbed through the pages of Simon Wiesenthal's *Murderers among Us* (1968), becoming more and more captivated with each fragment I read, I could not have envisioned how this chance encounter was to impact my life. Had the carousel of books been turned a bit more to the right or left, chances are things would have been much different. Today that same volume, now worn and well read, sits modestly among many others of its kind, a silent testimony to a long-standing commitment.

Occasionally Wiesenthal's book catches my eye, and my thoughts drift back to that day in the late 1960s. I was a history major at Upsala College in East Orange, New Jersey, where I was about to receive a degree and totally ignorant of a series of events that had occurred less than 30 years before. Growing up in the shadow of New York City, I have no memory of any class offering, discussion, or assignment that had the slightest connection to Nazi Germany's onslaught against European Jewry. I do recall reading about the Adolf Eichmann trial and vividly recollect the photo of someone holding up a pair of children's shoes as evidence; but this fragment of memory is all that remains about a period now known as the Holocaust.

Graduate school would have to wait, for these were the days of the military draft and the war in Southeast Asia, which put more than a few plans on hold. Yet the dark images Wiesenthal's words had created would not leave me. Although at that time books on the subject were certainly not numerous, a copy of Gerald Reitlinger's *The Final Solution: The Attempt to Exterminate the Jews of Europe, 1939–1945* (1961) would eventually find its way into my hands. Reitlinger's work was the first scholarly account of the period I had read, and I remember being immediately caught up in the overwhelming scope and horrific nature of the events. It is a bit embarrassing to admit, but I found my first encounter with Nazi racial theory rather compelling. I do not mean to imply that I was somehow "won over" to this kind of thinking, but reading of the uniqueness and superiority of a racial group, to which I happened to belong, made me curious and caused me to inquire further. However, the sobering reality of how such thinking would contribute to the demise of millions quickly put an end to any initial enthusiasm I might have had surrounding this philosophy. Nevertheless, my commitment to more study had been made.

Finding a graduate program with an emphasis on Holocaust studies was no simple task in the early 1970s. I was most fortunate to learn that two professors in the history department at the University of San Francisco—Dr. George Lerski, a Righteous Gentile, and Dr. James Shand—were offering a number of related courses in the field. So with the ink on my discharge papers barely dry, I found myself in the Bay Area, becoming personally acquainted with Raul Hilberg, George Mosse, Henry Feingold, Lucy Dawidowicz, and others.

As a young graduate student, being able to have Hilberg's monumental *The Destruction of the European Jews* (1985) at my fingertips provided the firm foundation needed for serious study. But now after so many years, I look back and realize the profound influence his words have had on my work and thoughts relative to the field of Holocaust studies.

Hilberg's work was extensive and inclusive, and he dealt with issues and content that other scholars would not address for years, for example, the aryanization process. One particular point he consistently made, which would eventually become an area of focus for my teaching, was that the Holocaust was the result of conscious decision making by many individuals, not all of whom were black-booted fanatics. Hilberg caused us to reexamine more traditional ideas relative to collaboration and culpability. Murder could be orchestrated from behind desks where civil servants silently acquiesced in efficiently processing the paperwork that neatly deprived people of their property and rights and ultimately their lives. This grassroots involvement by rather ordinary people became a theme I consciously wove throughout my lessons.

From the practical standpoint of incorporating content into classroom lessons, Mosse's work on German ideology has never proven to be invaluable. His treatment of the concept of the *Volk*—the people—is a rather sophisticated line of thinking that most students would find hard to digest. For the most part my students seemed to come away with a fairly good grasp of the components and evolution of German antisemitic thinking without my having to expose them to the complexities of *volkisch* ideology. However, on a personal level Mosse's work held far more significance. In his *Crisis of German Ideology: Intellectual Origins of the Third Reich*, Mosse (1964), like Hilberg, deals with subject matter that few scholars address. What impressed me most was his explanation of a German sense of uniqueness and how this self-concept was grounded in a "rootedness" epitomized by the *Volk*. The metaphor of a mature tree with its roots deep in the German soil clearly conveyed to me the image that National Socialists would use and exploit—an image that focused on some mist-shrouded past when simple people's sweat mixed with the very earth they tilled. An image that evoked sentiment for a time when the German people needed neither the example nor the assistance of those beyond the borders of the Fatherland. *An image that at its very core celebrated the prominence of the state above the individual.* This view and sense of what lay at the heart of German ideology provided me with a clear understanding of the "crisis" Mosse spoke of—a way of thinking that would provide the philosophical underpinnings for a regime whose legacy would be genocide.

EARLY ATTEMPTS TO TEACH ABOUT THE HOLOCAUST

A few years later, with an MA in history in hand, I decided to take a job turning a group of mostly disinterested and sometimes unruly young people into interested, productive, and disciplined learners. Yes, I had become a teacher. A junior high history teacher at that! Those acquainted with that type of student know that tears and hormones flow freely, and what appears to be a perfectly normal and functioning human being one moment may be transformed before your eyes (and class) into a life form yet to be categorized. It has been well over 20 years since I began. It has not always been easy, but it has always been meaningful and rewarding.

Oddly enough, many of the concerns and problems I faced as a new teacher with teaching the Holocaust still confront educators today. Poorly written standards and documents with vaguely worded goals and objectives left me wondering what exactly I was to teach. Social studies and history classes had no formal curriculum document developed for them, and where such did exist, there was no mention of content about teaching the Holocaust. Textbooks barely mentioned this genocide, and supplementary material was virtually nonexistent.

Initial frustration soon gave way to the realization that certain advantages came with curricular disarray, for it allowed me the opportunity to create and incorporate a unit of study on the Holocaust with very few constraints. The main concern was with materials; they simply did not exist. Today there are catalogs that are dedicated solely to curricular materials on teaching this history. In the early 1970s I considered myself fortunate to get my hands on a few tattered copies of Anne Frank's diary. Out of necessity, those of us in the field created our own materials and activities; we wrote curriculum and developed goals and objectives particular to Holocaust studies. We found out what worked and what did not; we built on the former and discarded the latter. Very slowly a pedagogy surrounding this area of study was developing. Methodologies were being formulated and fine-tuned in classrooms across the country. Most of this work at first was done in isolation, and there were few, if any, opportunities for educators to share and network.

One thing I eventually learned from my colleagues in the field was something I had noticed early on in my teaching—how riveted students' attention became when the classroom focus shifted to lessons on the Holocaust. No other topic seemed to interest them more. Had I stumbled upon an innovative technique or was there an inherent appeal that was inexplicable? Considering my students' responses to most of the content areas we explored, I quickly came to the conclusion that it no doubt was more of the latter and not much of the former. Students simply did not want to let the subject go. As I became more experienced, I realized that this intense interest could at least partially be explained by the fact that the study of the Holocaust raised issues for these young people that they themselves dealt with on a daily basis: conformity, peer pressure, indifference, fairness, obedience. The magnitude of the event—the fact that so many individuals and groups made decisions to act or not to act—also seemed to impress students and contribute to the compelling nature of the subject.

Each academic year I looked forward to that time when my Holocaust unit would begin. The enthusiastic response by the students encouraged me to explore a variety of methodologies as well as to revise course content and classroom activities. As new books and videotapes slowly became available, I tried to incorporate as many of the best as I could to make the study even more meaningful.

Even though I felt confident that my students were learning the "whos," "whys," "whats," and "whens" of the Holocaust, and they seemed excitedly involved, I had the uneasy feeling that something was missing. I was providing them perspective, but it just did not seem enough. I was not sure that they viewed the millions of victims as anything other than a set of overwhelming statistics, or the events and places as just some more vague and distant facts that "came with the turf" when you took a history class. Was the Holocaust for them just another tragedy, difficult to distinguish from others that appeared almost daily in newspapers and on television? Could the true significance of the Holocaust be conveyed to students by somehow personalizing it? But how to do this? Due to the enormity of the event, personalizing this history was no easy task. Was there an approach that could make the critical connection between the statistics and the human beings represented by those numbers? Unless my students could see the individuals within those piles of corpses and unless they understood the impact of the destruction of a single shtetl on the lives of the individuals who lived there, could I truly say with any degree of certainty that my students had achieved a meaningful understanding of the significance of this history?

PERSONALIZING THE HISTORY

I knew from my own experience how powerful the personalization of this history could be. I came to this realization during my first visit to Auschwitz in 1976. The emotion of actually being there—at a place symbolic of, if not synonymous with the Holocaust—was distracting to the degree that I almost left without gaining a true feel for the dreadfulness that had transpired there. I was so caught up in the process—this happened here, they did that over there—that the tragedy of the victims was obscured. It was not until I climbed the stairs of one of the redbrick former barracks (now museums) to a second-floor exhibit that the true horror of a Nazi death camp was impressed upon me.

I will never forget the hair. Under glass, running one entire side of the building, all colors and shades heaped together. I was not prepared for such a display, nor was I prepared for my reaction. It caused me to take a step back, and only after several deep breaths could I reenter the room. Viewing the plunder of the Final Solution was like being struck across the face.

Among the tangled assortment you could easily identify the braids of young girls. After so many years the carefully worked hair remained in place, as if a mother's hand had lovingly just completed its task. The image of an older woman, humming as she ran a comb through her child's hair, leapt before me. Who were they? Did they have any inkling as to their fate?

The image only intensified as I walked the length of the barracks. Eventually I found myself standing before some neatly packaged bundles that at first glance appeared to be carpet rolled up in brown paper. Numbers, indicating the weight of each, were scribbled on the side. A slit had been made in several of the bundles to reveal the contents. These were no carpets. This was the method the Germans used to transport human hair back to the Fatherland for processing into felt or perhaps to be used in mattresses. The openings in the brown wrappers allowed for the wretched remnants to spill outward; and once again there were the braids.

To say what I experienced that day was sobering would be an understatement. Viewing the pitiful remains of a proud people personalized for me the tragedy of the event and provided a focus that had been absent. The Holocaust was no longer simply pages of statistics or mountains of unidentified bodies; no longer remote places with indecipherable names, or countless walking skeletons stumbling about camp compounds or staring through barbed wire. A little girl with braids had broached the impersonal facade created by the enormity of the event. A little girl who no doubt trustingly left home one day holding on to her mother's hand, about to enter a time that can only be described as "unimaginable." She could never know the effect she would have upon me so many years later.

Since few students would ever have the opportunity to visit Auschwitz, I wrestled with the issue of personalizing this history for quite some time; indeed, all the way up until the summer of 1986 when I was fortunate enough to take part in the "Teaching the Holocaust and Jewish Resistance" program in Israel.

TAKING PART IN THE "TEACHING THE HOLOCAUST AND JEWISH RESISTANCE" PROGRAM IN ISRAEL

Having access to some of the top scholars and educators in the field at Israel's Yad Vashem, The Holocaust and Martyrs' and Heroes' Remembrance Authority, in Jerusalem and the Ghetto Fighters' House in Western Galilee, I felt optimistic that the "connection" I was searching for would be found.

Prior to commenting on the connection, let me say this about my experience with the program. The opportunity to immerse oneself in such an intensely focused area of study with individuals who had similar interests was an invaluable intellectual experience. What proved extremely beneficial was the interaction among program participants. The program afforded us not only the opportunity to discuss the implications and meaning of the material we were being exposed to, but also the time to thoughtfully consider how this content might be skillfully formatted into challenging, dynamic, and meaningful lessons. This interaction gave rise to the need for an ongoing dialogue, which eventually took the form of "reunions" held every other year in Washington, D.C. Friendships were not only rekindled but also our teachers' "batteries" received a thorough "recharging" as scholars and educators shared and presented the latest research and methodology. Professionally reinvigorated, and with our commitment reaffirmed, we scatter back to every corner of the nation and into its classrooms, well equipped to meet the challenges of this most demanding of content areas.

While in Israel I was fortunate to meet and spend a significant amount of time with Nili Keren, an Israeli educator and historian. She was well acquainted with the dilemma I faced with my teaching, for apparently it was a concern shared by many educators in the field. Over lunch we were discussing the merits of a variety of methodologies, when she happened to mention a particular approach that had shown some promise. She was just a few sentences into her explanation, and I knew I had found what I had come looking for. In my mind's eye I could already see myself in front of my students. I could not wait to get started.

What she suggested was that I should perhaps try a literary approach. A short story, for instance, whose main characters were the approximate age of the students. As the story unfolds, students often begin to identify with the characters and get caught up in the narrative. They are led through the complex historical reality of the period through the actions of characters their own age. What made this idea seem even more viable was the fact that by the mid-1980s there was a growing body of Holocaust literature that could support such an approach. Books such as *Friedrich* by Hans P. Richter (1987) and *Stolen Years* by Sara Zyskind (1981) seemed to be ideal for such an approach.

Well, it worked. It has been an effective strategy that has served my students and me for quite a few years. Good literature can illuminate historical content and engage students in ways that traditional histories do not. The history becomes more personalized and thought provoking. And if the history becomes more than simply a series of facts, then perhaps it can very well touch students in ways that may cause them to reflect more meaningfully upon the significance of these events. Literature provided the connection I was searching for—the bridge between the magnitude of the event and the individual tragedies that made up the Holocaust. The little girl in braids no longer was lost among a mountain of statistics, but stood out in clear relief to help my students with personalizing the "unthinkable."

I should note that my decision to adopt a literary approach to teaching the Holocaust perhaps had the greatest practical impact on what I was doing in the classroom. Classroom instruction took on a totally different format. As groups of students read various pieces of literature, this approach required me to present content that would not only fill in the gaps but at the same time provide the context necessary for as complete an understanding of the historical realities as was possible.

A classroom concern that was a constant source of frustration was the little amount of time I could devote to a study of the Holocaust. Like most history teachers, the breadth of the curriculum was a challenge. I always felt torn in regard to just how detailed a unit I should teach on the Holocaust. Given the time constraints, how many days could I devote to the unit and how deeply could I delve into the subject? I certainly wanted to provide more than just a cursory treatment. Yet the demands of the curriculum made a long-term study unfeasible.

NATIONAL HISTORY DAY

What proved to be a godsend in this regard was discovering the National History Day (NHD) program, which was (and is) an exciting way for students to study and learn about historical issues, ideas, people, and events. The yearlong educational program fostered academic achievement and intellectual growth. It provided the opportunity for students to research a topic by investigating its historical significance and relationship to a yearly theme and to present their findings in exhibits, documentaries, research papers, and dramatic performances. And perhaps just as importantly, the NHD Program provided me with a format where I could extend what might be a two-week unit into a yearlong study of the Holocaust. As the focus of the classroom instruction shifted to different content areas throughout the academic year, students became actively involved with research on Holocaust topics as they developed their entries. (For those interested in obtaining more information about this program, write to: National History Day, University of Maryland, Cecil Hall, College Park, MD, 20742.)

I noticed that as students became more successful at the state and national competitions, especially those who had undertaken research on the Holocaust, discussions with new students about what areas of history they would like to research became shorter and shorter. The word was out that the Holocaust was "the" topic. The kids were "hooked" on the subject and anxious to begin working. Those of us who have been teaching for awhile can testify that this behavior is not always characteristic of junior high students.

Students consistently chose the dramatic performance category to showcase their research. Historical analysis literally came to life with presentations that had as their focus such topics as the Kovno *Judenrat*, the Eichmann trial, the Warsaw ghetto, the role science played in the Final Solution, antisemitic legislation in Germany, the reaction of the Catholic Church, and the response of the United States. The quality and sophistication of the students' work, along with their enthusiastic involvement, provided all the encouragement I needed. Incorporating the NHD program into my methodology allowed for the detailed coverage I was looking for and at the same time made it possible for me to adequately address the remaining objectives in the curriculum.

As my knowledge base expanded, the challenge of how to incorporate more and more content into a time frame and curriculum that was already bursting at the seams caused me to rethink and restructure my lesson planning. Given the time constraints, my lessons, out of necessity, became much more focused on the most essential topics of Holocaust history—such as the historical roots of antisemitism, Germany between the wars, the establishment of the concentration and death camps, and the role played by bystanders—at the expense of issues that could be considered ancillary, issues such as resistance and medical experimentation.

Having my students involved in the NHD program provided me with the most rewarding experiences I have had as an educator. As my students were exposed to the complexities of historical research, the program allowed me the opportunity to expand and extend my teaching of the Holocaust beyond the constraints of time and the extant curriculum.

Taking a Critical Stance toward Holocaust Curricula

As I became more involved with curriculum development and the pedagogy and methodology surrounding the subject, I became aware of a particularly troubling trend that seemed to have found its way into many teachers' lessons. What I am referring to is, for lack of a better term, the "de-Judifying" of the Holocaust. In recent years the term "Holocaust" seems to have become a generic metaphor for every conceivable form of human suffering. We read about the Native American Holocaust, the Cambodian Holocaust, the Rwandan Holocaust, and more recently the Bosnian Holocaust. Many of us in the field bristle at this rather cavalier use of the word. For us, the "Holocaust" refers to a very specific period of time and series of historic realities in which Jews, while not the only victim group, were the primary target of the Nazis' Final Solution.

Directly related to this trend is the argument that the emphasis on the plight of European Jewry minimizes the sacrifices made by the non-Jewish victim groups. Many suffered, not just Jews. That some five million non-Jews perished in the Holocaust is a story that needs to be told, and for those teachers who have the time to devote lessons to it, they most certainly should. But, again, we can never lose sight of the fact that the primary victims in the Holocaust were Jews. If any true understanding of the Final Solution is to be realized, the latter must be understood and appreciated. Well-planned and focused lessons help to assure that this is the eventual outcome.

The Power of Survivor Testimony in the Classroom

As my lessons evolved and I became more comfortable with teaching the subject, I expanded the scope of the unit by incorporating survivor testimony. As these "living links" to the past slowly make their way to podiums and begin to speak, all those present are transported back to a time that we cannot fully understand. The survivors' soft accented voices conjure up images of loving families, tight-knit communities, friends at school, and holidays at home. Yet within the span of just a few seconds, those same voices are capable of creating the most dramatic of mood swings as they painfully relate the horrific realities they experienced. We stand with them as they pass before Dr. Mengele; we walk with them through ghetto streets and concentration camp gates; we weep with them as their loved ones are murdered; and in the end we can only marvel at their strength.

One particular meeting between some of my students and a survivor is noteworthy. It involved Meyer Dragon, a Polish survivor who spent over three years in Auschwitz. Even though half a century has gone by, he still finds it much too difficult to relate to others the details of his experiences. I always made it a point for students involved in the NHD program to attend the annual Yom Hashoah commemoration, so as to provide them an opportunity to meet and interview Holocaust survivors. I would tell them in advance that there was one survivor I would be introducing them to who would be very pleasant but would not agree to an interview. I was even less prepared than my students for what was to happen.

As the students began to speak with survivors, I noticed Meyer in the crowd. He agreed to say hello to my students before he left, and as I gathered them together I reminded them of who they would be meeting. Meyer wished them well in their research into the Holocaust. However, when he learned they had done some work that involved Dr. Mengele's experimentations at Auschwitz, his expression suddenly changed.

He took a few steps away as if he was leaving when he suddenly turned back and said, "Let me tell you something." The kids all glanced toward me as if to ask, "What's going on here?" I was as shocked as they were as Meyer told them of his experiences with the "Angel of Death." He spoke of Mengele arriving for selections in his shiny black Mercedes, motioning people to the right or left with a flick of his riding crop while brushing lint from his uniform. In that same car he would drive unsuspecting children to the gas chambers.

For the next hour he spoke in what was now the empty synagogue. It had been the first time he had done so since those horrific years. The time had come for him to share and unburden himself of the sorrow and grief he had carried within himself for so long. My students and I were the beneficiaries of those truly special moments—ones that would remain with us forever.

He spoke of ghetto life and witnessing his infant niece being thrown through the window of their third-floor apartment onto the street below, where German soldiers collected the small broken bodies and pitched them into trucks as so much refuse. He told of an SS officer who served as a concentration camp dentist and took particular pleasure in extracting inmates' teeth without the use of anesthesia. If the prisoner made the slightest whimper in pain, another tooth was removed, then another and another until death mercifully ended the ordeal. This same man would make daily inspections of the camp's "hospital" barrack, slashing with his scalpel ulcerous growths that appeared on any unsuspecting prisoner's body.

Before they move on to high school, all of the students in our school district have the opportunity to personally meet and hear a survivor of the Holocaust. This has become part of an integrated approach that I have helped initiate as district social studies coordinator. What never ceases to amaze me is how the survivor's message seems to be able to touch students in a personal way. We know this from the letters the students write expressing thanks for the speaker and from class discussions that follow. Each year as the survivor paints the dramatic landscape that was the Holocaust, students sit riveted to every word. Indeed, year in and year out, you can hear a pin drop as these elderly witnesses captivate and astonish their young audiences, who in some ways, become their emotional partners as the historic realities unfold before them. They travel together to a time and world that truly was the "other kingdom."

The effectiveness of using survivor testimony has much to do with the preparation that goes on in the classroom. Hearing a survivor is usually the culmination of the unit of study. The students have gone through a good number of lessons that have addressed a broad spectrum of issues and content surrounding the history, so the "stage" is set, so to speak, for the survivor's presentation. In cases where students have not been adequately prepared, where a sound foundation, built on the facts, has not been presented, educators are likely to experience problems. Lacking the background and context needed to appreciate the true nature and scope of the events, students become confused. I have also witnessed a number of unfortunate instances where inadequate preparation by certain teachers has resulted in such a distorted view, that the history has been trivialized to the point that students view it as insignificant and even humorous.

Those of us in the field of Holocaust studies have a deep respect for all survivors. For many of us, it borders on the reverential. We realize how difficult it is for them to put into words what they experienced. Through their tortured expressions we can almost feel the personal anguish they carry with them. For many of us, they embody an era that dominates our professional lives and to which we have committed ourselves. And yet the high regard we hold them occasionally can lead to some rather awkward moments.

Survivors are not necessarily teachers, nor are they historians. Memories fade and oftentimes are at variance with the facts. Even though an obvious error or inconsistency may arise during a survivor's presentation, I must admit that I am most reluctant to offer any suggestion that things may have been otherwise. I once heard a survivor tell students that before German guards were transferred from Auschwitz they were poisoned to keep them from telling what they had witnessed. He finished his remarks by boasting to the students that, "You don't find those stories in the history books."

We all know why stories like that are not in the history books, but in the students' eyes, who is the expert? I certainly was not there and possess none of the cachet of a survivor. Yet when situations like this present themselves, teachers must find the proper time to discreetly deal with them. What I find even more troubling are instances where survivors become insistent on matters of pedagogy. In other words, "This is what you should say and this is how you should do it."

As a board member of the local survivors' association and chairman of their education committee, I have run into this attitude from time to time. Survivors have strong opinions on how this history should be taught. Room to negotiate is usually quite limited. It does not take long for discussions on the topic to become animated. All survivors have an opinion, and they want to make sure that you are especially aware of theirs. I have had to deal with individuals who were of the opinion that unless classroom lessons focused on content that was directly associated with their experience, you were not teaching the history properly.

Although conflicts such as these may arise, they are not truly characteristic of the relationship the survivor community has with the educational establishment. Survivors have a tremendous respect for teachers who take on this subject. The obligation to speak for those who no longer can, to keep this history and the memory of the six million alive, is a responsibility all survivors live with. Yet many are unable to speak—the pain is still too great. This at least partially explains why survivors hold teachers in such high regard. For they view us as sharing in this duty that is virtually a heavenly mandate; a mandate that within a very short period of time will be totally our responsibility.

Additional Studies and Expanded Work in the Field

In addition to my study in Israel, I took part in two National Endowment for the Humanities programs, both of which focused on particular approaches to the study of the Holocaust. One was entitled "The Literature of the Holocaust" and was taught by Dr. Allie Frazier at Hollins College; the other, "The Drama of the Holocaust," was taught by Dr. Robert Skloot at the University of Wisconsin-Madison. The former seminar allowed me the opportunity to explore a variety of genres related to a methodology that I have alluded to above. The latter course was of particular interest since so many of my students were involved with dramatic performances associated with the NHD program.

After my study in Israel and attendance at the two aforementioned National Endowment for the Humanities programs, I began to present at local and state conferences, and before long I was receiving requests from school districts to provide in-service opportunities for their staffs. Regional and national conferences, especially those of the National Council for the Social Studies (NCSS), provided additional forums for sharing and networking. At one NCSS conference, I was asked by Dr. Robert Stahl, then president of NCSS, to design and to present at a session dealing with Holocaust studies in light of all the publicity *Schindler's List* had created. Dr. Stahl was aware of my work in the field since we had served together for a number of years on the Arizona Council for the Social Studies. The resulting two-hour session, in which a panel of survivors (Sam Soldinger, a Schindler Jew; Helen Handler, a Hungarian Jew; and educators, including myself) explored a wide range of topics, drew some 800 people.

With the opening of the United States Holocaust Memorial Museum (USHMM), support for the efforts of educators across the nation took on a new dimension. As millions of visitors filed through its doors, education department staff members were developing materials and activities that teachers across the nation could access. Perhaps even more valuable were the workshop opportunities the museum created. Educators from every state now had the opportunity to study and share their expertise within the walls of one of the world's finest museums.

As one of the first graduates of the Mandel Teacher Fellowship Institute, I can testify to the quality of program to which teachers are exposed. This fellowship is designed for experienced secondary school educators who have an extensive knowledge of Holocaust history and who are active in community and professional Holocaust-related organizations. Participants spend a two-week period at the USHMM where they interact with its historians, curators, archivists, educators, and librarians as they further their knowledge about this history. The selection process for this particular fellowship was based upon the development of individual projects, judged significant for their potential to impact classroom instruction and to add to the body of knowledge surrounding the pedagogy of this subject. Utilizing the museum's extensive resources helped to facilitate this project development.

I now teach for the USHMM as part of its Belfer National Conference for Educators. This program is primarily structured for educators with less than five years' experience in teaching the Holocaust. My teaching responsibilities cover a wide range of subjects from methodology to specific areas of historical content, which oftentimes is determined by a particular theme that has been adopted for the program.

As further evidence of the marked increase in interest in the subject, I have found myself conducting an ever-growing number of workshops across the country, primarily for teachers. Typically, the topics focus on the methodology and pedagogy related to the Holocaust: how to teach the history, what to teach, potential problems to be aware of, and so on. The latter are among the most requested topics at workshop sessions.

Sometimes the requests are very specific. For example, a school district in rural Illinois that I have worked with through the years has asked me to tailor my remarks to such topics as the Nazis' euthanasia program, antisemitic legislation, and the American response to the Holocaust.

As the subject of the Holocaust continues to grow in popularity and finds its way into an ever-increasing number of curricula and classrooms across the country, there is a growing need for sound pedagogical practices that help to ensure that the historical events are presented in an accurate, meaningful, and challenging manner. My work seems to focus on this end more and more as I am asked to conduct seminars and inservices for educators who are becoming involved with this history for the first time.

OBSTACLES AND FRUSTRATIONS

The one thing that continually frustrates me relative to my work in the field is the severe time limitations teachers operate under. It has been my experience that administrators and teachers are most receptive to include this history as part of their curricular programs; yet, as I conduct inservice after inservice that focus on methodology, I find myself tailoring my remarks to fit the demand of teachers for practical suggestions on how to teach the Holocaust in the five days they have to accomplish the task. How students are to reach any meaningful understanding of this most complex subject after just a few lessons is beyond me. To even think about it is frustrating. To attempt it is pedagogically unsound.

I am fully aware that this nation's history and social studies curricula are the "target" for a myriad of groups who want "their piece of the curriculum" to tell their story. This is understandable, but with so much content to be "covered," some rather difficult choices have to be made. Oftentimes, indeed most times, at least from my perspective, it is the story of the Holocaust that suffers. Another obstacle that has been thrown in front of Holocaust education are the mandates some states have instituted. On one level, requiring all of a state's students to be taught lessons on the Holocaust appears to be a move in the right direction. And yet, it has created some real concerns—especially as it relates to issues of appropriateness and quality of instruction. To properly prepare teachers in every school district within a state to conduct challenging, thought-provoking, and meaningful lessons in this complex content area is no easy task and it certainly cannot be accomplished overnight. This lack of preparation, plus teacher resistance to add "something else" to an already "full plate," has resulted, in many cases, in creating much confusion and frustration. Ultimately, the material is being "covered," but based upon my observations, it is being covered in rather haphazard and uninspired ways. That does not mean there are not outstanding examples of exemplary teaching, just that the overall impression one gets is of a curriculum and instructional program characterized by inconsistency and lack of "buy in" by the teaching staff.

As alluded to above, appropriateness of content for younger students, K–6 especially, is a prime concern for teachers who find themselves facing a mandate. Many, if not most educators in the field of Holocaust studies, feel that the nature and sophistication of the subject matter requires a developmental level beyond the middle school years. Personally, I would not attempt to teach lessons on this history to students below junior high school age. Certainly students, even the youngest, can empathize with the victims, but a true understanding of these historical realities involves so much more. We, as educators, simply cannot expect younger students to grasp the extremely complex issues that are necessary if any meaningful and substantive comprehension is to be achieved. It is a tough enough task for high school students, not to mention adults.

A DEVOTION TO TEACHING ABOUT THE HOLOCAUST

Often I am asked why I have devoted so much of my life to this subject; all of the teaching, the lesson development, the presentations at conferences and inservices, the research and writing, and the endless reading just to keep current. More often than not this question comes from survivors or others who wonder why there is such a commitment from someone who is not Jewish. The answer is not very complex, and I usually make it part of my closing comments when before an audience. It involves a small part of a survivor's testimony that was told to me in Israel. It will be forever a part of me.

Anushka Frieman was a young mother living in Kovno, Lithuania, when the Germans invaded in 1941. Her husband, along with all Jewish men, was forced to labor outside the ghetto on projects the Germans viewed as essential to the war. Thus, when the order came to move into the newly created ghetto, the back-breaking task of moving one's possessions fell primarily on the shoulders of the women.

The Germans had given Kovno's Jews a month to make the move. Every day, Anushka and her neighbor used their baby carriages not only to convey their young children, but also as means to transport their households. The women utilized every available space to pack in those items that were essential. So with sacks tied to their backs and carriages overflowing with their belongings, they would make several daily trips to the site of their new homes.

On one such trip they were stopped by a Ukrainian who was guarding a bridge that they needed to cross. When he ordered Anushka's friend to remove her boots and give them to him, she began pleading with him. Out of all the things she had, was there nothing he could satisfy himself with besides her boots? The guard began rummaging through the bundles she was carrying, when suddenly, with one quick motion, he reached into the baby carriage, grabbed her child, and flung it off the bridge. Anushka stood terrified, gripping the handle of her carriage, certain her child would be taken next. Yet, without the slightest show of emotion, the guard matter-of-factly waved them forward across the bridge.

The Frieman family survived in the ghetto until the order for deportation came in 1944. Even though the Jews were allowed to take so very little with them, Anushka's husband insisted on taking his beloved cello. He had been unable to play the instrument for years since his hands were so terribly battered and swollen. At night he would caress it like he would his child, no doubt thinking of those glorious days when he played for the national symphony. And so, with cello in hand, the Friemans walked to the assembly point where they would be taken to be "resettled."

They had not walked far when a guard noticed the frail man carrying the cello. As the guard wrenched it from his grip and smashed it before his eyes, the musician stood by stoically. There were no tears left to shed. What truly mattered stood by his side. Silently they walked on.

Men were separated from the women and children as the Germans loaded the ghetto's inhabitants into trucks. This was the last Anushka would see of her husband, but she had no way of knowing that as she held tight to her daughter. As the trucks began to fill she began to slowly work her way toward the back of the line. If the trucks were full, then perhaps they would be sent back to the ghetto. To live another day was all that mattered.

Why her daughter began to cry at this moment, the very moment that a brief glimmer of hope presented itself, she could not explain. The child cried uncontrollably. As her small cries turned to screams many in the queue grew angry with her. The last thing they wanted was for attention to be drawn to where they stood. Anushka did everything she could to quiet the child. The screams only became louder. Then, no doubt out of frustration and fear, she slapped her daughter across the face. In that same instant, a hand reached down from the back of the truck, tearing the child from its mother's arms. With a wave of the hand, the German dismissed the wretched remnants. They would "live" for awhile longer.

As Anushka told this story it was as if it had happened only yesterday. With tears streaming down her face, her last words were from a time and place I could only imagine. "Since that day, I dream the same dream every night. That the last thing I did to my child was to strike it."

When I speak or write, Anushka's face is before me; her sorrow and pain impressed upon my memory forever. What better reason do we need to teach this history? Not simply to preserve the memory of the millions who perished, but for those who survived. For those who never had the chance to say good-bye. As Holocaust scholar Deborah Lipstadt (1994) has so aptly stated, "The still, small voices of millions cry out to us from the ground demanding that we do no less." (p. 222)

REFERENCES

Hilberg, Raul (1985). *The Destruction of the European Jews*. New York: Holmes and Meier.

Lipstadt, Deborah (1994). *Denying the Holocaust: The Growing Assault on Truth and Memory*. New York: Plume Books.

Mosse, George (1964). *The Crisis of German Ideology: Intellectual Origins of the Third Reich*. New York: Gosset and Dunlap.

Reitlinger, Gerald (1961). *The Final Solution: The Attempt to Exterminate the Jews of Europe, 1939–1945*. Cranbury, NJ: Thomas Yoseloff.

Richter, Hans P. (1987). *Friedrich*. New York: Puffin Books.

Wiesenthal, Simon (1968). *Murderers among Us: The Simon Wiesenthal Memoirs*. New York: Bantam Books.

Zyskind, Sara (1981). *Stolen Years*. Minneapolis, MN: Lerner Publications Co.

Selected Bibliography
of Contributors' Works

Chosen by the writers themselves, the books and articles listed below identify publications that each author places among his or her most significant contribution to Holocaust education. Books and articles appear together, and each person's writings are listed alphabetically.

REBECCA G. AUPPERLE

Aupperle, Rebecca G. "Face to Face: The Study of *Friedrich*, A Novel about the Holocaust," pp. 73–102 in Samuel Totten (Ed.) (2001). *Teaching Holocaust Literature*. Boston, MA: Allyn and Bacon.

Flaim, Richard F.; Aupperle, Rebecca G.; Cervi, Douglas; Gwin, Christopher; Holden, Robert; Pordy, Barbara; Rosen, Philip; and Shenkus, Arlene. (2001). *The Holocaust and Genocide: The Betrayal of Humanity — A Curriculum Guide for Grades 7–12*, 2nd ed. Trenton, NJ: New Jersey Commission on Holocaust Education.

STEVE COHEN

Cohen, Steve and Johnson, Mary. "Kristallnacht: A Documentary — Discussion Guide." *Dimensions: A Journal of Holocaust Studies*. 4(2) (fall 1998):G1–G16.

Cohen, Steve and Michalczyk, John. (1992). *The Cross and the Star: A Study Guide*. Wayland, MA: Albion Press.

———. "Expressing the Inexpressible through Film," pp. 203–222 in Samuel Totten and Stephen Feinberg (Eds.) (2000). *Teaching and Studying the Holocaust*. Boston, MA: Allyn and Bacon Publishers.

Facing History and Ourselves. (1994). *Facing History and Ourselves: Holocaust and Human Behavior*. Brookline, MA: Facing History and Ourselves. (Note: Steven Cohen served as chief researcher.)

ELAINE CULBERTSON

Culbertson, Elaine. "*The Diary of Anne Frank*: Why I Don't Teach It," pp. 63–69 in Samuel Totten (Ed.) (2001). *Teaching Holocaust Literature*. Boston, MA: Allyn and Bacon Publishers.
———. "The Difference That It Makes: Holocaust Education in the Public Schools." *Teaching and Thinking and Problem Solving* 16(2) (1994): 1–4. (Note: This is a publication of Research for Better Schools based in Philadelphia, Pennsylvania.)
Culbertson, Elaine and Libowitz, Richard. "Teaching the Teachers: Asking Questions," pp. 19–29 in Douglas F. Tobler (Ed.) (1998). *Remembrance, Repentance, Reconciliation: The 25th Anniversary Volume of the Annual Scholars' Conference on the Holocaust and the Churches*. Lanham, MD: University Press of America.

CAROL DANKS

Danks, Carol. "Choiceless Choices and Illusions of Power: A Study of *Throne of Straw in the Lodz Ghetto* in an Advanced Placement Class," pp. 197–214 in Samuel Totten (Ed.) (2001). *Teaching Holocaust Literature*. Boston, MA: Allyn and Bacon Publishers.
———. "Teaching Holocaust Literature." *English Language Arts Bulletin* 29(2) (fall/winter 1988/1989):26–32.
———. "Using Holocaust Short Stories and Poetry in the Social Studies Classroom." Special issue ("Teaching About the Holocaust" edited by Samuel Totten and Stephen Feinberg) of *Social Education*, 59(6) (October 1995): 358–361.
———. "Using the Literature of Elie Wiesel and Selected Poetry to Teach the Holocaust in the Secondary School History Classroom." *The Social Studies* 87(3) (May/June 1996):101–105.
Danks, Carol and Rabinsky, Leatrice (Eds.) (1999). *Teaching for a Tolerant World, Grades 9–12*. Urbana, IL: National Council of Teachers of English.
———. (Eds.) (1994). *The Holocaust: Prejudice Unleashed*. Columbus, OH: State Department of Education.

HAROLD LASS

Lass, Harold, Poizner, Malca, and Segal, Nadine. "Teaching the Holocaust in Ontario." *Multiculturalism* 12(1) (April 16–22, 1989):16–19.
Lass, Harold and Reed, Carole. "Racism Today—Echoes of the Holocaust." *Canadian Social Studies: The History and Social Science Teacher* 29(4) (summer 1995):140–142.

LEATRICE B. RABINSKY

Danks, Carol and Rabinsky, Leatrice B. (Eds.) (1999). *Teaching for a Tolerant World, Grades 9–12*. Urbana, IL: National Council of Teachers of English.

Rabinsky, Leatrice. "Holocaust Education: Reaching Students and Students Reaching Out." Special issue ("Teaching Social Issues in the English Classroom" edited by Samuel Totten) of *The Arizona State English Journal* 29(1) (fall 1987):99–109.

———. "Holocaust Education: Reaching Students and Students Reaching Out." Special issue ("Genocide: Issues, Approaches, Resources" edited by Samuel Totten) of *The New York Social Studies Journal* 24(2) (fall 1987):52–55.

Rabinsky, Leatrice and Danks, Carol (Eds.) (1989 and 1994). *The Holocaust: Prejudice Unleashed*. Columbus, OH: Ohio Council on Holocaust Education.

Rabinsky, Leatrice and Mann, Gertrude (1979). *Journey of Conscience: Young People Respond to the Holocaust*. Cleveland, OH: William Collins Publishers.

KAREN SHAWN

Shawn, Karen. "Choosing Holocaust Literature for Early Adolescents," pp. 139–155 in Samuel Totten and Stephen Feinberg (Eds.) (2001). *Teaching and Studying the Holocaust*. Boston, MA: Allyn and Bacon.

———. "Current Issues in Holocaust Education." *Dimensions: A Journal of Holocaust Studies* 9(2) (1995): 15–18.

———. (1994). *The End of Innocence: Anne Frank and the Holocaust*, 2nd ed. New York: Anti-Defamation League of B'nai B'rith.

———. (1991). "Goals for Helping Young Adolescents Learn about the Shoah." *Ten Da'at* vol. 2, pp. 7–11.

———. "The Liberation of Europe and the Concentration and Death Camps: A Documentary Discussion Guide." *Dimensions: A Journal of Holocaust Studies* 8(3) (1995): G–1 to G–23.

———. "Literary Commentary: A Transactional Approach to Holocaust Literature." *Jewish Library Association Journal* 8(1–2) (1995): 91–94.

———. "Virtual Community, Real-Life Connections: A Study of *The Island on Bird Street* via an International Reading Project," pp. 103–124 in Samuel Totten (Ed.) (2001). *Teaching Holocaust Literature*. Boston, MA: Allyn and Bacon.

———. "The Warsaw Ghetto: A Documentary Discussion Guide to Jewish Resistance in Occupied Warsaw, 1939–1943." *Dimensions: A Journal of Holocaust Studies* 7(2) (1993): G–1 to G–15.

———. "What Should They Read and When Should They Read It? A Selective Review of Holocaust Literature for Students in Grades Two through Twelve: Part Two." *Dimensions: A Journal of Holocaust Studies* 11(2) (1997): A-1 to A-23.

Shawn, Karen (Ed.) (1995). *In the Aftermath of the Holocaust: Three Generations Speak*. Englewood, NJ: The Moriah School of Englewood.

SAMUEL TOTTEN

Parsons, William S. and Totten, Samuel. (1993). *Guidelines for Teaching About the Holocaust*. Washington, D.C.: United States Holocaust Memorial Museum. (Note: Major contributors included: Grace Caporino, Stephen Feinberg, William Fernekes, and Sybil Milton.)

Totten, Samuel. "The Critical Need to Teach the Holocaust in a Historically Accurate and Pedagogically Sound Manner," pp. 342–361 in F.C. Decoste and Bernard Schwartz (Eds.) (1999). *The Holocaust's Ghost: Writings on Art, Politics, Law and Education*. Alberta, Canada: The University of Alberta Press.

———. "Diminishing the Complexity and Horror of the Holocaust: Using Simulations in an Attempt to Convey Historical Experiences." *Social Education* 64(3) (April 2000):165–171.

———. "A Holocaust Curriculum Evaluation Instrument: Admirable Aim, Poor Result." *Journal of Curriculum and Supervision* 13(2) (winter 1998):148–166.

———. (2002). *Holocaust Education: Issues and Approaches*. Boston, MA: Allyn and Bacon Publishers.

———. "How They Taught the Holocaust to High School Students: A Semester-Long Course Cotaught by a University Professor and a High School English Teacher." *The Journal of Holocaust Education*. In press.

———. "Should There Be Holocaust Education for K–4 Students? The Answer Is No!" *Social Studies and the Young Learner*, 12(1) (September/October 1999): 36–39.

Totten, Samuel and Feinberg, Stephen. "Teaching about the Holocaust: Issues of Rationale, Content, Methodology and Resources." Special issue ("Teaching about the Holocaust" edited by Samuel Totten and Stephen Feinberg) of *Social Education*. 59(6) (October 1995):323–327, 329, 331–333.

Totten, Samuel (Ed.) (2001). *Teaching Holocaust Literature*. Boston, MA: Allyn and Bacon Publishers. Note: This book contains four essays by Totten: "Incorporating Fiction and Poetry into a Study of the Holocaust," "Analyzing Stories About the Holocaust via a Multiple Intelligences and Reader-Response Approach," "'Written in Pencil in the Sealed Railway Car': Incorporating Poetry into a Study of the Holocaust via a Reader-Response Theory Activity," and "Encountering the 'Night' of the Holocaust: Studying Elie Wiesel's *Night*.")

Totten, Samuel and Feinberg, Stephen (Eds.) (2001). *Teaching and Studying the Holocaust*. Boston, MA: Allyn and Bacon Publishers. (Note: This book contains four chapters authored or coauthored by Totten: "Rationales for Teaching the Holocaust," "Incorporating First-Person Accounts into a Study of the Holocaust," "Incorporating Literature into a Study of the Holocaust," and "Incorporating Primary Documents into a Study of the Holocaust.")

PAUL WIESER

Wieser, Paul. "The American Press and the Holocaust." Special issue ("Teaching about the Holocaust" edited by Samuel Totten and Stephen Feinberg) of *Social Education*, 59(6) (1995): C1–C2.

———. "Anti-Semitism: A Warrant for Genocide." Special issue ("Teaching About the Holocaust" edited by Samuel Totten and Stephen Feinberg) of *Social Education* 59(6) (1995): C4–C6.

———. "Hitler's Death Camps." Special issue ("Teaching About the Holocaust" edited by Samuel Totten and Stephen Feinberg) of *Social Education* 59(6) (1995): 374–376.

———. "The Holocaust: Turning Point in History." *National History Day Theme Supplement* (1999) 53–59.

———. "Instructional Issues/Strategies in Teaching the Holocaust," pp. 62–80 in Samuel Totten and Steve Feinberg (Eds.) (2000). *Teaching and Studying the Holocaust*. Boston, MA: Allyn and Bacon.

Index

About the Editor and Contributors

The contributors are an eclectic group: men and women; Jewish, Christian, and unaffiliated; teachers of social studies, English, and teacher education; site administrators; and midcareer and retired. All but one live and teach in the United States.

REBECCA G. AUPPERLE is a reading and language arts teacher at the Mary E. Volz School in Runnemede, New Jersey. The school is also a Holocaust Demonstration Site, and Aupperle is its director.

STEVE COHEN lectures on education at Tufts University in Medford, Massachusetts, and is a longtime associate of Facing History and Ourselves. For many years, he taught history at the high school level in Weston, Massachusetts.

ELAINE CULBERTSON is the principal of Philadelphia Regional High School. A long-standing teacher of the Holocaust, she is the former curriculum and workshop coordinator for the Teachers Summer Seminar on the Holocaust and Jewish Resistance in Poland and Israel.

CAROL DANKS, an English teacher at Roosevelt High School in Kent, Ohio, is a codeveloper of Ohio's Holocaust curriculum, *The Holocaust: Prejudice Unleashed*.

HAROLD LASS teaches history and English at Northern Secondary School in Toronto. He is the codeveloper of the curriculum, *Racism Today: Echoes of the Holocaust*.

LEATRICE B. RABINSKY is a retired, longtime English teacher in the Cleveland Heights-University Heights school system. She codeveloped Ohio's Holocaust curriculum, *The Holocaust: Prejudice Unleashed*.

KAREN SHAWN is the assistant principal at the Moriah School in Englewood, New Jersey, and an instructor at the Yad Vashem Summer Institute for Educators from Abroad in Jerusalem, Israel.

SAMUEL TOTTEN is a professor of curriculum and instruction at the University of Arkansas in Fayetteville, and a curriculum specialist in the areas of the Holocaust, genocide, and human rights education. Totten has taught English and social studies in Australia, Israel, and the United States.

PAUL WIESER is a staff member at Phoenix's Anti-Defamation League. He is a former social studies teacher, and social studies coordinator for the Pendergast School District in Phoenix, Arizona.